BETWEEN THE PSYCHE AND THE POLIS

Between the Psyche and the Polis

Refiguring history in literature and theory

Edited by
MICHAEL ROSSINGTON and ANNE WHITEHEAD
University of Newcastle upon Tyne

Ashgate

Aldershot • Burlington USA • Singapore • Sydney

Published by
Ashgate Publishing Ltd
Gower House
Croft Road
Aldershot
Hants GU11 3HR
England

Ashgate Publishing Company
131 Main Street
Burlington, VT 05401–5600 USA

Ashgate website: http://www.ashgate.com

British Library Cataloguing in Publication Data
Between the psyche and the polis: refiguring history in literature
    and theory.
    1. History in literature 2. History–Philosophy.
    I. Rossington, Michael II. Whitehead, Anne
    809. 9'3358

Library of Congress Control Number: 00–108822

ISBN 0 7546 0228 1

Printed in Great Britain by
Antony Rowe Ltd, Chippenham, Wiltshire

Contents

Acknowledgements   vii
Notes on Contributors   ix
Preface   xii

Introduction: Between the Psyche and the Polis   1
Michael Rossington and Anne Whitehead

PART I: HISTORY IN THEORY: AFTER MARX AND FREUD

1   Old Idolatry: Rethinking 'Ideology' and 'Materialism'   21
    Simon Jarvis

2   History and the Sacred in de Man and Benjamin   38
    Nigel Mapp

3   Freud and the Force of History: *The Project for a Scientific
    Psychology*   59
    Clare Connors

PART II: TRAUMATIC HISTORIES

4   Parting Words: Trauma, Silence and Survival   77
    Cathy Caruth

5   Reading Trauma: Charlotte Delbo and the Struggle to Represent   97
    Victoria Stewart

6   Trauma, Testimony and the Survivor: Calling Forth the Ghosts of
    Bosnia-Herzegovina   108
    Stephenie Young

PART III: MEMORY AND CULTURAL HISTORY

7 In the Penal Colony 123
John Frow

8 Séance Fiction: Confronting the Ghost(s) of the Mexican
Revolution in *Madero, el otro* by Ignacio Solares 143
Robin Fiddian

9 The Angel of Memory: 'Working Through' the History of the
New South Africa 157
Christopher J. Colvin

PART IV: *NACHTRÄGLICHKEIT*: HISTORY AND AFTERWARDSNESS

10 History and Trauma: Reviewing *Forrest Gump* 177
Susannah Radstone

11 Traumatic Memories of Remembering and Forgetting 191
Elizabeth Cowie

12 Aftermath: Pastiche, the Postmodern and the End of History in
Angela Carter's *Nights at the Circus* 205
Rachel Carroll

Bibliography 219

Index 232

Acknowledgements

Most of the essays in this volume were first presented as papers at a two-day international conference, 'Refiguring History: Between the Psyche and the Polis', organized by the editors and hosted by the Department of English Literary and Linguistic Studies at the University of Newcastle upon Tyne in May 1999. We acknowledge financial support from our Department, Faculty of Arts, and University Research Committee Small Grants Research Fund without which the conference could not have taken place. Several colleagues and many postgraduates in our Department assisted in its organization including Marie Addyman, Linda Anderson, Celeste-Marie Bernier, Janice Burrow, Jerome de Groot, Suzanne Fairless, Christopher Goulding, Claire Lamont, Marita le Vaul-Grimwood, Andrew Moor, Tracy Olverson, Jennifer Richards, and Terry R. Wright. Special thanks to Rowena Bryson, the Department Secretary, Rachel Woolley, the Conference Secretary, and to all the delegates who gave papers. The idea for the conference developed out of the 'Rethinking History' reading group, established in the Department in 1997. It gives us pleasure to acknowledge here the energy and commitment of the group's members: Linda Anderson, Victoria Bazin, Rachel Carroll, Jerome de Groot, Neil Hairsine, Nick Montgomery, Andrew Moor, Jennifer Richards, and Rieko Suzuki.

The essay by John Frow in this volume was first published in *Journal of Australian Studies: The Beautiful and the Damned*, no. 64 (2000) and Cathy Caruth's essay here is also published in *Cultural Values*, vol. 5, no. 1 (2001). Grateful acknowledgement is made by Cathy Caruth and Clare Connors to Sigmund Freud Copyrights, The Institute of Psychoanalysis, The Hogarth Press and Basic Books for permission to quote from *The Standard Edition of the Complete Psychological Works of Sigmund Freud*, translated and edited by James Strachey (translation modified as stated in the case of Cathy Caruth's essay), and by Victoria Stewart to Yale University Press for permission to quote from Charlotte Delbo, *Auschwitz and After*. The cover image, 'Granada, Spain, 1933', is courtesy of Henri Cartier-Bresson/Magnum Photos. Every effort has been made to trace all copyright holders of quoted material, but if any have inadvertently been overlooked, they should contact the publishers

viii   *Between the Psyche and the Polis*

in the first instance to make any necessary arrangements. The editors thank Professor Linda Anderson, Head of the Department of English Literary and Linguistic Studies at the University of Newcastle upon Tyne, for her support and encouragement of this project throughout. Cathy Caruth, John Frow, Simon Jarvis, Nigel Mapp and Lyndsey Stonebridge offered much appreciated critical engagement at various stages in the volume's inception. Special thanks to each and all of our contributors for adapting so readily to a tight production schedule, to Colette Anderson, Rowena Bryson, Pat FitzGerald, Tom Norton and the Department of English Literary and Linguistic Studies at the University of Newcastle upon Tyne for various kinds of assistance in producing the book, and to Erika Gaffney and Ruth Peters at Ashgate for their help and advice.

Michael Rossington and Anne Whitehead
Department of English Literary and Linguistic Studies
University of Newcastle upon Tyne
May 2000

Notes on Contributors

Dr Rachel Carroll is Lecturer in English at the University of Teesside. Her research interests include modernity, the postmodern, feminist literary theory and twentieth-century women writers. She has published articles in *Critique: Studies in Contemporary Fiction*, *The Yearbook of English Studies*, and *Textual Practice*.

Professor Cathy Caruth is Director of the Comparative Literature Programme at Emory University. She is the author of *Empirical Truths and Critical Fictions: Locke, Wordsworth, Kant, Freud* (Johns Hopkins University Press, 1991), and *Unclaimed Experience: Trauma, Narrative and History* (Johns Hopkins University Press, 1996). She has also edited *Trauma: Explorations in Memory* (Johns Hopkins University Press, 1995) and co-edited, with Deborah Esch, *Critical Encounters: Reference and Responsibility in Deconstructive Writing* (Rutgers University Press, 1995).

Christopher J. Colvin is a doctoral student in cultural anthropology at the University of Virginia. His research is on the use and transformation of psychologically-inspired models of conflict resolution and reconciliation in post-apartheid South Africa.

Clare Connors, a lecturer in English at The Queen's College, University of Oxford, is currently completing a PhD on theorizations of 'force' in the works of Nietzsche, Freud, Heidegger, Arendt, Foucault and Derrida.

Dr Elizabeth Cowie is Reader in Film Studies at the University of Kent at Canterbury. She is the author of *Representing the Woman: cinema and psychoanalysis* (Macmillan, 1997), and co-edited, with Parveen Adams, *The Woman in Question* (Verso, 1990). Most recently she has published essays in Stephen Neale and Murray Smith (eds), *Contemporary Hollywood Cinema* (Routledge, 1998) and Jane Gaines and Michael Renov (eds), *Collecting Visible Evidence* (University of Minnesota Press, 1999).

Dr Robin Fiddian is Reader in Spanish at the University of Oxford and Fellow and Tutor in Spanish at Wadham College. His research interests include the literature and cinema of Spain, Spanish American fiction, and postcolonial studies. His most recent books are *García Márquez* (Longman, 1995) and (co-edited, with Ian Michael), *Sound on Vision: Studies on Spanish Cinema* (Carfax Publishing, 1999). His volumes *Between Paradigms: An Intertextual Study of the Novels of Fernando del Paso* and *Postcolonial Perspectives on the Cultures of Latin America and Lusophone Africa* (ed.) are currently in press.

Professor John Frow is Regius Professor of Rhetoric and English Literature at the University of Edinburgh. He is currently working on cultural memory and the moral economy of everyday life. Recent publications include *Cultural Studies and Cultural Value* (Clarendon Press, 1995) and *Time and Commodity Culture: Essays in Cultural Theory and Postmodernity* (Clarendon Press, 1997).

Dr Simon Jarvis is Gorley Putt Lecturer in English Literary History at the University of Cambridge and a Fellow of Robinson College. His publications include *Scholars and Gentlemen: Shakespearian Textual Criticism and Representations of Scholarly Labour, 1725–1765* (Clarendon Press, 1995) and *Adorno: A Critical Introduction* (Polity Press, 1998). He is currently working on a study of Wordsworth.

Nigel Mapp teaches in the Department of English Literary and Linguistic Studies at the University of Newcastle. He has published on various literary-theoretical topics and is co-editor, with Christopher Norris, of *William Empson: The Critical Achievement* (Cambridge University Press, 1993).

Dr Susannah Radstone teaches cultural studies and media studies at the University of East London. She is currently completing a monograph *On Memory and Confession* (to be published by Routledge) and is editor of a collection of essays, *Memory and Methodology* (Berg, 2000). She organized the international *Frontiers of Memory* conference at the University of East London in September 1999.

Dr Victoria Stewart is Lecturer in the School of English at the University of the West of England. Her research interests include Holocaust testimony and representations of the Second World War in drama. She has forthcoming articles on war crimes trials in the plays of Ronald Harwood (*Modern Drama*) and on Michael Frayn's play *Copenhagen* (*New Theatre Quarterly*).

Stephenie Young is a PhD student in the Comparative Literature Program of the State University of New York, Binghamton. Her research interests include representations of trauma in the literature of post-boom women writers from Latin America, translation practice and theory, and French and Latin American Feminist Theory. She has recently published in *PALARA* (Publication of the Afro-Latin/American Research Association) and in *Beacons* (a publication of the American Translators Association).

The Editors

Dr Michael Rossington is Senior Lecturer in the Department of English Literary and Linguistic Studies at the University of Newcastle upon Tyne. His publications include editions of Mary Shelley's *Valperga* (Oxford University Press, 2000) and Percy Shelley's *The Cenci* in *The Poems of Shelley, Volume 2*, eds Kelvin Everest and Geoffrey Matthews (Longman, 2000), and he is co-editor, with Gill Perry, of *Femininity and Masculinity in Eighteenth-Century Art and Culture* (Manchester University Press, 1994). He is currently completing a monograph on the past in the writings of Percy Shelley.

Dr Anne Whitehead is Lecturer in the Department of English Literary and Linguistic Studies at the University of Newcastle upon Tyne. She has had articles published in *Modern Fiction Studies* and *Textual Practice* and is currently completing a book on trauma theory.

Preface

This volume of essays aims to show how history is being refigured in contemporary literary, cultural and theoretical studies. Its project can be situated in relation to a chronological account of theoretical debates about the past from the mid-nineteenth century to the present, organized around key thinkers and movements: Marx, Freud, and Nietzsche; Adorno, Benjamin and the Frankfurt School; Foucault, Derrida and Lacan; North American deconstruction and new historicism and British cultural materialism; and, most recently, debates about the postmodern and postcolonial conditions. However an exclusively historicizing orientation of this kind, in which genealogy is the guiding rhetorical figure, is as restrictive as it may be instructive. Shifting to a spatial, as opposed to a temporal, structuring metaphor, this volume seeks to explore the ways in which current thinking about the past operates within a dialogic space and can be located in relation to multiple perspectives. Thus cultural memory can be seen not just as a recent development within the field of cultural studies but as constructing a between-space which also draws in aspects of psychoanalysis. Similarly, trauma theory may usefully be conceptualized as operating in a rich and complex dynamic between deconstruction and the work of Freud. The purpose of this volume is not to claim that it is desirable or possible either for there to be a synthesis of the diverse critical positions under review, nor that a chronological account – of the kind outlined above – in which one way of thinking is placed alongside another in succession can *explain* such positions. Rather, temporality, memory and the past are often attended to here in terms of the dislocations of narrative, of resistances to linear genealogies. It is hoped that within this space the reader will be liberated into making unanticipated connections between theories and cultures, and between the demands of the psyche and the polis.

Introduction: Between the Psyche and the Polis

MICHAEL ROSSINGTON AND ANNE WHITEHEAD

Remaking the past is an indispensable feature of cultural life. Art promotes the recognition that history is not only remembered events but the endless process of refiguring the temporal through narrative. The contributors to this volume – whose expertise ranges across theory, cultural studies and literary studies – invite the reader to attend to the forms – linguistic, visual, monumental – by which a connectedness with, or separation from, the past takes place. Their criticism is situated in an uneasy space between the demands of the psyche and the polis or, to use Gillian Rose's words, 'the soul' and 'the city'. For Rose, it is possible that:

> Plato is as 'realistic' about power, violence and domination as Thucydides; and Thucydides' history serves as ethical an impulse as Plato's philosophy. Ethics and metaphysics are torn halves of an integral freedom to which they have *never* added up.[1]

This diagnosis of a dialectical relationship or, more accurately, fissure, between the twin imperatives of metaphysics ('the soul') and ethics ('the city') can be extended to a further terrain which may be seen as 'broken' in a productive sense, that identified by Pierre Nora as 'between memory and history'.[2] It is with current thinking about memory's relationship to history, and the ongoing critical reassessment of historicism that many of the following essays are preoccupied.[3] First, from within the traditions of Marxism and deconstruction there is a questioning of the grounds of 'ideology-critique' in historicist criticism which announces itself to be 'materialist'. The view that absolute disenchantment is illusory, that metaphysics cannot be banished from history – as Rose suggests in the above quotation – may be seen to permeate other, quite distinct areas of the volume, in particular the emphasis in trauma theory on the catastrophic, which finds expression in a language of witnessing that frequently has recourse to sublime and apocalyptic imagery. Secondly, there is analysis of the means by which collective cultural memory is forged in

1

societies addressing crises in national identity, in some cases precipitated by the legacy of colonialism. Thirdly, issues of temporality – more specifically, of temporal belatedness – are raised across the essays in the volume. In relation to postmodernity the ascendancy of memory in current historical discourse may be seen as a belated response to the shock of modernity while in relation to psychoanalysis – in an era structured by trauma – it may be seen as symptomatic of a return of the repressed.[4] Finally, in considering the relation of memory and history, the volume is sensitive to the imbrication of such issues in a discourse which is primarily literary – the essays not only offer a range of readings across literary and filmic texts, but are also interested in a memorialized historicism which is necessarily bound up with narrative structures. Viewed in this light, the volume offers a series of narrative alternatives for the ways in which we have come to think through our relations to the past.

I

The volume begins with a section which addresses theories of history – broadly defined – in the work of Marx, Benjamin, de Man and Freud. From distinct perspectives the opening three essays scrutinize the vocabulary of temporal relations in traditions associated with these thinkers, and in so doing deepen and extend our understanding of the historical. Both Simon Jarvis and Nigel Mapp in different ways take off from Marx's statement that 'All criticism begins with the criticism of religion', and show how what goes under the name of 'materialism' and 'ideology-critique' leaves behind a stubborn residue of enchantment. In addressing discourses of religion and the sacred their aim, however, is determinedly *not* to fashion new idols, rather to suggest more self-critical conditions in which an analysis of illusion may take place. Clare Connors's essay, in examining the material and temporal ordering of force in Freud's discussion of the psyche, shows how psychoanalysis both disables and is enabled by history. All three essays invoke Rose's idea of 'torn halves which have *never* added up', and figure history in aporetical rather than deterministic terms.

Simon Jarvis's essay provides a historiography of ideology, idolatry and ideology-critique by means of interconnected readings of Marx, Hobbes, Althusser, and de Man and culminates with a proposal for a new conception of materialism. It is Marx's withering critique of Feuerbach and other 'German Ideologists' which impels his argument. Marx's writings, Jarvis reminds us, claim that idol-breaking 'is *itself* to be unmasked as a form of superstition' not, as some hasty readings would have it, that science or materialism may *dispel* the social illusion we have come to term 'ideology'. Just as Marx ridicules the Young Hegelians' apparent belief that by linguistic fiat we can be divested of illusion, so Hobbes's *Leviathan* is found to be thwarted in its effort to demystify patristic demonology by the very idol-worship it seeks to root out. Althusser's well-known essay, 'Ideology and Ideological State Apparatuses', may seem to offer more promising territory in the search for an absolutely disenchanted account of social illusion, but in the famous statement *'individuals are always-already subjects'* lies a reductive ontological claim – itself an ideology rather than its diagnosis – which closes off the possibility allowed for by Marx that illusion arises in the space between 'suffering-thinking-desiring bodies and the representations and personifications which such bodies are made to inhabit'. Finally, in his analysis of Paul de Man's reading of Kant's *Critique of Judgement*, Jarvis sees de Man's view that Kant is invoking an undeceived 'sheer materiality' as another case of the *mistaken* identification of perfected disenchantment. The implications of this essay for contemporary critical theory hardly need spelling out. It is not only the work of the critics most commonly invoked in the cause of ideology-critique but also some of the most dominant tendencies in contemporary critical theory – historicism, cultural materialism, and post-modernism – which risk performing not 'salutary demystification' but idolatry. In part, this essay contributes to a critique of a potent narrative of our times – the 'Despairing rationalism without reason' which Gillian Rose describes as 'the story of post-modernism ... the story of what happens when "metaphysics" is barred from ethics'. It ends by urging the rethinking of 'materialism': in a dialectic of disenchantment, materialism cannot be considered as void of idealism and, as such, the very metaphysical categories so routinely banished from it – 'nature', 'subjectivity' and the somatic – require re-admission.[5]

Nigel Mapp's essay shares with Simon Jarvis's a clear affiliation to the critical philosophy bequeathed by Kant, to thinking aporetically rather than deterministically, but its destination is different. In its analysis of a 'brokenness in the middle'[6] of language itself, his essay identifies a convergence of deconstruction and Marxist dialectical thought. Mapp begins with Paul de Man's reading of *The German Ideology* and finds in it just that recognition of the impossibility of removing idealism from materialism with which Jarvis's essay is preoccupied. But where Jarvis sees de Man as promoting the view that deconstruction can demystify language by arguing that it is *just* formal and material – even 'inhuman'[7] in its literality – Mapp argues that the linguistic in de Man's late work is to be seen in terms of a dialectical engagement of the material and ideal. A distinctive contribution of Mapp's essay, then, is its willingness to address the core of many readers' discomfort with, not to say resistance to, de Man's contribution to critical theory – the sense that he sets up deconstruction as itself capable of removing illusion or unmasking ideology. For Mapp this is to ignore de Man's understanding of Marx, manifest in his refusal to be seduced by any critical language which partakes of the ideology of either religion ('the sacred') or 'history'. In de Man's lecture on Walter Benjamin's 'The Task of the Translator', we are shown – through an examination of his compelling analysis of the inadequacies of English and French translations of Benjamin's essay – that the *impasse* between languages to which translation attests demonstrates the dialectical state of between-ness which is always the condition of language. While de Man sees Benjamin as arguing that translation teaches us that there can be no authoritative, whole, or pure language in a sacred sense, it would be misleading to see him as suggesting that language can be purified, so to speak, of its aspiration to be pure. There can be neither the pathos of messianic redemption – the nostalgic invocation of an originally pure, whole language – nor a glib disenchantment which fetishizes sheer fragmentedness or the brute materiality of the letter. Translation tells of a dynamic disturbance in which the boundaries between what is inside and outside language are continually ruptured.

Clare Connors ends this section with an essay which draws attention to dialectical contradictions and irruptions in Freud's early work on the material economy of the psyche, the *Project for a Scientific Psychology*. Connors's essay is framed by the metacritical problem – addressed elsewhere in the volume – of an antagonism between the discourses of history and psycho-analysis which is dramatized in Freud's thwarted attempt to provide a developmental narrative of neurological forces within the psyche. Her focus is upon both the material impossibility of force's 'drive' to inertia in the psychic economy and the temporally impossible way in which the principle of inertia in the psyche is described by Freud as 'broken through from the first'. Moreover in her analysis of Freud's account of force's breaching of 'impermeable' neurones, his account of the origin of memory itself is shown to be articulated in terms of an act of wounding. The sense of force and time being conditioned by rupture in Freud's *Project* reverberates through other essays in the volume.

II

The second section in this collection draws together the theoretical interests of the first section through the writers' engagement with the area of trauma theory. In broad terms, trauma theory combines a historicized reworking of deconstruction with psychoanalytical thought. The two figures who arguably lead the current field of trauma theory, Shoshana Felman and Cathy Caruth, have emerged from the Yale School, and both are particularly indebted, in differing ways, to the work of de Man.[8] Trauma theory reworks deconstruction in line with a notion of history or temporality which is profoundly psycho-analytical, and which is based on notions of repetition, return and belatedness.

The essays on testimony and violence draw on the increasingly influential corpus of Cathy Caruth. Caruth opens this section with an essay which complements, in its meticulous analysis of *Beyond the Pleasure Principle*, Connors's close reading of Freud in chapter 3. The title of Caruth's piece, 'Parting Words', signals that the essay is both a return to, and a departure from, Caruth's own former work on *Beyond the Pleasure Principle*, which was itself based on an analysis of the notions of departure and return. In the 'Introduction' to her edited volume, *Trauma: Explorations in Memory* (1995), Caruth's analysis of the nightmare in *Beyond the Pleasure Principle* provided her with the notion of trauma as a 'pathology ... of history',[9] in which the surprisingly literal return or repetition of the event signalled the trauma as a missed experience. Caruth's reading of *Beyond the Pleasure Principle* in *Unclaimed Experience: Trauma, Narrative and History* (1996) placed the text alongside *Moses and Monotheism* and argued that it was necessary to read the significance of individual trauma in the light of a broader cultural memory.[10] The nightmare was read not only as a missed experience to be interminably repeated but also as an awakening to consciousness or an attempt to claim one's own survival. In *Unclaimed Experience*, Caruth also analysed the significance of the child's game of *fort-da*, and argued that it introduced to Freud a pattern of departure and return which he was to elaborate fully in *Moses and Monotheism*. The significance of the game in *Unclaimed Experience* lies in its role as a bridge, or a textual point of connection, between *Beyond the Pleasure Principle* and *Moses and Monotheism*, between Freud's theorizing of the battle nightmare and Jewish historical experience, between individual trauma and cultural memory. Caruth's 'Parting Words' is both a culmination of her earlier work and an attempt to resituate current thinking on trauma.

Caruth's analysis of *Beyond the Pleasure Principle* in 'Parting Words' is concerned to read the significance of the battle nightmare in relation to the child's game of *fort-da*, or to write the game into the tradition of trauma theory. Where the nightmare points backwards and is connected with the death drive, the game represents for Caruth a creative act, and witnesses the past by pointing to the future. Caruth regards current trauma theory as too concerned with the death drive, or the centrality of death in culture, and contends that the life drive, represented by the game, is equally central to Freud's conception of trauma.

Caruth explores the trauma of late twentieth-century American urban violence, through her analysis of a testimonial exchange between Bernadette, the mother of teenager Kahlil, who was shot dead in Atlanta, and Kahlil's best friend, Greg.[11] Caruth traces through the exchange the passage from the death drive to the life drive. The transition is accomplished through a playful act of departure, in which the clothing of Greg's shirt and Kahlil's cap substitute for the child's reel, in a game of positioning and repositioning, 'here' and 'there'.[12] The game represents the possibility of a new history of survival, which is enacted through the encounter between Bernadette and Greg, and which is marked by a creative act of address to the living, instead of the dead.

Caruth's essay seeks to renegotiate the current boundaries of trauma theory in relation to Freud's notions of the death drive and the life drive. Victoria Stewart's analysis of memory in the writing of Holocaust survivor, Charlotte Delbo, complements Caruth in analysing trauma as an encounter with death and the ongoing experience of survival, but also questions Caruth's resituating of trauma in relation to the life drive. In a footnote to chapter 4, Caruth argues that Delbo testifies to survival as the life-in-death of the death drive. Drawing on Delbo's own analysis of memory in *Days and Memory* (1990),[13] Stewart distinguishes between 'external memory', or the processes of thought, which are connected by Delbo with the act of testifying, and 'deep memory', which is intensely physical and based on sense impressions. Stewart suggests a correspondence with Beckett's analysis of Proust's distinction between voluntary and involuntary memory. While voluntary memory can be connected with 'external memory', Stewart indicates that there is a crucial distinction between involuntary memory and 'deep memory'. Involuntary memory can be allied to the creative act of parting or separation from the dead, which inaugurates the life drive: Stewart cites the example of Proust's recognition of his grandmother's death. However, 'deep memory' can generate no such act of departure, and operates exclusively in the death drive.[14] Stewart's chapter questions whether the theorization of the life drive can be transferred from the analysis of the individual trauma of bereavement, to the analysis of such an overwhelming historical trauma as the Holocaust.[15]

Moving forward in time, Stephenie Young's essay explores the themes of testimony and violence in relation to *Calling the Ghosts* (1997), a film which explores the lives of two female survivors of the Omarska camp in Bosnia. Young's essay draws attention to a film which is not yet widely known or read, but which deserves greater attention, especially in the field of trauma theory. The film comprises an important act of testimony, not only on the subject matter of rape in Bosnia, highlighting the previously unacknowledged presence of female prisoners in the camps, and particularly at Omarska, but also in its reflections on the nature of testimony itself. In its self-reflexive nature, *Calling the Ghosts* recalls Lanzmann's *Shoah* (1985), and Young's analysis of the film draws on Lanzmann's notion of blindness, or the refusal of understanding, in relation to his own role as filmmaker.[16] However, where Lanzmann has been criticized as an interviewer of survivors for pushing his witnesses to a point of breakdown,[17] Young's analysis of *Calling the Ghosts* reveals the sensitivity of the filmmakers to their subject(s) and suggests a new point of departure for testimonial filmmaking. The inextricability of language and the body at the opening of *Calling the Ghosts* anticipates Cowie's essay on *Hiroshima Mon Amour* and gestures, in the creative interplay between the voiceover and the camera's self-conscious engagement with the body, towards a means of transmitting the impact of trauma which does not involve the survivor's re-enactment or reliving of the (unlived) event.

Young's essay comprises a close analysis of the opening sequence of *Calling the Ghosts*, which is concerned to position the survivor in relation to the viewer, through the movements of the camera. In the 'water sequence' at the beginning of the film, the camera traces the movements of the female survivor, Jadranka, as she enters the sea and begins to swim. The camera is positioned and repositioned in relation to Jadranka's movements, in a creative and playful act of departure and return, which explores the possibilities of identification and the limits of understanding. Young analyses the playful interaction between the movements of the camera and the words of Jadranka on the voiceover of the film, which speak of the simultaneous danger and necessity of testifying. The creative act of the filmmaker is demonstrated in Young's analysis to lie precisely in the game of 'here' and 'there', departure and return, which is revealed by Caruth to lie at the heart of Freud's theorization of trauma.

For both Stewart and Young, the act of testimony raises important questions about the nature of its own address. Both Delbo's writing and *Calling the Ghosts* meditate on the identity of the addressee.[18] The testimonies also raise suggestions about the ways in which we conceptualize the act of testimony, complicating the temporal dimension of before/after, exploring the spatial dimension of inside/outside,[19] and questioning the possibilities of the linguistic dimension of silence/speech. Throughout the section, the essays seek, through the analysis of testimony and violence, to negotiate the relation between the death drive and the life drive, and to explore the connections between individual trauma and a broader, historical experience of trauma. The essays in the next section are concerned to develop the theorization of the cultural assimilation and memorialization of the past, and reflect an emergent interest within the academy in the area of cultural memory.

III

Pierre Nora's essay 'Between Memory and History: *Les Lieux de Mémoire*' begins with the concept of a 'rupture of equilibrium', a turning point in the history of a culture 'where consciousness of a break with the past is bound up with the sense that memory has been torn'.[20] This tearing, according to Nora, occurs in such a way that the embodiment of memory attaches to sites (*lieux*) where a sense of historical continuity persists: the very concept of *lieux de mémoire* is thus borne of a breach of one mode of temporal organization, memory, by another, history. *Lieux de mémoire* exist in a secular culture to satisfy the vestigial remnants of the auratic, sacralizing gestures of memory (they are both material and symbolic), moreover 'all are objects *mises en abîme*'.[21] Although Nora's model of memory being culturally superseded by history has been criticized for its aridly linear conception of temporal relations,[22] his invocation of *lieux* as 'mixed, hybrid, mutant, bound intimately with life and death, with time and eternity ... the sacred and the profane'[23] offers fruitful dialectical possibilities. And, in this regard, his investigation of the 'realms of memory' out of which a modern national identity has been shaped in France serves as a way of introducing the question of 'the periodicity of a nation' investigated by the three contributions in this section.

John Frow's essay departs from Nora by emphasizing discontinuities in the historical time of the nation. It focuses on the multiple histories of the site of Port Arthur in Tasmania, established in the nineteenth century by the British as a penal settlement. Frow's interest in the relationship between memory and inscription[24] in the history of institutionalized punishment in a colonial context is pursued alongside a reading of Franz Kafka's story, 'In the Penal Settlement'. Port Arthur is shown to embody the contested, fissured character of its memorializing which is disciplinary in that it both tells the story of punishment and frames different imperatives which make that story. Rather than seeing spontaneous 'lived' memory of the kind that Nora associates with archaic cultures as being superseded by the more organized, modern making of historical memory around the site, Frow's account details the necessarily dialectical nature of the disciplining of this 'disciplinary' arena and the complex of functions that are demanded of it. His essay is a critique of an impoverished historicism which would seek to 'preserve decay' or to immunize the past against itself (a temporal impossibility of the kind with which several essays in the volume are intrigued). Through an analysis of the debate about whether and how to keep Port Arthur as an aesthetic ruin, and whether the ruins of the penitentiary can both retain and criticize the site's disciplinary past, Frow provides an enriched sense of the workings of cultural memory in which the heterogeneity of the past is to be understood as resistant to singularization and monumentalization. For Frow, the study of memorializing must account for forgetting and the resistances within and between periodicities of remembrance.

The other two essays in this section also invite attention to the subversion of normative models of historical understanding in the figuring of national pasts. Robin Fiddian uses Michel de Certeau's critique of historiography – with its emphasis on the need to challenge the artificial division between fiction and history and to admit psychoanalysis into history – to explore a novel by the contemporary Mexican author, Ignacio Solares, concerning Francisco I. Madero, a leading figure in the history of the Mexican Revolution. For Fiddian, Solares's fidelity to Madero's interest in ghosts, spirituality and the paranormal demonstrates the possibility of an enriched sense of history which arises through its integration of psychoanalysis and in this respect his essay looks forward to Rachel Carroll's reading of Angela Carter's fiction later in the volume.[25] The final essay in this section, by Christopher J. Colvin, analyses a therapeutic ethic which he sees at the heart of the Truth and Reconciliation Commission in South Africa. Colvin's account of the desire on the part of the ANC to have the recent history of South Africa shaped by memory may be seen in productive comparison with John Frow's account of resistances which have emerged in the shaping of the past in another colonial society. Colvin's analysis draws attention to the explicit and implicit comparison of apartheid to the Holocaust by the ANC, and its goal – in the excavation of repression and terror under apartheid – of a 'fully citable past' in contrast to the contextual, historicist perspective of the National Party submission. His essay communicates a sense of the precariousness of a project which on the one hand seeks to place the memory of victims of apartheid at the centre of the historical imagination of the new South Africa and on the other to endeavour to 'transmute' trauma into narrative, to separate past and present.

IV

The essays in the final section are grouped around the Freudian concept of *Nachträglichkeit*[26] (translated by Jean Laplanche as 'afterwardsness'),[27] which has proved to be a useful concept for those seeking to rethink the relation between memory and trauma, and to construct models of historical temporality which depart from the strictly linear. The theorization of *Nachträglichkeit* has itself exemplified the problem of 'afterwardsness', the concept having assumed significance largely through the French rereading and translation of Freud, and it is associated with such key figures in French psychoanalytical thought as Lacan, Laplanche and Pontalis.[28] Arguably the most important text in defining the concept of *Nachträglichkeit* is Laplanche's 'Notes on Afterwardsness', and it is on Laplanche's analysis that the following discussion of the term is based.

Laplanche argues that *Nachträglichkeit* describes a complex and ambiguous temporal trajectory. Strachey's English translation of Freud renders *Nachträglichkeit* as 'deferred action', thereby establishing a temporality which refers from the past to the present, in a model of progression. A deposit within the individual acts belatedly, so that that which comes before determines that which comes after.[29] However, other translations of the term have suggested an alternative temporality, based on retroactivity. Helmut Thomä has translated *Nachträglichkeit* as 'retrospective attribution':[30] his model refers back from the present to the past, so that while events may be registered a first time, they are only later given a retroactive significance. In order to clarify the distinction between the two temporalities, Laplanche draws on Freud's illustration of the concept of *Nachträglichkeit*.[31] A young man, talking of the attractive woman who had acted as his wetnurse when he was a child, regrets that he did not make better use of his opportunity. In a deterministic interpretation of this scene, traces of infantile sexuality awaken the adult sexuality of the man at the thought of the infant at the breast, so that the childhood deposit produces a belated affect. In a retroactive interpretation, however, the young man, thinking of the suckling child, retrospectively reinterprets the function and significance of breastfeeding, according to his adult interests and concerns.

Laplanche is concerned that both of the suggested translations of the term *Nachträglichkeit* not only act to translate, but also to interpret, the concept.[32]

Laplanche therefore suggests 'afterwardsness' as a more adequate translation, inasmuch as it captures the ambiguity and complexity of a temporal trajectory, which combines a progressive and a retrogressive momentum. Laplanche's reworking of the term *Nachträglichkeit* has generated a dynamic concept for recent writing on the refiguring of memory and temporality. Writing in 1992, Sue Vice described *Nachträglichkeit* as 'a literarily promising concept': her comment referred directly to Peter Nicholls's innovative reading of Toni Morrison's novels *Beloved* (1987) and *Jazz* (1992).[33] Another highly influential demonstration of the literary potential of the term was provided by Jacqueline Rose, in her reading of Sylvia Plath's 'Daddy' in *The Haunting of Sylvia Plath* (1991).[34] The essays in this section demonstrate the ways in which the potential of the term has been realized not only in the reading of literature, but also in relation to film criticism and cultural theory.

Susannah Radstone combines theories of *Nachträglichkeit* with questions of cultural memory. Addressing the imaginative and psychic investment in the past, Radstone indicates how these issues are not confined to the theoretical sphere, but entail a wider cultural resonance. Exploring the emergence of trauma theories within the humanities, Radstone argues that, while there are disciplinary and theoretical arguments which can partially account for the current popularity of these theories within academia, their dominance can also be linked to a broader psycho-political context and symptomatology. Radstone proposes that the rise of trauma theories within the academy can be explained by their consonance with certain postmodern conceptualizations of history; however, she also engages with broader cultural questions, arguing that contemporary postmodern culture represents a fragmented and uncontaining psycho-political context, which inhibits our capacity to assimilate the past.

Nachträglichkeit represents for Radstone an enlivening act of revision, which is able to transform an inert, traumatic past, and is central to our ability to assimilate recent events. A psychoanalytic understanding of the temporalities of memory, based on *Nachträglichkeit*, is thus distinguished from approaches to trauma founded in psychiatric models, which ignore the role of fantasy in relation to memory, and draw on survivor culture, and its attendant emphases on the fully knowable past, and the implantation of false memory. Radstone's reading of *Forrest Gump* (1994) demonstrates that much mainstream criticism of the film was based in the psychiatric model of trauma, in critics' belief in the film's capacity to implant in its audiences false memories of recent American history. Radstone's own reading of the film is based in the concept of *Nachträglichkeit*. Arguing for the latency of cultural memory, Radstone regards the film as providing a point of identification (in the figure of Forrest

Gump), through which its audiences can begin to work through the recent past. Theories of *Nachträglichkeit* transform the significance of the film, so that it engages its viewers in an act of psychical revision, through which the recent traumas of American culture may be revisited and assimilated.[35]

Radstone's discussion of the relation between film and the temporalities of memory establishes a theoretical model, in which the cinematic representation of the past can allow a deferred act of psychical revision to occur. This notion is elaborated in Elizabeth Cowie's analysis of the film *War Neuroses* (1918), a medical documentary which traces the treatment of 'shell-shocked' soldiers in two British military hospitals in 1917 and 1918. Cowie's reading of the film emphasizes the dual and contradictory nature of *Nachträglichkeit*, which radically disrupts the possibility of a fixed or determinate meaning. In the coda to the film, a group of medically treated soldiers re-enact trench warfare. On the one hand, the soldiers' performance enacts a demonstration of successful soldiering, so that the scene signifies a retroactive mastery of the past. On the other hand, the soldiers re-enact the scene of their trauma; in this reading, the film stages the belated emergence of the past, and emphasizes the symptom, rather than the cure. Cinematic representations of the traumatic past engage the ambiguous temporality of *Nachträglichkeit*, so that the after-effects of trauma are uncertainly suspended between remembrance and repetition.

Cowie's reading of *Hiroshima mon amour* (1959) engages not only with Laplanche's reworking of the temporality of *Nachträglichkeit*, but also with his interests in the inter-subjective nature of trauma and the concept of translation. Laplanche's reading of Freud's illustration of *Nachträglichkeit* emphasizes the presence of the wetnurse in Freud's scenario, as a desiring subject. Trauma arises as the suckling child perceives the nurse's desire as an enigmatic message, which he is unable to fully interpret, and to which he will subsequently return, in a complex process of detranslation and retranslation. Trauma is thus not connected to the nature of an event, but to the subject's way of knowing or registering that event. Laplanche also reintroduces into the theorization of trauma the inter-subjective relations of desire. Cowie's reading of *Hiroshima mon amour* centres on the problematic relation between the woman's individual trauma of the loss of her German lover in Nevers, and the cultural trauma of the bombing of Hiroshima. The representation of trauma in the film is overlaid by two love affairs: the woman's past relationship with the German soldier in Nevers, and her present relationship with the Japanese man in Hiroshima. Cowie argues that the film resonates with Laplanche's understanding of *Nachträglichkeit*, both in its imbrication of trauma in the inter-subjective realm of desire, and in its exploration of the traumas of Hiroshima and Nevers, not as events which are comparable in nature, but as events which cannot be fully known or registered by the subject, and which therefore set in motion complex processes of revision and retranslation. Cowie's analysis of the film in terms of *Nachträglichkeit* complements Radstone's, in its emphasis on the cinematic staging of a gap between seeing and knowing, which provides the film's audiences with a crucial point of identification, through which they are able to begin to address and work through the traumatic events of the recent past.[36]

Radstone's interest in the postmodern is elaborated in the final chapter of the collection, Rachel Carroll's analysis of the relation between the modern and the postmodern in terms of *Nachträglichkeit*. Carroll argues that current discourse on the relation between the modern and the postmodern is caught in a conceptual *impasse*, which corresponds with Laplanche's analysis of the problems of translating the term *Nachträglichkeit*. The relation between the modern and the postmodern is either viewed in terms of determinism (for the modernist, the modern is the originating cause of the postmodern), or in retrospective terms (for the postmodernist, the anticipatory signs of the postmodern in modernism legitimize the concept in the present). Carroll proposes Laplanche's concept of 'afterwardsness' as a possible solution to this *impasse*: the complex temporality which Laplanche's translation embraces avoids either an appeal to a notion of authentic origin, whose loss is to be endlessly mourned, or a retrospective projection in which the past is interminably re-enacted. Carroll figures the relation between the modern and the postmodern in terms of *Nachträglichkeit*: the modernist shock of the new is seen as analogous to the Lacanian missed encounter with the real, so that it is only in traumatized repetition that the encounter can be registered. The chapter challenges the standard view that the 'grand narratives' of modernism gave way to the fragmented forms of postmodern culture, by suggesting a more complex temporal relation between modernism and postmodernism, in which the key texts of modernism contain an unresolved element, so that postmodern gestures of recovery and return can be theorized as a form of deferred revision.

Carroll's reading of Angela Carter's *Nights at the Circus* (1985) analyses the text in relation to the complex temporality of *Nachträglichkeit*. Carroll argues that readings of *Nights at the Circus* which explore the text either as a representation of the birth of the modern age, or as an exemplary postmodern text, focus on the novel's representation of history, and conclude that Carter is concerned with a forgetting or repressing of the past. Carroll's analysis of *Nights at the Circus* suggests that the interest of the novel may lie not so much in its representation of history, as in the complex temporality which it enacts. The return to the past which the novel portrays does not represent a regressive or nostalgic gesture, but is a transformative preparation, and a gathering of energies, for a departure into the future. Carroll's elucidation of the narrative trajectory of *Nights at the Circus* is once more suggestive of the literary potential for the concept of 'afterwardsness': the novel looks backwards, but explodes the possibility for fixation on the past inherent to retrospective attribution; the movement forwards of the novel does not represent the deferred action of trauma, but a truly revolutionary projection into the future.[37] A reading of *Nights at the Circus* in terms of *Nachträglichkeit* transforms the significance of the novel's relations to the past, so that it is no longer read as a travestied representation of history, but becomes a vehicle through which an ethical encounter with the otherness of the past may be thought.

Carroll's chapter closes the volume on a flight of prose, in which the character of Fevvers morphs into Benjamin's 'Angel of History',[38] a figure which embodies a double temporal trajectory, in facing the devastation of the past, while being projected into the future. Carter's novel represents a suitable conclusion to the collection, for the narrative does not close, but ends on the threshold of the turn of the nineteenth century. Our own collection has been written at the 'cusp' or 'hinge' of the twentieth century, and the double trajectory of Benjamin's Angel of History seems an appropriate figure for the turn of the millennium.[39] At such an imaginatively and psychically invested (some would argue, overdetermined) historical juncture, the writing in this volume explores theorizations of the temporalities of history and memory, across the disciplinary boundaries of post-Marxism, trauma theory, cultural memory and psychoanalysis. Like Benjamin's Angel of History, the essays enact a double trajectory, in seeking to think through new, ethical relations to history and the past, and to explore the ways in which the reconstructions of the past are able to project into and shape the future.

Notes

1 Gillian Rose, *Mourning Becomes the Law: Philosophy and Representation* (Cambridge: Cambridge University Press, 1996), p. 9. The editors are grateful to Simon Jarvis for pointing out that the phrase 'Both are torn halves of an integral freedom, to which however they do not add up' is initially Adorno's (see Adorno's letter to Benjamin of 18 March 1936 in *Aesthetics and Politics*, Afterword Fredric Jameson [1977; London: Verso, 1980], p. 123).
2 Pierre Nora, 'Entre Mémoire et Histoire: La problématique des lieux' (1984), in *Les Lieux de Mémoire*, ed. Pierre Nora, 3 vols (Paris: Éditions Gallimard, 1997), i, pp. 23–43. This essay has been translated by Marc Roudebush under the title 'Between Memory and History:

Les Lieux de Mémoire' in *Representations* 26 (1989), pp. 7–25, and as 'General Introduction: Between Memory and History', in *Realms of Memory: rethinking the French past*, under the direction of Pierre Nora, English-Language Edition edited and with a foreword by Lawrence D. Kritzman, trans. Arthur Goldhammer, 3 vols (New York: Columbia University Press, 1996–8), i, pp. 1–23. Citations here are from Roudebush's translation.

3   For a critical account of historicism, see Paul Hamilton, *Historicism* (London: Routledge, 1996). For a sceptical view of the ascendance of memory in current literary and cultural studies, see Kerwin Lee Klein, 'On the Emergence of *Memory* in Historical Discourse', *Representations* 69 (Winter 2000), pp. 127–50.

4   On the relation of memory to postmodernity, see Andreas Huyssen's excellent 'Monument and Memory in a Postmodern Age', in *The Art of Memory: Holocaust Memorials in History*, ed. James T. Young (Munich: Prestel-Verlag, 1994), pp. 9–17. For a recent situating of trauma theory, see Mary Jacobus, Preface, 'Trauma and Psychoanalysis' Special Issue, *Diacritics* 28:4 (Winter 1998), pp. 3–4.

5   For a rethinking of materialism in the Italian Marxist tradition, see Sebastiano Timpanaro, *On Materialism*, trans. Lawrence Garner (London: NLB, 1975).

6   Rose, p. 10.

7   See de Man's exchange with Neil Hertz in the discussion following his lecture on Benjamin in Paul de Man, 'Conclusions: Walter Benjamin's "The Task of the Translator"', *The Resistance to Theory*, Foreword Wlad Godzich (Minneapolis: University of Minnesota Press, 1986), pp. 95–7.

8   Shoshana Felman has explicitly acknowledged her debt to de Man's work in her essay 'After the Apocalypse: Paul de Man and the Fall to Silence', in Shoshana Felman and Dori Laub, *Testimony: Crises of Witnessing in Literature, Psychoanalysis and History* (New York: Routledge, 1992), pp. 121–64. See also Shoshana Felman, 'Postal Survival: The Question of the Navel', *Yale French Studies* 69 (1985) pp. 49–72. De Man is a felt presence throughout Caruth's writing, and she explicitly engages with his work in her essay on falling, see Cathy Caruth, 'The Falling Body and the Impact of Reference', *Unclaimed Experience: Trauma, Narrative, and History* (Baltimore: Johns Hopkins University Press, 1996), pp. 73–90. Felman is particularly interested in de Man's writing on Rousseau and the nature of confession, while Caruth's work on memory and temporality is informed by de Man's writing on Wordsworth.

9   Cathy Caruth, *Trauma: Explorations in Memory* (Baltimore: Johns Hopkins University Press, 1995), p. 5.

10   Cathy Caruth, 'Traumatic Departures: Survival and History in Freud', *Unclaimed Experience*, pp. 57–72.

11   Caruth explains that the exchange comprises part of a testimonial video archive, established by Bernadette in her work with traumatized children who had witnessed violence.

12   Caruth's emphasis on clothing, and particularly on Greg's shirt, resonates with de Man's analysis of the shirt of Nessus in 'Autobiography As De-Facement', *The Rhetoric of Romanticism* (New York: Columbia University Press, 1984), p. 80. De Man's essay comprises a reading of Wordsworth's *Essays upon Epitaphs*, a text which is precisely concerned to analyse 'parting words' (see *The Prose Works of William Wordsworth*, Vol. II, eds W.J.B. Owen and J.W. Smyser [Oxford: Clarendon Press, 1974], pp. 45–122). In the third of his *Essays*, Wordsworth argues that the language of epitaphs should unite reason and passion, and should act as an 'incarnation' of thought, rather than as 'clothing' for it (p. 84). Wordsworth underlines his negative association of language with clothing by asserting

that if language is a mere clothing for thought, it acts as a 'poisoned vestment' (p. 84). Wordsworth has in mind here a garment such as the shirt of Nessus, which was given to Hercules by his wife as a token of love, but which represented a murderous gift (see Sophocles, *Trachiniae*). De Man deconstructs Wordsworth's opposition of body and clothing, pointing out that all language is figurative (clothing). De Man concludes his essay by defining death, not as a deprivation of life, but as a 'linguistic predicament': death is the loss of 'the shape and sense of the world', and if language is able to perform a restorative function, this is always combined for de Man with its power to deprive and disfigure (p. 81). Caruth is interested in death as a 'linguistic predicament' for those who have survived, and it is for her precisely the figurability of language (language as 'clothing'), which restores the function of autobiography: through his playful positioning and repositioning of the shirt (and subsequently the cap), Greg is able to distinguish his own life from Kahlil's death, and to claim his own survival into the future.

13 Charlotte Delbo, *Days and Memory*, trans. Rosette Lamont (Vermont: Marlboro Press, 1990).

14 Stewart quotes Delbo from *Days and Memory* on the operation of deep memory: 'I feel death fasten on me, I feel that I am dying' (p. 3).

15 Debates such as these are central to current work in the area of trauma theory. For an alternative formulation of similar ideas, see Dominick LaCapra on the representation of the Holocaust in terms of 'acting out' and 'working through'. Dominick LaCapra, 'Conclusion: Acting-Out and Working-Through', *Representing the Holocaust: History, Theory, Trauma* (Ithaca: Cornell University Press, 1994), pp. 205–24.

16 See Claude Lanzmann, 'The Obscenity of Understanding: An Evening with Claude Lanzmann', *Trauma: Explorations in Memory*, ed. Cathy Caruth (Baltimore: Johns Hopkins University Press, 1995), pp. 200–20. Lanzmann's refusal of understanding, in relation to the Holocaust, refers to a specific conception of understanding, namely causal explanation. Lanzmann's refusal of understanding is based on a working-through of understanding to its limits, and it is identifiable with, and inseparable from, a creative act. Young is primarily interested in the implications of the refusal of understanding as a creative act, and her essay links to Caruth's writing in its emphasis on a creative act of departure. Lanzmann's emphasis on the 'refusal of understanding' has been challenged in Dominick LaCapra, 'Lanzmann's *Shoah*: "Here There Is No Why"', *Critical Inquiry* 23 (1997), pp. 231–69. LaCapra's essay takes issue, in particular with Felman's writing on *Shoah*. See Shoshana Felman, 'The Return of the Voice: Claude Lanzmann's *Shoah*', in *Testimony: Crises of Witnessing in Literature, Psychoanalysis and History*, pp. 204–83. See Elizabeth Cowie, in chapter 11 of this volume, for an exposition of LaCapra and for an essay which is broadly sympathetic to LaCapra's position.

17 See LaCapra, 'Here There Is No Why', p. 255. LaCapra relates his criticism of Lanzmann's desire for survivors to relive the past to the question of identification. If the survivors act out the trauma in front of the camera, they provide a point of identification for the filmmaker. Young's analysis is sensitive to the limits imposed on identification between filmmaker and survivor by the techniques which are adopted by Jacobson and Jelinic in *Calling the Ghosts*.

18 For Stewart, Delbo's later self encounters her earlier self, and the reader also acts as a proxy witness; for Young, *Calling the Ghosts* mediates between the survivor, the filmmaker and the viewer.

19 In relation to the spatial dimension of inside/outside, compare for example Stewart's analysis of Delbo's imagery of memory as a snake skin, and Young's elaboration of the camera's movements in relation to Jadranka.

20 Nora, 'Between Memory and History', p. 7.
21 Nora, 'Between Memory and History', p. 20.
22 This is an aspect of John Frow's detailed critique of Nora's essay at the opening of his chapter, '*Toute la mémoire du monde*: Repetition and Forgetting', in *Time and Commodity Culture: Essays in Cultural Theory and Postmodernity* (Oxford: Clarendon Press, 1997), pp. 218–46 [pp. 218–23].
23 Nora, 'Between Memory and History', p. 19.
24 The relationship between memory and writing is the main theme of his chapter, '*Toute la mémoire du monde*: Repetition and Forgetting', in *Time and Commodity Culture*, pp. 224ff.
25 On ghosts, see Peter Buse and Andrew Stott, eds, *Ghosts: Deconstruction, Psychoanalysis, History* (Macmillan, 1999).
26 The key Freudian texts in relation to the concept of *Nachträglichkeit* are as follows: Sigmund Freud, *The Interpretation of Dreams*, trans. James Strachey, ed. Angela Richards, Penguin Freud Library 4 (Harmondsworth: Penguin, 1991); Sigmund Freud, 'Analysis of a Phobia in a Five-Year-Old Boy ("Little Hans")', *Case Histories I*, trans. James Strachey, ed. Angela Richards, Penguin Freud Library 8 (Harmondsworth: Penguin, 1977), pp. 167–303; Sigmund Freud, 'From the History of an Infantile Neurosis (The "Wolf Man")', *Case Histories II*, trans. James Strachey, ed. Angela Richards, Penguin Freud Library 9 (Harmondsworth: Penguin, 1991), pp. 227–366.
27 See Jean Laplanche, 'Note on Afterwardsness', in *Essays on Otherness*, ed. John Fletcher, (London: Routledge, 1999), pp. 260–5.
28 See Jacques Lacan, 'The Function and Field of Speech and Language in Psychoanalysis', *Écrits: A Selection*, trans. Alan Sheridan (London: Routledge, 1985), pp. 30–113. Lacan's analysis of the term is largely discussed in terms of Freud's case history of the Wolf Man. See also Jean Laplanche and J.-B. Pontalis, *The Language of Psycho-analysis*, trans. Donald Nicholson-Smith, introd. Daniel Lagache (London: Hogarth Press, 1973) and Jean Laplanche, *Life and Death in Psychoanalysis* (Baltimore: Johns Hopkins University Press, 1970).
29 Laplanche points out that Freud's use of the term *Nachträglichkeit* largely favours such a deterministic model.
30 See Helmut Thomä and Neil Cheshire, 'Freud's *Nachträglichkeit* and Strachey's "Deferred Action": Trauma, Constructions and the Direction of Causality', *International Review of Psychoanalysis* 18 (1991), pp. 407–27. The retroactive model of *Nachträglichkeit* emphasizes the hermeneutic process, or the attribution of meaning and significance to the past.
31 See Freud, *The Interpretation of Dreams*, Penguin edition, p. 295.
32 For Laplanche, this is demonstrated by the fact that the two translations are not interchangeable in usage.
33 Sue Vice, 'Introduction', *Psychoanalytic Criticism: A Reader*, ed. Sue Vice (Cambridge: Polity, 1996), p. 4. Nicholls's essay was especially commisioned for Vice's volume. See Peter Nicholls, 'The Belated Postmodern: History, Phantoms and Toni Morrison', in Vice, pp. 50–67.
34 Jacqueline Rose, 'Daddy', *The Haunting of Sylvia Plath* (London: Virago, 1991), pp. 205–38.
35 Examples of recent traumas which are addressed in *Forrest Gump* include the Vietnam conflict, the Kennedy assassination and Watergate.
36 Compare Cowie's analysis of the opening shots of *Hiroshima mon amour* with Radstone's interest in the gap between seeing (the filmed representation of the past, often based on

contemporary footage of events) and knowing (Forrest's subjective viewpoint) in relation to *Forrest Gump*.

37 Carroll argues that the double trajectory of *Nachträglichkeit* is figured in *Nights at the Circus* by the motif of the train, which, on the one hand, inaugurates a seemingly irresistible forward momentum, as a symbol of modernity and progress, but, on the other hand, becomes associated with the traumatic return to and re-enactment of the past in the train crash, which resonates with Freud's description of trauma in *Moses and Monotheism*. Carroll's discussion of the significance of the train in *Nights at the Circus* alludes to Caruth's analysis of *Moses and Monotheism* in 'Introduction', *Unclaimed Experience*, pp. 3–12.

38 Walter Benjamin, 'Theses on the Philosophy of History', *Illuminations*, trans. Harry Zohn (London: Fontana, 1992), p. 249.

39 For example, the marking of the millennium in South Africa represents an interesting coda to Colvin's analysis of the representation of the trauma of apartheid in South Africa, in the work of the Truth and Reconciliation Commission. Mandela returned to his cell on Robben Island, and lit a candle in the window of the cell, at once a light of remembrance for the devastation of the past, and a projection of hope into the future.

PART I
HISTORY IN THEORY:
AFTER MARX AND FREUD

1 Old Idolatry: Rethinking 'Ideology' and 'Materialism'

SIMON JARVIS

Wordsworth's 'poem to Coleridge' ends with a figure drawn from sacred history. The two friends are compared to 'Prophets of Nature' who, even though the age may 'fall back to old idolatry', will jointly build a lasting inspiration able to counteract such idol-worship.[1] In this essay I want to examine the intimate connection between this notion of 'idolatry' and a concept in more current use, that of 'ideology'. In what follows I examine certain central problems in the theory of ideology, and try to show how they are illuminated by a study of the connection between 'ideology' and 'idolatry'. In particular I argue that the opposition between 'ideology' and 'materialism' may be misleading in so far as it is premised upon a materialism conceived of as absolute disenchantment. This is because, despite the ways in which it is often understood, ideology is itself a form of disenchantment.

I

The opening lines of *The German Ideology* have often been quoted, but they have sometimes been read too quickly:

> Until now human beings have always formed false ideas about themselves, and about what they are or should be. They have ordered their own relations according to their ideas of God, of normal human beings, etc. The progeny of their heads have got out of control. They, the creators, have bowed down before their own creations. Let us free them from the chimeras, the ideas, the dogmas, the insane imaginations under whose yoke they are wasting away. Let us rebel against this dominion of thoughts. Let us teach them to exchange these imaginations for thoughts which correspond to the essence of humanity, says one; to conduct themselves critically towards them, says another; to get them out of their heads, says another, and – existing actuality will collapse.
>
> These innocent and childish fantasies form the core of recent young-Hegelian philosophy, which is not only received by the German public with horror and

21

awe, but which is also proclaimed by the *philosophical heroes* themselves with a solemn consciousness of its world-shattering danger and criminal ruthlessness. The first volume of this publication aims to unmask these sheep in wolves' clothing ...[2]

'They, the creators, have bowed down before their own creations.' This sounds rather like what is often taken to be Marx's own view. Human beings misrecognize their own products as though they had an autonomous life of their own. They worship as 'natural' social relations which they themselves have produced. But here, of course, the words are a quotation. They offer, not Marx's views, but those of the thinkers who are to be 'unmasked' in the coming text as the German ideologists: the German successors to the French ideologists led by Destutt de Tracy. Marx sees these ideologists not as idol-worshippers but as idol-breakers; but idol-breaking is *itself* to be unmasked as a form of superstition. The idol-breaker is superstitious in so far as he thinks that breaking the idol will dispel the worship of it. He superstitiously attributes to the idol a real power over its worshippers. Just so, for Marx, the ideologists – Feuerbach, Bauer, Max Stirner – are in fact, to borrow an expression from the French scholar Patrick Tort, ideolators.[3] In so far as they think that breaking the *ideas* of transcendence will produce demystified social relations, they superstitiously attribute to those ideas a power of their own, a kind of power which in truth belongs, for Marx, only to living human individuals.

Marx uses the term 'ideology' in an equivocal sense in this text. He goes on to apply the concept very widely, as a figure for systematic social illusion. Yet at the same time readers are not to forget what the term meant to its inventor, Destutt de Tracy: 'the science of ideas'. This doubleness, I want to suggest, is quite deliberate; it is part of the essentially comic mode of *The German Ideology*. We are jolted into a realization that social illusion repeatedly takes the form, not of simple mystification, but of *disenchantment as mystification*. This can be illustrated by a use of the term 'ideologists' which crops up later in Marx's text: 'The division of labour only becomes truly a division from the moment when a division of mental and material labour appears. [Marginal observation:] The first form of ideologists, *priests*, is concurrent.'[4] Marx's reference to '[t]he first form of ideologists, *priests*' sounds rather unsurprising if we simply take ideology to mean 'mystification'. When we remember that Marx has at no stage explicitly distinguished his use of the term 'ideology' from de Tracy's, it becomes more startling. The comparison of priests to ideologists is a deliberate contrast in registers. The 'scientists' of ideas are compared to a priesthood, superstitious in the powers which they attribute to the ideas whose hold they intend to break. Yet the priest, conversely, is compared to a scientist of ideas. His monopoly on ideas is achieved not through mystification alone, but through mystifying *de*mystification: as, for example, when priests provide supernatural *explanations* for natural phenomena. Thus is illustrated what becomes for Marx the central point, that it is not mystifying *theories* that cause systematic social illusion. 'Demystification', then, may not dissolve such illusion; indeed, 'demystification' may very easily be the preferred activity of its beneficiaries.

The idea that ideology is disenchantment is not a result produced merely by a passing reading of this single text. We can see it at work in so central a passage of *Capital* as the discussion of 'the fetishism of the commodity and its secret'.[5] The way in which illusions arise from disenchantment is well illustrated in the analysis of the actions of partners in commodity exchange. At first sight, there could hardly be a less undeceived form of action. It is no part of Marx's analysis here to show that partners in exchange are acting in the service of, say, illusory higher values. Rather they are acting in the most disabused way known to them: a calculation of their own best interests. The point of the analysis is to show how what Marx thinks of as the central illusion of capitalist society – the apparent naturalness and self-determiningness of social relations and 'laws' of the market, etc. – is produced, not by a fidelity to mystifying higher values, but by the most disenchanted behaviour available. Through this behaviour relations between people come to appear as though they were properties of things. The chapter is trying to explain how it happens that human beings can live in the grip of a particular systematic social illusion, an illusion which not only appears dismayingly resistant to mass disenchantment, but which operates by means of that disenchantment. It is then central to *Capital* to undertake the aporetic task of disenchanting us about our veneration for disenchantment.

As with so many other central motifs of Marx's thought, it has been the unfortunate fate of 'ideology' to be taken for a technical term in the imaginary pseudo-science of 'Marxism'. Of course it is true to say that Marx uses the term in a much wider set of contexts than, say, de Tracy. He does this, not because he has invented a new meaning for the word, which would henceforth have some esoterically 'Marxist' signification, but as a continual corrective: wherever we would be tempted to set *our* scientists against *their* priesthood, *our* secular reason against *their* superstition, the very use of the word 'ideology' as a name for social illusion reminds us that this is, precisely, the kind of illusion that cannot be obviated by having the right opinions. The name 'ideology' keeps reminding us that escaping from social illusion can never be merely a matter of specifying the correct method for thinking – including

Marx's own materialist 'method'. This does not mean that Marx does not think that his own account is true; it means that the truth of his account would not of itself suffice to dispel social illusion.

Two important consequences follow from this. Firstly, what passes today for 'ideology-critique' is what Marx understood as 'ideology'. Feuerbach was *already* undertaking what is now called 'ideology-critique'. Secondly, straight oppositions between 'science' and 'ideology', or between 'materialism' and 'ideology' are necessarily misconceived, because it is not the truth or falsity of ideas that decides whether they form part of 'ideology', but their relation to monopolies over whatever is needed for life.

This is much more than a merely pedantic point. It concerns, for example, the whole way in which the historicist criticism of aesthetic artefacts is understood as salutary demystification. If it is the case that ideology is itself a form of demystification, but a mystifying one, then scepticism is called for about the emancipatory effects of an assault on ideas of the beautiful. The critique of the 'ideology of the aesthetic' is ideology no less than Feuerbach's critique of religion. Marx sees that the ruthless critics of religion and their horrified opponents in the Germany of the 1840s actually live rather contentedly together. The idol-worshippers resist the idol-breakers, but console themselves that they are at least in possession of something which is thought to be worth smashing up. The comic mode of *The German Ideology* is essential to it, not a rhetorical ornament. It is not disgraceful criminals who are here to be unmasked, but sheep in wolves' clothing.

For this reason it could not be my hope here to unveil (yet another) recipe for final disenchantment; to say, as though it had not been said sufficiently, and indeed tediously, often that critics ought to stop being like Feuerbach and start being like Marx. As it happens, I think neither that Marx ever solved the problems which he discovered in writing the book, nor that 'ideology' is a rubric under which they can be solved. His use of the term is a cunning lexical warning, but is not usefully thought of as the inaugural term of a special domain of social science. In particular, whenever a materialism, Marxist or otherwise, sets to work to dismantle an ideology, there we have ideology in its classical form. What Marx's text puts its finger on is how he, and we, are caught up in the illusions which are to be dispelled. But as a matter of fact some aspects of Marx's own farewell to philosophy have much in common with ideology in both its de Tracyan and Feuerbachian shapes, as a unilateral farewell to metaphysics. It has been one achievement of a number of different philosophical authorships in this century to have shown how much more difficult it is really to achieve such a farewell than it is to announce it.

In my view, then, the resources provided by the term 'ideology' for thinking about cultural artefacts have been overestimated. The unfortunate idea that the word is a special or technical term has detached it from its long prehistory in patristic and, later, Enlightenment discourse about idolatry. It is useful to reconsider this prehistory when thinking about current applications of the term 'ideology'. The problems addressed in Marx's book are not a special wisdom, but are instead very closely connected to the debate out of which they emerge: the Enlightenment account of the origins and function of 'religion', and its ancestors, the deist attack on revealed religion and, ultimately, the patristic attack on idol-worship. Indeed we could here go back still further to consider, for example, Xenophanes' attack on religious anthropomorphism. This indicates that the problems which Marx raises in *The German Ideology* cannot in fact be detached from a lengthy philosophical and cosmological tradition. They cannot be treated as though they concerned a special offshore zone in which social theorists had been granted a dispensation from considering any excessively obscure difficulties; they are, rather, problems which can *only* be understood if social (or 'human', or 'cultural') 'science' is not too hastily detached from what is called metaphysics. Ideology, now in the guise of 'ideology-critique', continues to perform the manoeuvre for which it was invented: the separation of sciences of society, and later of humanities or human sciences, from 'metaphysics' and, in the end, from philosophy as such. This is a separation which has been profoundly damaging, as well as locally enabling, to the disciplines in question. The next parts of my argument resist this damage in two ways: firstly, by investigating – all too briefly, and, it will be understood, in no sense exhaustively – some of the contours of the link between 'idolatry' and 'ideology'; secondly, by reconsidering the relationship between ideology and disenchantment in the work of two leading ideologists, ideologists chosen not for the ease with which they can be dispatched but for their acute sensitivity to the difficulties involved.

II

The aporias of ideology and idolatry have a long history. Their fundamental shape emerges early on, with the notion of idolatry itself. Two especially important moments in this *longue durée* are represented by those apparently diametrically opposed book-polities, Augustine's *City of God* and Hobbes's *Leviathan*. The latter offers an especially acute case of what Marx was later to call ideology. In its third book, 'Of a Christian Commonwealth', Hobbes appeals to the notion of idolatry in order to press home his contention that incorporeal substances are chimerical. Hobbes overcomes the difficulty that Scripture seems to refer to such spirits by arguing that there the term is used simply to refer to non-solid substances such as air. These 'aeriall substances' differ from patristic and scholastic notions of incorporeal substance:

> But for those Idols of the brain, which represent Bodies to us, where they are not, as in a Looking-glasse, in a Dream, or to a Distempered brain waking, they are (as the Apostle saith generally of all Idols) nothing; Nothing at all, I say, there where they seem to bee; .... [6]

Spirit, in the sense of incorporeal substance, is expelled from Hobbes's cosmos. But there is a symptomatic redundancy here. If idols are nothing, how are they to be broken? How, indeed, can they be described as 'idols' at all? These difficulties become acute in the final book, 'Of the Kingdome of Darknesse'. Here Hobbes, having explained the necessary laws of political nature, attempts to explain how it has nevertheless come about that these laws have not been recognized as such. The problem, he argues, has been a widespread worship of (nonexistent) idols. An important instance arises towards the end of the book, where Hobbes discusses what he thinks of as the worship of images in the post-apostolic church. He is reluctant to think of this as having resulted from a misunderstanding of Scripture. This would imply that Scripture itself might be dangerously unclear on this point. Instead, image-worship is said to be the result of

> ... not destroying the Images themselves, in the conversion of the Gentiles that worshipped them.
> The cause whereof, was the immoderate esteem, and prices set upon the workmanship of them, which made the owners (though converted, from worshipping them as they had done Religiously for Daemons) to retain them still in their houses, upon pretence of doing it in the honor of *Christ*, of the *Virgin Mary*, and of the *Apostles*, and other the Pastors of the Primitive Church; as being easie, by giving them new names, to make that an Image of the *Virgin Mary*, and of her *Sonne* our Saviour, which before perhaps was called the Image of *Venus*, and *Cupid*; and so of a *Jupiter* to make a *Barnabas*, and of a *Mercury* a *Paul*, and the like.[7]

This powerful story of the survival of the pagan gods conceals an important difficulty, because the apparently sober explanation is not devoid of superstition. The persistence of idolatry is explained from the persistence of the worshipped objects themselves. Because they remain in place, so does idolatry. It is hard to escape the implication that these objects have a power of their own.

Although this implication is most unlikely to have been intended by Hobbes, it is more than an accidental slip. It is the trace of a central problem for his political science. How could irrational misrecognitions of the supposedly self-evident natural laws of politics and religion have become so widespread? Hobbes argues that the true faith of Scripture became corrupted in a number of ways during the patristic period. It was at this time that pagan mythology and pagan philosophy were grafted on to the scriptures. Here Hobbes has recourse to a very un-secular hypothesis indeed: that of demonic interference.

> The Enemy has been here in the Night of our naturall Ignorance, and sown the tares of Spirituall Errors; and that, First, by abusing, and putting out the light of the Scriptures: For we erre, not knowing the Scriptures. Secondly, by introducing the Daemonology of the Heathen Poets, that is to say, their fabulous Doctrine concerning Daemons, which are but Idols, or Phantasms of the braine, without any reall nature of their own, distinct from human fancy; such as are dead mens Ghosts, and Fairies, and other matter of old Wives tales. […][8]

'The Enemy' has been among us: the adulteration of apostolic truth with pagan philosophy and superstition alike is the work of the devil. Indeed, it is the work of presumably demonic *spirits*: 'we come to erre, by *giving heed to seducing Spirits*, and the Daemonology of such *as speak lies in Hypocrisie* …'.[9] The explanation given for our belief in spirits is that spirits have led us to believe in them. The first demonology, that of the Fathers, is supplemented by a second demonology, Hobbes's own.

Patristic philosophizing and early medieval 'idolatry' are thus not in the event given a merely diffusionist explanation, but rather a particular kind of Christian explanation. They are given an explanation which is itself, ultimately, patristic in origin. Unlike Hobbes, the Fathers did not regard the notions of demons and spirits (or the witches or mediums who could raise them) as unscriptural. Their view of pagan religion was not that it lacked access to supernatural powers, but rather that the power which the pagans attributed to their deities was in fact exercised by demons. As Augustine notes in his *City of God*, 'although man was the creator of his gods, he was not, their very maker, any the less possessed by them when he was delivered by his worship into their fellowship; a fellowship, I mean, not with stupid idols, but with wily demons'.[10] It becomes important to understand, both that the power associated with idols is real, and that it is not really exercised by the idols. For this reason scriptural passages in which mediums appeared successfully to raise spirits could become acutely sensitive areas. The Old Testament narrative of the raising of Samuel's spirit at Saul's behest by the 'witch' or rather medium of Endor makes no mention of Satan. The medium is herself implied to have the ability to raise spirits. In patristic exegesis the medium's powers are transferred to Lucifer, who is declared either to have produced the real Samuel or a diabolical illusion of him.[11]

Just as Hobbes's demystification of the patristic demonology leads him into a further demonology of his own, so that patristic demonology itself is founded on a demystification: that of the anthropomorphic 'pagan' deities. (Just so, for Marx, Feuerbach will later superstitiously attribute a power to the ideas he would break.) These correlations are significant, not because they could somehow show that Hobbes's thought is rather like Augustine's or has little new to add on the topic of political illusion, but, instead, just *because* Hobbes was a thinker who set himself so vigorously against patristic and scholastic thought, which he tended to regard as a unified continuum. Seventeenth-century exponents of natural and rational religion played a crucial role in handing over the concept of idolatry invented in patristic theology and exegesis to the 'science' of ideology when it was born. The discourse of idolatry had the outstanding advantage of being both pious and philosophical. It could be turned not merely against obvious targets, such as the Roman church, but also, at need, against more surprising ones; Henry More understood even Calvinism as a form of idolatry. The concept of idolatry is greatly extended, so as to refer not merely to the worship of non-scriptural deities, but also to a wide range of other perceived irrationalities.[12]

An illustration of the very wide range of referents which the concept of idolatry could be made to take is provided by a figure who often found himself in disagreement with Hobbes, Robert Boyle. His *Free Enquiry into the Vulgarly Received Notion of Nature* regarded, for example, the scholastic notion that *Natura est sapientissima* not merely as mistaken but as a form of 'idolatry':

> According to the foregoing hypothesis, I consider the frame of the world already made as a great and, if I may so speak, pregnant automaton, that like a woman with twins in her womb, or a ship furnished with pumps, ordnance, etc. is such an engine as comprises or consists of several lesser engines ... if I mistake not, the looking upon merely corporeal and oftentimes inanimate beings as if they were endowed with life, sense and understanding, and the ascribing to nature and some other beings (whether real or imaginary) things that belong but to God, have been some (if not the chief) of the grand causes of the polytheism and idolatry of the Gentiles ...[13]

Once the demand for a wholly disenchanted concept of nature is imagined as a reproof of idols, it can be represented not merely as a scientific, but also as a theological, imperative. What has taken place is perhaps less a real demystification than the replacement of one set of anthropomorphic imaginations about nature with another, hardly less exotic, mechanical set: the 'pregnant automaton'.

III

What is beginning to come into view is the way in which ideology-critiques, that is, ideologies, as well as their ancestors, the demonologies, must at all turns be intimately connected with much broader ontologies. The attempt to say what an idol or an ideology is, like any attempt to dispel an illusion, always implies an account, whether explicit or not, of what there is. This is why the 'science of ideas', like its descendant, the science of society, risks blocking the exit which it claims to be seeking. The philosophical problems have not been solved, but set aside. They have been suppressed. So they continue to inhabit the supposedly undeceived 'science' of ideas.

One of the most acute instances of these difficulties occurs in the work of Louis Althusser. Althusser was by no means a thinker who was naïve about the kinds of problem set out above. Indeed, his work does much to lay them bare. At the centre of ideology for Althusser is the interpellated 'subject', that is, a compulsory illusion of free agency. '[E]very "subject" endowed with a "consciousness", and believing in the "ideas" that his "consciousness" inspires in him and freely accepts, must "*act* according to his ideas", must therefore inscribe his own ideas as a free subject in the actions of his material practice. If he does not do so, "that is wicked"'.[14] For Althusser the theory of our freedom is the means of our real subjection. Subjectivity, by which he means this subjection, *is* ideology.

The idea that we can get outside illusion is, for Althusser, an essential element of ideology. Yet he naturally wishes to offer an undeceived account of its workings. Hence such formulations as the following:

> those who are in ideology believe themselves by definition outside ideology: one of the effects of ideology is the practical *denegation* of the ideological character of ideology by ideology: ideology never says 'I am ideological'. It is necessary to be outside ideology, i.e. in scientific knowledge, to be able to say: I am in ideology (a quite exceptional case) or (the general case): I was in ideology. As is well known, the accusation of being in ideology applies only to others,

never to oneself (unless one is really a Spinozist or a Marxist, which, in this matter, is to be exactly the same thing). Which amounts to saying that ideology *has no outside* (for itself), but at the same time *that it is nothing but outside* (for science and reality).[15]

The Marxist is distinguished from the Feuerbachian by being able to admit that he is inside ideology, and has no access to a position 'outside' ideology. Yet he is also to be the scientist who is to diagnose ideology not merely as illusory, but as 'nothing but outside'. For science, ideology is nothing real at all. Nevertheless, for us, nothing else is real. The availability of a perspective of 'science' makes Althusser's recognition of our own entanglement in illusion a formality. It is not acknowledged as having consequences for science, but only for the scientist.

The idea that ideology is subjection introduces a key difference from Marx. As the phenomenologist Michel Henry pointed out nearly a quarter of a century ago, in a magnificent study still too little known in the Anglophone world, Marx does not in fact make comfortable reading for anti-individualist social theorists.[16] His hopes are for a noncontractual community of free individuals. This is an unsurprising consequence of his ontology, which is not at all collectivist, but individualist. It is individualist in the specific sense that for Marx the experience of 'living human individuals' is what is real. In one sense there is indeed no such *thing* as 'society' for Marx, because society is not a thing, but the relations between living human individuals. Althusser can be understood as having seen this point. But the exhaustive and literal application which he makes of Marx's ironic and restricted concept of ideology changes everything. At first Althusser acknowledges a distinction between the 'concrete individual' and the 'subject'. This door, however, then swings slowly shut:

> As ideology is eternal, I must now suppress the temporal form in which I have presented the functioning of ideology, and say: ideology has always-already interpellated individuals as subjects, which amounts to making it clear that individuals are always-already interpellated by ideology as subjects, which necessarily leads us to one last proposition: *individuals are always-already subjects.*[17]

The idea that 'ideology is eternal' is an acknowledged divergence from *The German Ideology*.[18] Marx's claim that 'ideology has no history' means that ideology has no history of its own, only that created for it by living human individuals, the ideologists and their predecessors, priests and ideology-critics alike, and those who believe them. It is this divergence which here leads 'science' to speak with the voice of 'ideology'. Individuals *are* always-already subjects. The gulf is crossed as soon as the idea that 'individuals are always-already interpellated by ideology as subjects' is allowed to lead into this emphatic ontological claim, that individuals just are subjects (even though there are, for science, no such things as subjects). The distance taken from Marx's 'positivism' in *The German Ideology* is crucial. What Althusser means by calling Marx 'positivist' there is that Marx thinks he can say something about what these living human individuals are, independently of ideology. The distinction which Marx always keeps open, between suffering-desiring-thinking bodies, on the one hand, and the representations and personifications which such bodies are made to inhabit, on the other, is allowed to close. There is real experience, but not for us.

Althusser's ideology is powerful because it testifies to a real loss of experience. But this closure – individuals *are* always-already subjects – confirms that loss of experience, if not as absolute, then as something whose remedy remains unthinkable, short of *something turning up* in the form of millennial or lucky rescue. The discourse of ideology has been the means by which a series of unresolved philosophical problems has been ruled out of court. In so far as there is really a 'positivism' to be complained of in Marx, it results not from his refusal to regard the idea of real human experience as an 'ideology', but rather from the idea of a unilateral farewell to philosophy; a farewell to which his work in practice only in part aspires, but which, in so far as it does, he shares with the first 'positivist', Auguste Comte. The damage of this fantasized departure is everywhere evident in the widespread assumption that the difficulties associated with such aporetic categories as nature, subjectivity, beauty, goodness and truth can be overcome simply by suppressing, avoiding, or junking those categories – or by subjecting them to 'ideology-critique', that is to say, to ideology.

IV

It should be clear by now that I do not think that this damage can be mended simply by coming up with a better theory of ideology. Rather, the literal and exhaustive application given to that initially comic and restricted concept is itself part of the problem. One of the outstanding strengths of deconstructive reading has been its caginess about the kind of abrupt idol-breaking which I have so far been examining. Deconstructive readers have wanted to distinguish their operations from 'ideology-critique', not because they are uncritical, but because of their caution about the difficulty of saying goodbye to philosophy.

A special interest therefore attaches to the late Paul de Man's late reflections on this subject. De Man understands at once that the motif of 'ideology' can never properly be addressed if it be abruptly detached from philosophy in advance. He chooses, in the essay 'Phenomenality and Materiality in Kant', to approach the motif through the very promising avenue of a reflection upon transcendental thought. He explains the relation between criticism and 'ideologies' (a word which, although he refers briefly to de Tracy, he is using here in its looser twentieth-century sense) through an analogy with the relationship between Kant's critical thought and the metaphysical speculation which it wishes to limit. The point of the analogy is that criticism is interdependent with the ideology which it criticizes. The attempt finally to separate them produces idealism, even where materialism is loudly proclaimed. The effects of any final distinction between science and ideology are equally pronounced on both sides of the equation. Science can no longer account for its own entanglement in ideology ('idealism'); ideology now appears as mere 'error' rather than as a set of illusions occurring for reasons which may not easily be set aside. Unlike simple error, ideology does not disappear just because the mistake is pointed out. In the same way, Kant does not think that the *Critique of Pure Reason* is likely to put an end to reason's metaphysically speculative excursions. These are illusions which are inseparable from human reason itself.[19]

The counterweight to ideology here is provided by de Man's claim to have uncovered what he calls 'Kant's materialism'; and it is here that his argument becomes still more innovative. Its aim, like that of several other pieces in the book, is to detach a more austere Kantian *critique* of aesthetic judgement from the more metaphysically compromised account of aesthetic experience offered by Schiller and numerous points downstream. The reading corrects the assumption that a vast range of what is called 'aesthetic ideology' can rapidly be labelled 'Kantian'. Instead, de Man begins to uncover what he regards as a 'materialism' at work in Kant's 'analytic of the sublime'.[20] There is a materialism, de Man claims, because we arrive in the course of Kant's analytic at a moment when a sheer materiality, devoid of mediation by spirit, is invoked. Indeed de Man argues that it is for Kant essential to the effect produced that 'no mind is involved' at this stage. Kant is arguing that when we find the starry sky sublime it is essential that we do not think of astronomical laws – this would produce only a 'teleological' and hence a non-aesthetic judgement – but must regard it just as we see it:

To find the ocean ... sublime we must regard it merely as poets do, merely by what the eye reveals – if it is at rest, as a clear mirror of water only bounded by the heavens; if it is stormy, as an abyss threatening to overwhelm everything.[21]

It is at this point that de Man turns to a contrast with Wordsworth, the better to illuminate Kant's materialism.

> ... one thinks of the famous passage from 'Tintern Abbey':
>> And I have felt
>> A presence that disturbs me with the joy
>> Of elevated thoughts; a sense sublime
>> Of something far more deeply interfused
>> Whose dwelling is the light of setting suns,
>> And the round ocean and the living air
>> And the blue sky, and in the mind of man: ...
>
> The sublimity of the round ocean, horizon-bound as a vast dome, is especially reminiscent of the Kant passage. But the two invocations of sublime nature soon diverge. Wordsworth's sublime is an instance of the constant exchange between mind and nature, of the chiasmic transfer of properties between the sensory and intellectual world that characterizes his figural diction, here explicitly thematized in the 'motion and spirit that impels/ All thinking things, all objects of all thoughts/ And rolls through all things.' No mind is involved in the Kantian vision of ocean and heaven. To the extent that any mind, that any judgement, intervenes, it is in error – for it is not the case that heaven is a vault or that the horizon bounds the ocean like the walls of a building.[22]

In one sense de Man is right to say that '[n]o mind is involved in the Kantian vision of ocean and heaven'. The vision must not be submitted to a concept of any particular purpose, otherwise it could provoke only a teleological judgement, never a judgement of taste. In order to work, the claim would need to exclude 'reason' from 'mind'. Kant is working here with an architectonic parallel and distinction between the feeling associated with judgements of the beautiful and that associated with judgements of the sublime. The former are associated with a presentation which provokes the harmonious play of the faculties – imagination and understanding – necessary for cognition. The latter, on the other hand, are associated with the attempt and failure of imagination to provide an intuition adequate to *reason* (in the case of the 'mathematical' sublime, pure reason in its theoretical application, in the case of the 'dynamic' sublime, pure reason in its practical application). Our attempt and failure to imagine God is an instance of the imagination's sublime failure to provide an intuition adequate to reason. Sheer *Augenschein*, what appears to be the eye, as invoked by de Man, can never for Kant provoke the feeling which is associated with the judgement of the sublime unless it provoke this sublime failure, whose value is that it is a failure which *reinforces* our sense, precisely of 'mind': '*Sublime is what even to be able to think proves that the mind has a power surpassing any standard of sense*'.[23] So that while mind in the sense of understanding may not be present when we look at the ocean as the poet does in order to be sublime, reason certainly is.

What is important to me here, however, is less the accuracy or otherwise of de Man's reading of Kant, than what is here imagined to be characteristic of 'materialism'. Materialism is seen as what we get when a pure appearance to the eye in whose appearance 'no mind is involved' is invoked. In order to arrive at materialism, we are to delete any mediation of sheer *Augenschein* by our consciousness or by affectivity. On these criteria, Wordsworth's passage could not qualify because it thinks of 'the round ocean' as a 'dwelling'. Materialism is made to depend upon the dispelling of anthropomorphic illusions, pathetic fallacies, about what we see. Materialism, in other words, is a perfected disenchantment.

This is a curious terminus for a thinking so alert to the difficulties of separating the figurative from the literal as de Man's is to have arrived at. For the demand that the materialist may not think of the earth, for example, as a dwelling, but must think of it, instead, as data, has as one of its implications the purging of figures from the materialist's literal language: a 'materiality of the letter' which is held to be '[t]he bottom line, in Kant as well as in Hegel'.[24] As soon as Wordsworth thinks of ocean, air and sky as a 'dwelling' for anything, the literal *Augenschein* receives an idealizing figurative addition. The difficulties of such an approach can be seen if we return to the Kantian passage which de Man sets against Wordsworth. Is it really only the 'eye' and nothing else which 'reveals' the ocean 'as a clear *mirror* of water'? As 'an abyss *threatening* to overwhelm everything'? Are these not themselves already ways of *understanding* the ocean, through a language whose figures and concepts cannot but be contaminated with human experience?

V

If Marx is right to understand *ideology* as a form of disenchantment, there may be a difficulty in understanding materialism and ideology as necessarily opposed polarities. It is often just where materialism is most zealously and literally pursued that its involuntary kinship with idealism is most in evidence.

Two points are especially striking here. Firstly, the rise of what might be called materialism-without-nature. Boyle's assault on the vulgarly received conception of nature as idolatrous has cast a long shadow over subsequent materialisms. Any idea of nature as signifying more than the sum total of entities is thought of as a form of anthropomorphic projection, and hence as idolatrous, superstitious, or, more recently, and less trenchantly, as 'ideological'. The development of oxymoronic programmes such as a cultural materialism in the humanities is an extension of this logic. It pursues the deletion of nature so far that materiality itself is deleted, in the sense that any notion of the real unmediated by culture is prohibited as, of course, 'ideological'.[25]

Secondly, we are offered the dismantling of subjectivity. Only when we can arrive at an invocation of a materiality free from contamination by subjective 'consciousness', affectivity, or interpretation, can we speak of materialism. But this scepticism about the subject is in fact an important feature of the development of idealism. It is not quite correct to think that idealism consists primarily in the absorption of everything by the subject. It is central to idealist conceptions of experience that the subject is *nothing at all* without its mediation by the object. This is clear enough in Kant's insistence that the pure concepts of the understanding produce no knowledge at all unless they are combined with an intuition; clear in Hegel's subject which *is* nothing at all by itself, without the self-relinquishment in the realm of objects to which alone it owes its experience. The notion that what is characteristic of idealism is the monopoly of the subject over everything else is almost the opposite of the true situation. Rather, it is precisely because of idealism's allergic sensitivity to charges that it is relapsing into metaphysical soul-talk that it takes such pains to expel all ontological reality from the category of the subject. It is by just this means that the subject becomes pure consciousness; pure, that is, nothing at all until it gives itself away to objectivity.

I want now to turn, then, to consider some alternative ways of understanding materialist thinking. What will be important here will not be the label itself, so much as the attempt to articulate a kind of thinking which could at once fulfil two desiderata. Firstly, it would need to reconsider its relation to the category of 'subjectivity'. In order to do this it would need to be able to do justice to the somatic element in thinking, the sense in which all thinking is entangled with affectivity and is itself a kind of affectivity. Such an account would not regard the claim of thinking to *be* thinking as dependent on, say, stripping thinking of its entanglement with somatic affectivity, for example by representing it as 'pure' consciousness. Accordingly it would demand a revised phenomenology of the body, one which could understand the body not as an originally insignificant and qualityless dataset – materialism as the unwitting shadow of idealism – but rather as always already cognitive. The body is not merely a set of givens like any other processed by consciousness; it is itself also what must *know* any such phenomena. Secondly, such a materialism would need to reconsider its relation to the very category of 'nature'. Nature is a category which materialism deletes at its peril. If it does delete it, it cannot avoid becoming a degraded idealism. Yet nature is also a category which it cannot currently define. So materialism must understand itself as caught up in, rather than exempt from, a dialectic of disenchantment. Historically changing ways of conceiving nature could not legitimately be thought of as outworn superstitions unless we were confident of having a fully undeluded category available with which to replace them.

Because materialism is currently entangled in a dialectic of disenchantment, rather than standing at some wholly undeluded vantage point, its most valuable insights take a fragmentary and aporetic form. They cannot take the form of a 'materialist method'; the phrase is an oxymoron, because any method which remains the same whatever its object must be idealist, even if it calls itself materialist. They have not yet been able to take the form of a body of doctrine, because none has yet succeeded in stripping language utterly of its non-literal aspects. Nor is it certain that, were this possible, it would be desirable, or would be in any sense 'materialist'. 'Materialism', unlike, say, undeluded happiness, cannot in any case properly count as an end in itself. What we may learn from the historiography of idolatry, ideology, and 'ideology-critique' is the impossibility of a painless exit from the logic of disenchantment. Whether there can be such an exit does not depend only upon the discovery of the right method, doctrine, or lexicon – the idea that this is decisive is just what ideology thinks – but also upon the nature of the problems themselves, which are not yet exhaustively known. This means that the logic of social illusion cannot be delegated to a special science which has simply decided to say farewell to metaphysics, the science of ideology-critique, but will remain tied up with the persisting difficulties presented by the problem of cognitive illusion in general. It means that the logic of aesthetic illusion cannot be delegated to a sub-branch of that special science, a critique of aesthetic ideology, but will remain tied up with the persisting difficulties presented by the tasks of an aesthetic theory.

Notes

1 William Wordsworth, *The Thirteen-Book Prelude*, ed. Mark L. Reed, 2 vols (Ithaca: Cornell University Press, 1991), i, pp. 323–4.

2 Karl Marx and Friedrich Engels, 'Die Deutsche Ideologie', in *Werke*, 42 vols (Berlin: Dietz, 1962–71), iii, p. 13 (my translation).

3 Patrick Tort, *Marx et le problème de l'idéologie. Le modèle Égyptien* (Paris: Presses Universitaires de France, 1988), pp. 9–47, p. 25.

4 Marx and Engels, 'Die Deutsche Ideologie', p. 31 and n.

5 Marx, *Capital*, Vol. 1, trans. Ben Fowkes (Harmondsworth: Penguin, 1976), pp. 163–77.

6 Thomas Hobbes, *Leviathan*, ed. Richard Tuck (Cambridge: Cambridge University Press, 1991), p. 270.

7 Hobbes, p. 455.

8 Hobbes, pp. 418–19.

9 Hobbes, p. 418.

10 Augustine, *The City of God against the Pagans*, 7 vols (Cambridge, Mass.: Harvard University Press and London: William Heinemann, 1988), iii, pp. 121–3.

11 See Valerie I.H. Flint, *The Rise of Magic in Early Medieval Europe* (Oxford: Clarendon Press, 1991), p. 18.

12 See Peter Harrison, *Religion and 'Religions' in the English Enlightenment* (Cambridge: Cambridge University Press, 1990); for More on Calvinism, cf. Henry More, *Divine Dialogues*, 2 vols (London, 1668), i, p. 411; quoted in Harrison, p. 57.

13 Robert Boyle, *A Free Enquiry into the Vulgarly Received Notion of Nature*, ed. Edward B. Davis and Michael Hunter (Cambridge: Cambridge University Press, 1996), pp. 40–41.

14 Louis Althusser, 'Ideology and Ideological State Apparatuses (Notes towards an Investigation)' in *Mapping Ideology*, ed. Slavoj Žižek (London: Verso, 1994), pp. 100–40, pp. 126–7.

15 Althusser, p. 131.

16 Michel Henry, *Marx*, 2 vols (Paris: Gallimard, 1976).

17 Althusser, p. 132.

18 Althusser, p. 122: 'Now, while the thesis I wish to defend formally speaking adopts the terms of *The German Ideology* ("ideology has no history"), it is radically different from the positivist and historicist thesis of *The German Ideology*.'

19 Paul de Man, 'Phenomenality and Materiality in Kant' in *Aesthetic Ideology*, ed. Andrzej Warminski (Minneapolis: University of Minnesota Press, 1996), pp. 70–90.

20 De Man, *Aesthetic Ideology*, p. 88.

21 De Man, *Aesthetic Ideology*, p. 80.

22 De Man, *Aesthetic Ideology*, p. 82.

23 Immanuel Kant, *Critique of Judgment*, trans. Werner S. Pluhar (Indianapolis: Hackett, 1987), p. 106 (Kant's emphasis).

24 De Man, *Aesthetic Ideology*, p. 90.

25 This final section draws above all on two sources: first, an interpretation of Theodor W. Adorno's 'non-dogmatic materialism' as set out in my study, *Adorno: A Critical Introduction* (Cambridge: Polity Press, 1998), chs 6–8; and second, the thought of the French phenomenologist Michel Henry, most recently set out in his *Phénoménologie matérielle* (Paris: Presses Universitaires de France, 1990).

2 History and the Sacred in de Man and Benjamin

NIGEL MAPP

> The crows maintain that a single crow could destroy the heavens. There is no doubt of that, but it proves nothing against the heavens, for heaven simply means: the impossibility of crows.
>
> *Franz Kafka*

Paul de Man once remarked that he intended 'to take the divine out of reading'.[1] Of course, this does not mean that he aims to free the sacred from sublunary determination – to make room, as Kant wished, for *faith*.[2] Despite the rumours, de Man was atheistical to the end. And while he invokes the Kantian filiation for his criticism, it seems that he does so in order to emphasize the purging of reading of any bogus appeals to grounds transcending its text (whether in the phenomenal world or beyond it), grounds whose principles cannot be assumed to apply to linguistic entities.[3] When interpretation stops reading and rests on an uncriticized meaning it is *ipso facto* religious, though the religious is only one form this meaning will take. But the intended critical reduction of the transcendent, if such it is, may be as aporetic as Kant's effort to separate off the divine for its own preservation.

The challenges and possibilities of this situation are legible – in a way that the direct critique of religion may obscure – in the problems that Kant runs into when he tries critically to mark off the transcendent and (redundantly?) to veto all efforts of understanding to trespass into its realm. For Kant cognitively crosses his own limit in drawing it, as Hegel points out, and this must change our understanding of what lies on both sides.[4] The critical philosophy ultimately takes as given the historical experience whose possibility it is trying to explain, and wrongly ratifies it as changeless and unchangeable. Yet this experience, which excludes through the constraints of intuition the knowledge of freedom, God and an immortal soul, *is* historically, if not transcendentally, binding.[5] In underwriting it, Kant is true to its historical force – its real fixity – whose overcoming depends on a change in society

38

itself. The metaphysical elements can neither be dispensed with, nor rescued as they are already (contradictorily) posited as virtual objects. For Adorno, who pursues this implication of materialism with metaphysics, Kant's transcendent thinking promises rather the possibility of a changed experience, and makes room, this side of death, for a different future. Kant's antinomical delimitation, then, implies a critique of transcendent religion as well as of the immanence transcendentally purified of it. It reveals the predicament of an experience which has virtually withered away into its social mediation by enciphering a hope for its overcoming.[6] (Benjamin, too, characterized his speculative thinking as a revision of Kant, and from early on this was explicitly formulated as an attempt to rescue theological significance for experience.)[7]

In fact, de Man draws attention to similar difficulties; and, as I discuss below, one symptom is his distancing his work from what might be understood – religiously, once more – as a linguistic metacritique of experience or metaphysics, a laying bare of new foundations. For example, reading's persistent search for its immanent foundation in an implicit or explicit thematization of its operation in the work commands that that theme, too, and its figural status, be *read*. De Man's reflections on allegory as an (allegorical) name for the intrication of referential demand with the possible figurality of reference suggest this complication: allegories become allegories of the impossibility of reading, incomplete, open, changeable.

I

De Man finds inspiration in Marx's *German Ideology* for his explorations of ideology, which are therefore to be understood in some sort of connection with the critique of religion (and Marx's critique of that critique).[8] More particularly, he is no doubt familiar with Marx's demolition of secularizing thinking that blithely opposes all those words about God with other words – this time about human beings – and which, despite its trumpeted radicality, changes nothing but its lexicon:

> Since the Young Hegelians consider conceptions, thoughts, ideas, in fact all the products of consciousness, to which they attribute an independent existence, as the real chains of men [...] it is evident that [they] have to fight only against these illusions of consciousness. Since, according to their fantasy, the relations of men, all their doings, their fetters and their limitations are products of their consciousness, the Young Hegelians logically put to men the moral postulate of exchanging their present consciousness for human, critical or egoistic

consciousness, and thus of removing their limitations. This demand to change consciousness amounts to a demand to interpret the existing world in a different way, i.e., to recognize it by means of a different interpretation. The Young-Hegelian ideologists, in spite of their allegedly 'world-shattering' phrases, are the staunchest conservatives. The most recent of them have found the correct expression for their activity when they declare they are only fighting against '*phrases*'. They forget, however, that they themselves are opposing nothing but phrases to these phrases, and that they are in no way combating the real existing world when they are combating solely the phrases of this world.[9]

This species of would-be materialism, which directly proclaims the safe return of alienated human meaning to the here and now, repeats the illusions of religious transcendence rather than binning them. If the overcoming of religion and the subsequent transformation of the world – everyone's being born again – requires no more than the issuing of a new, human phrasebook, then that religious language is being credited with a real power over people's minds – power that the critique declares illusory, empty. But to maintain that religious phrases can be deleted or replaced through mere exertion of thought, and at the same time to state that this critical effort will definitively break the religious charm, is actually a 'fantasy' akin to the one it claims to destroy: belief in the power of incantation. In uttering fresh words to disenchant the world, the German ideologists just cast the old spell once more. Religion cannot therefore be spirited away by one or other of the more up-to-date 'human' sciences: the exorcism relapses into superstition.[10] The ideologists' critique is defined by its contradictory exclusion of religion, and is involved, like the life in whose name it wishes to speak, in the metaphysics that is supposedly being despatched – its 'humanity' is not as human as it should be. This co-implication of categories does not placate their antagonism, but it does rule out its cure through cerebration alone.

So by seeing what matters as something purely conceptual or linguistic, the Young Hegelians achieve only linguistic changes, and unwittingly reveal that what they want to attack is *not* just a matter of phraseology – that getting rid of illusion must be more than a question of coming up with the right words. God is not returned to humankind through the divination of His code-book. Mental substitutions of this sort are in fact easily reversible, and they offer little more than a thesaurus of indifferent alternatives, spells and counter-spells. And the hopes of changing the society that underlies these solidary phrases are buried even more deeply by the ideologists than they are by religion.

The conversion of religious categories into human ones leaves untouched the same forces underlying *both*; the critique misrecognizes the reality that alienates itself in this way. The religious illusion (or the 'metaphorical' transcendence) that masks 'literal' reality is part of that reality, and merely conceptual (or tropological) exchanges within this system will neither fix nor grasp historical antagonisms.[11] Rather, they reproduce them. Materialism of this stripe, like all unadmitted idealisms, blinds itself to its real dependencies and violences. It ends up not thinking at all (which is not the answer, either), trapped in the consciousness promoted by the social totality; one averted, precisely, from these real conditions.

This argument impacts on the false literalness of the ideologists' language as well as on the idea of an illusionless theoretical language itself. In Marx's characterization of his target ideologists' ineffectually mental or linguistic criticisms (which, notoriously, interpret the world rather than changing it), he criticizes their separation of the mental from the material as a cardinal instance of the illusion it wants to eradicate. Like Feuerbach and the others, Marx can *change* nothing by merely reflecting on it; but that is the point. The ideologists conceive the problem of religion as a mental one, their target a pure metaphor, but that is exactly the delusorily *literal* conception of society that shores it up. Their inadequate theory of language and consciousness is coterminous with a deluded view of the world that underwrites it.

Consciousness is bound to the material, and its material life is language, says Marx.[12] Tracing the way thought is determined by social reality demands that the aporetic character of its own effort be faced, for that reality stipulates thought's independence. That illusion, fixed by the division of manual and mental labour, cannot be dissolved by the type of thinking it sponsors. The ideologists' sharp distinctions between the mental and the material, God and man, illusion and reality, language and life – in order to empty one into the other – are real, then, but illusory. The abortive attempt to retrieve human meaning from its religious trappings exposes this predicament. A separation of word from meaning that would jettison the offensively religious *labels* – as in mere interpretation, or secular paraphrase – reproduces a central component of the ideology it wants to strip away, assigning substantial, misleading effects to what is meant to be an impotent and immaterial husk, no more than an arbitrary and discardable nomenclature. If critique is implicated in such aporias, perhaps its effort should be towards redeeming, rather than deleting, the insight they may provide.

II

Presumably no one ever thought that de Man's criticism concerns itself with some kind of Young Hegelian re-homing of an alienated human essence. The question is, rather, whether de Man falls foul of a comparable error by projecting another false immanence onto the skies, thus deludedly blotting out transcendence *as* transcendence, and historical hopes with it. So what of de Man's attention to language? Does his 'formal materialism' ditch one uninspected category merely to exalt another?[13] Is 'language' one more swappable label here for the divine, changing nothing? Does he just translate God-talk into a new code, leaving both languages undisturbed? Or does his work have something to say about such re-badging, such linguistic substitutions, because it is about language?

De Manian critique is after all often presented – then indicted – as hopelessly formalist. Myopically linguistic, de Man (for many) is mired in the aporias that issue from his assumption of an inert separation of language from world – as if the impossibility of sealing a text off from the world were already reason enough to shun the 'formalism' of 'critical-linguistic' analyses.[14] If, for de Man, displacing religious categories into historical ones leaves untouched and uninspected the enabling rhetorical conditions of that conversion, getting snarled up in language may be no more appealing. And there is no doubt that de Man does characterize the valuable, and indeed *subversive*, aspects of theory as having to do with the introduction of a linguistic terminology into the analysis of texts.[15] While the illusory dimensions of reading are not to be dispelled by switching words about God for words about words, something occurs in de Man's readings that goes beyond this endless shuffling of *meanings*: the recognition of an error, if not its end.

The necessity, viability and completability of critique are all central issues for de Man. The critical moment must always be *read* in his writings, where critique is configured with its own aporetic conditions and results (such as the stubborn perdurance of the transcendent urge and its indeterminability).[16] De Man's analyses criticize both religion – or religious humanism – and any plan rapidly to eliminate its claims.[17] Here is one of de Man's better-known formulations of 'ideology', where he is querying the a priori alignment of linguistic functioning with the logic of experience of the world:

> It would be unfortunate, for example, to confuse the materiality of the signifier with the materiality of what it signifies. This may seem obvious enough on the level of sight and sound, but it is less so with regard to the more general

phenomenality of space, time or especially of the self; no one in his right mind will try to grow grapes by the luminosity of the word 'day', but it is very difficult not to conceive the pattern of one's past and future existence as in accordance with temporal and spatial schemes that belong to fictional narratives and not to the world. This does not mean that fictional narratives are not part of the world and of reality; their impact upon the world may well be all too strong for comfort. What we call ideology is precisely the confusion of linguistic with natural reality, of reference with phenomenalism. It follows that, more than any other mode of inquiry, including economics, the linguistics of literariness is a powerful and indispensable tool in the unmasking of ideological aberrations, as well as a determining factor in accounting for their occurrence. Those who reproach literary theory for being oblivious to social and historical (that is to say ideological) reality are merely stating their fear at having their own ideological mystifications exposed by the tool they are trying to discredit. They are, in short, very poor readers of Marx's *German Ideology*.[18]

De Man operates with a distinction of language and world that appears to promise an illusion-free critique of their confusion – such as unreflectively organic models of linguistic functioning. But such a reading assumes that language and reference are determined in advance here – whereas it is their a priori resemblance to the principles of phenomenal experience that is in question. It is this criticism of de Man which behaves as if it already knows what language is.[19] And what de Man recommends to the critic, who otherwise might appear stuck in experiments as daft as any in Swift's Academy of Lagado, is anything but easy. The apparently magical effects of words are not always so simply dismissed. Reality is bound to the very illusion ideology-critique might oppose to it. The model that opposes text to world is also in question; it too may be deformed by confusion within and between these categories.

The installation or revelation of a new transcendental text in place of all other potential candidates is in fact criticized by de Man as one more idealizing, theological gesture. He is continuously alive to such transcendental contraband, as Derrida calls it, which must raise the problem of how the focus on apparently purely linguistic matters is to be understood.[20] De Man's criticism attempts to adumbrate a moment which is not just more trundling around within some closed textual interior, or from a bounded text to an equally determined outside, whether religious or historical – two aspects of the same ideology for him. Language is not here anything like a demarcated inside. For de Man, the realms of the linguistic and the world are related in a way which ruptures their constituted internality, and they are not articulable, or separable, in the too-readily understandable forms organized by such metaphors as inside and outside.[21] Language will bear the mutilation of its false separation from the world 'within' itself, so neither term can just be emptied into the other any more than they are presently to be glued back together. Language is not one more determinate concept that can be shuttled back and forth, because it resists reduction to the tropological, metaphorical systems such movements depend on – and which it is also able to construct.[22] Language is the disjunction of such models, which means it must also be a catachrestic name for the disjunction of any totalized model of language. Words about words are not just metaphors about metaphors any longer.

Formalist and historicist readings, resting on uninterrogated rhetorics of inside and outside, are each prone to chiasmic reversal into the other. An examination of the conditions of this predicament can criticize such models of separation – and totalization – without falling *blindly* prey, at least, to one more empty metaphorical transfer, such as a lurch into a history that may as well be called religion. It is part of de Man's aim to reveal the aporetic binding together and disjunction of such apparently literal concepts as history, text, and world.

In de Man's terms, a system of exchanges is left intact by transmuting religious language into social or economic language, for example by seeing the sacred as the deductible metaphor of the latter's literality. Such tropological systems articulate linguistic meanings and such meanings with a given knowledge of the world. But there cannot be such an easily achieved literalness. An example of how de Man goes about such an argument is his late (1983) reading of Baudelaire's sonnet '*Correspondances*'.[23] Here the symbolic '*transports*' of metaphor, apparently the poem's *modus operandi*, which promise the totalizing, synaesthetic ascent of the mind and senses, are directly thematized in the last line: '*l'expansion des choses infinies* [...] *Qui chantent les transports de l'esprit et des sens*'.[24] But de Man sees these transports decomposing through a syntactic ambiguity into a mechanical enumeration of sense-experiences – perfumes are like infinite things, says one reading; perfumes are *exemplified* by various smells, says the other – trapping the transports in the horizontal movement from one sense impression to another.[25] Such a grammatical critique of metaphor (or of the poem's totalizing similes, its reliance on the word '*comme*') is able perhaps to hear the Paris Métro rumbling beneath the 'symbolist' dream, to literalize these '*transports*' and see metaphors as mere tickets to ride along from stop to stop, transferable between lines (the word '*correspondance*' also means 'transfer ticket', de Man points out), and thus return metaphysics to the real world.[26] But metaphor as the determinate movement of meaning allows *all* such movements, whether between railway lines or between the city and the heavens. This shunting around, which has the gritty charm of any demystified reading, is perhaps no more than a marshalling to and fro of meanings, a process as inconsequential as their disposable labels are meant to be. It does not escape, or alter, the system of such exchanges, but repeats its power. This reading keeps its feet on the ground of determinate metaphorical, and metaphysical, patterns in order to collapse the transcendent order into economic literalness, superstructure to base. Maybe de Man recalls that there is a lesson in the metaphorics of that infamous relation anyway, as Fredric Jameson has noted:

> [W]e must initially separate the figuration of the terms base and superstructure – only the initial shape of the problem – from the type of efficacity or causal law it is supposed to imply. *Überbau* and *Basis*, for example, which so often suggest to people a house and its foundations, seem in fact to have been railroad terminology and to have designated the rolling stock and the rails respectively, something which suddenly jolts us into a rather different picture of ideology and its effects.[27]

There is a solidarity, a mutual dependence, between economics and metaphysics. In economics, that abstract world dominated by the relations of exchange-value, we are still in the realm of a circulation of meanings of which metaphor is the key conceptual resource and literal measure; somehow we just know what is literal, what metaphorical, and how to get from one place to another. Nothing really happens in such reading; these 'historical' relationships are opened up by unquestioned tropological systems of semantic transportation, formal structures that organize their contents into indifferently reversible meanings.

By diagnosing metaphor so literally, these critical readings effect only metaphorical exchanges. But a different literalization of '*transports*' can reveal that what is called 'language' is not exhausted by such frictionless substitutions, is not projectable without disruptive remainder onto the second term of the history/consciousness or matter/mind binaries. This 'literalization' is more literal still than economic reading; it has to do with the semantic play of the syllable and letter within the very words '*transports*' and 'metaphor'. Because he has uncovered two syntactic subjects at a critical point in the poem, de Man inspects the potential syntax within the word *transports*, looks at the disposition of its subsemantic, fragmentary parts.[28] Perhaps, de Man suggests, reading can then can ask about a 'state that is beyond movement entirely', beyond (*trans*) carrying (*portare*), rather than yet another movement from one place to another.[29] He raises the *possibility* (it cannot be declared with certainty) that meaningful articulations are determined by such uncontrollable, accidental arrangements. Thus '*transport*' *translates* 'metaphor', disarticulating it, depositing it beyond metaphorical meaning (traditionally conceived 'metaphor'). It exemplifies and allegorically tells of a syntax no longer laid out in the purview of meaning, of somewhere beyond the limits of determinable semantic displacements. The word that is to name metaphorical synthesis, on which symbolist and historical readings rely, is pulled apart by the uncontrollable semantic effects of its syntax. Kevin Newmark writes: '[The text] prevents the carrying from ever becoming a homogeneous movement and thus cuts itself off from its own meaning as movement in the very moment it comes into being.'[30]

Language stymies any effort to articulate all its functions, which means it cannot be dismissed as some transferable set of meanings – by carting it off towards its historical conditions, for instance – or totalized. If it is seen as exclusively a tropology of meanings and their systematized exchanges, it will block such movements through its metonymic, grammatical, and material character – overdetermined semantic events and accidental contiguities. It criticizes, then, those formal gestures of the German ideologists, by pointing out that words are not just exchangeable meanings. If, on the other hand, it is approached as a purged syntax, its rhetorical potential will remain irreducible to any grammar. Grammar and rhetoric conflict with and denounce each other, but each leads into the other and wrecks its efforts at systematization.[31] Each ends in aporia, an aporia of language, a linguistic aporia of the concept of language. Grammar and rhetoric are not closed and exchangeable *meanings* like history and form, inner and outer.[32] Andrzej Warminski, who has made this argument, calls this language's referential aspect – by which is meant not the completed circuitry of metaphorical transportation beyond language into conceptual or worldly transcendence, but a 'carrying back' to something other than language which cannot be given a non-dogmatic meaning.[33]

III

Much of de Man's rhetoric seems to advert to a language freed of aberration, as if reading has indeed found resources for a deeper, disabused insight. But through the invocations of Kant and his stress upon 'critical-linguistic' analysis, de Man may be suggesting that language has a very disruptive role in the consciousness which tries to dominate it. His rhetorical critique of historicism and religion does imply that such reading has the best chance of seeing how tropological transfers work, and of finding the history that they occlude, precisely *because* it is suspicious of any literalness in language about language that does not face its aporetic upshot . So language is hardly a secured ground over which thinking can advance, once and for all, to a new critical level. De Man's late lecture on Walter Benjamin's 'The Task of the Translator' [*Die Aufgabe des Übersetzers*] – delivered in March 1983 – is, revealingly, set up as a problematization of Hans Georg Gadamer's attempt to define philosophical modernity as an increased self-consciousness, one that emphatically overcomes various kinds of naïveté by examining language as the critically purified condition of the categories of consciousness.[34] De Man objects both to the delusional epochal discernment of any 'modernity' itself and also, less predictably, to this sense of discovering a new foundation for criticism in the linguistic metacritique of Kant and Hegel.

Although there is no final authorized manuscript of de Man's lecture on Benjamin, it remains an essential text for the question of the relation between the sacred and what is called there, following Benjamin, 'pure language' (*reine Sprache*). The linguistic conditions at which (explicitly Kantian) critique, like translation, aims are examined for signs of a relapse into the sacred. From the concept of a pure poetic language, paradoxically, a blunt antagonism between the poetic and the sacred is developed – because poetic language, it emerges, is anything but pure.[35] The essay tracks how a language completely disburdened of meaning, from whose perspective translation reads, must in the end be read as a – or the *most* – sacred notion (p. 96). In a brief conference reply from 1981, de Man claims that 'it is possible that, of all human activities, literature is the one least compatible, in the final analysis, with religious experience – though it is also the activity that is easiest to confuse with that experience'.[36] By the time of the later piece, de Man at points is even less sanguine about the possibility of such a 'final analysis', of arriving at the end of the line.[37] Pure language seems altogether chimerical, along with the messianic hopes bound up with it; but neither is quickly extirpable, as de Man admits in the discussion session: '[Benjamin] succeeded so well in incorporating [messianic elements] in their displacement that you – it takes really a long practice – it's always lost again. Whenever I go back to this text, I think I have it more or less, then I read it again, and again I don't understand it. I again see a messianic appeal' (p. 103). The sacred's disappearance is a trick not easily brought off.

If de Man *wished* to excise the sacred from the poetic it seems that Benjamin's text is an odd place to go, unless he is just going to take it as a target, an egregious example of what he criticizes.[38] Benjamin invokes Kant in his discussion of translation to sketch how it does not try to resemble meaning, just as epistemological critique undoes models of knowledge organized in terms of imitation. So de Man's approach to Benjamin's understanding of translation can consider the possibility of a critical relationship that does not reproduce merely metaphorical substitutions. Metaphorically putting one meaning in place of another is distinct from translating one language into another. De Man develops Benjamin's strictures against resemblance of meaning intriguingly and paradoxically: although '*übersetzen*' (to translate) seems to mean 'metaphor', the sub semantic elements of the word '*übersetzen*' *translate* the Greek '*metaphor*', and that, de Man avers, is just not the same at all (p. 83). These words are not metaphors of each other, although they both mean 'metaphor'. 'The metaphor is not a metaphor, Benjamin is saying.' These words do not *resemble* each other. The relationship of translation is very different, and has to do with the split of meaning from form: translating the components of '*metaphor*' into '*übersetzen*' causes the original meaning to disappear.

But as intimated elsewhere in his work, such critical values are hardly anti-religious for Benjamin. In 1918 he had written: 'A concept of knowledge gained from reflection on the linguistic nature of knowledge will create a corresponding concept of experience which will also encompass realms that Kant failed truly to systematize. The realm of religion should be mentioned as the foremost of these.'[39] And the essay on translation appears to characterize 'pure language' in its full messianic dimensions through images of symbolic totalization, a totality it is translation's task to reveal. Liberated from its communicative function, pure, grammatical language, Benjamin's figures insinuate, is pieced together by translation in view of a metaphysical totality: the Idea or symbolic unity of all the different, and the most remote, relations within and between languages – which is brought forth in the *way* they mean, in the proliferating range of nuances of their linguistic devices.[40]

Translation, then, reads from the perspective of a hypothetical 'pure language', a language 'entirely freed of the illusion of meaning', as de Man defines it (p. 84), but this turns into a transcendent, symbolic idea of the unity of all languages. Translation, unlike poetry, for instance, is a relationship between two languages 'wherein the problem of meaning or the desire to say something, the need to make a statement, is entirely absent' (pp. 81–2). It is therefore aligned with critical poetics, the study of language prior to what de Man calls the 'extralinguistic', paraphrasable or imitable, meaning it carries. Translation proceeds by separating the meaning (*das Gemeinte*) and the devices of meaning, the way language means (*die Art des Meinens*) (p. 86). We receive the mode of meaning like the law, perhaps; but de Man sounds more colourful, emphasizing the possibility that language is not made by humans at all, as the idea of its God-given provenance can imply (p. 100) – nor is the essay at pains to avoid the pathos of language's *inhumanity*.[41] This offers a recasting of the human defined through its use of language; both that humanity and its language have been misrecognized (p. 96, pp. 99–102). Hanging on to language's inhumanity is a way of keeping a different humanity in play. This is clarified by the strange way in which translation, for de Man, must give up on its task, leave it incomplete – not only as a communication of meaning, perhaps, but also as a liberation from its constraints. *Aufgabe*, untranslatably, implies both task and failure (cf. p. 80).

De Man elaborates one of Benjamin's examples (and seems to regret it afterwards (p. 96)). The German '*Brot*' and the French '*pain*' appear to mean the same thing ('bread'), but translation reveals their incommensurability in the countervailing effects of the words as devices (p. 87). For the semantic play of these signifiers pulls in all different sorts of senses and connections (for de Man, '*Brot*' in this context echoes Hölderlin [who wrote *Brot und Wein*], while '*pain et vin*' reminds him of Paris cafés and, among other things, the word 'bastard' ['*bâtard*' is a type of bread roll]). Translating the German word into French upsets the homely way we live in language as a set of meanings; they are simply not the same. Meaning is disturbed by the means of constructing it, which is semantically overdetermined. Yet for Benjamin translation shows that the words do intend the same: pure language.[42] For Carol Jacobs this signifies 'that which is purely language – nothing but language. "What is meant" is never something to be found independently of language nor even independently in language, in a single word or phrase, but arises instead from the mutual differentiation of the various manners of meaning'.[43] The dispersal of totalizable meaning is precisely what guarantees the symbolic kinship of languages – beyond any communicable meaning. Purity emerges from impurity.

There is an implicit allegory in de Man's comments on this passage. The German word leads towards religious experience, intimating the totality of body and spirit in the (albeit interpretatively vexed) figure of the host, where bread is a synecdoche of the Son, God incarnate; while '*pain*' heads down town for a cheap meal, and suggests that meaning is some kind of bastard offspring of its material devices.[44] (And in English, 'bread' can stand in for 'money', too, de Man notes.) Translation exposes disjunction within and between the languages. The religious language is translated into the worldly, which is not the same as making one resemble the other, one the metaphor of the other. *Both* are disarticulated, illegitimate, in exile. Indeed, it is the most humdrum and concrete 'homeliness' of language, like the economic reality it shores up, that becomes alienatingly strange. Hard-headedly seeking to secure the provision of our daily bread was never the quickest exit from religious delusion.

De Man holds on to the fissile semantic effects as the condition of the deletion and supersession of semantics. The dispersal is not halted by a religious totalization. '*Aber es gibt ein Halten*', says Benjamin; there is an end to this – or there is a hanging on to it (p. 104).[45] De Man fixes Benjamin's text in the openness of its aporias by an abyssal, bottomless reading, taking its statements as examples of what they proclaim (p. 86).

IV

De Man presses his reading more closely through Benjamin's final version of the linguistic disjunction between logos and lexis, the nonadequation between 'trope as such and the meaning as a totalizing power of tropological substitutions' (p. 89). The passage at issue allegorizes the aporetic relations of sacred and prosaic, purity and impurity. It concerns Benjamin's image for this pure language, and its apparent figuring of a symbolic totalization – rather than de Man's atomized dispersal – of all the disarticulated texts and translations. But Benjamin's text acts and means in a compacted and paradoxical way. This is shown for de Man when Benjamin's English translator, Harry Zohn, gets the passage very wrong by going after the meaning, rather than translating the devices (pp. 89–92). Benjamin uses many tropes – organic ones, for example – which convey 'the illusion of totality', as de Man puts it, in a genitive it is tempting to read both ways (p. 89). But when read linguistically, they undo the intimation of a symbolic unification of traditional figure and meaning.

Benjamin's reflections on a 'pure language' and its connection to translation are presented in the figure of the broken amphora. Zohn makes Benjamin's figure into an argument for the ultimate unity of all languages expressed by translation:

> Fragments of a vessel which are to be glued together must match one another in the smallest details, although they need not be like one another. In the same way a translation, instead of resembling the meaning of the original, must lovingly and in detail incorporate the original's mode of signification, thus

making both the original and the translation recognizable as fragments of a greater language, just as fragments are part of a vessel. For this very reason translation must in large measure refrain from wanting to communicate. (p. 89)[46]

There is an original, pure language, each work being only a fragment of it, but through this fragment pure language can be rediscovered. Though unlike, all the parts match by 'incorporating' the original's mode of signification; through being distressed by pure language, fragments come to participate in what they are fragments of. The amphora is reconstructed by a translation which shows how everything *symbolically* matches, participating internally in this one language: 'as in the word *symbolon*, which states the matching of two pieces or fragments' (p. 90). De Man claims, flatly, that this is a religious theory of translation. He recalls the messianic figure of the mending of history's broken vessels, as in the Kabbalistic concept of the *Tikkun*. This symbolic 'Idea' is an all-too meaningful concept of the 'fundamental unity of language'.

But Benjamin states that symbol and symbolized do not correspond. An attentive translation bears out the way trope and what it seems to represent do not quite tally. Its grammatical construction unpicks its rhetorical totalizing:

> Wie nämlich Scherben eines Gefäßes, um sich zusammenfügen zu lassen, in den kleinsten Einzelheiten einander zu folgen, doch nicht so zu gleichen haben, so muß, anstatt dem Sinn des Originals sich ähnlich zu machen, die Übersetzung liebend vielmehr und bis ins Einzelne hinein dessen Art des Meinens in der eigenen Sprache sich anbilden, um so beide wie Scherben als Bruchstück eines Gefäßes, als Bruchstück einer größeren Sprache erkennbar zu machen.[47]

De Man, reading *verbatim*, sees a warning here: there is no messianic redemption to be had, any more than some purified prosaic realm it relies on. The fragments cannot be patched together. De Man refers to Carol Jacobs's translation: the fragments are to be 'articulated', not glued, and must 'follow one another in the smallest detail', not 'match' (p. 90).[48] They come along in metonymic sequence rather than merging in a symbolic unification. And the fragments of the vessel are no more than that – remaining, literally, *broken* parts. This is de Man's impromptu translation of the end of the passage:

> instead of making itself similar to the meaning, to the *Sinn* of the original, the translation must rather, lovingly and in detail, in its own language, form itself according to the manner of meaning [*Art des Meinens*] of the original, to make both recognizable as the broken parts of the greater language, just as fragments are the broken parts of a vessel. (p. 91)

Zohn responds to the meaning, seeing fragments as part of a vessel just as his translation makes the words match this symbolist meaning. For him the vessel is a synecdochic simile, part of one continuous, readily totalizable metaphorical system. It is a metaphor for the metaphorical relationship synecdoche promotes. Yet Benjamin's text teaches that the fragments are only fragments, just relating one to another as contiguous atoms. And de Man concludes, unpacking this allegorical message in a revealing indecision: 'there was no vessel in the first place, or we have no knowledge of this vessel, or no awareness, no access to it, so for all intents and purposes there has never been one' (p. 91).

This hesitation between nonexistence and transcendent existence is too interesting to dismiss as extempore incoherence. Reading pure language relies on this enabling religious fiction, but also upsets it. Pure language persists, but only as the disjunction between the sacred and the poetic – it is of the fractured essence of language – a fissure that runs through all languages (cf. p. 92), through the terms as well as between them. The figure has tied the sacred and the prosaic together aporetically. Benjamin's text says, then, that there is 'an initial fragmentation' – an oxymoron the idea of a pure language lands in – and that 'the work is totally fragmented in relation to this *reine Sprache*, with which it has nothing in common, and every translation is totally fragmented in relation to the original' (p. 91). The devices both disrupt and stand apart (de Man talks of 'the materiality of the letter, the independence, or the way in which the letter can disrupt the ostensibly stable meaning of a sentence' (p. 89)). In short, de Man's critical reading, which unavoidably goes through the thematic *meaning* of Benjamin's essay, preserves the disjunction between Benjamin's figure and its totalized meaning, and therefore reads its significance against the very notion of a pure language that allowed for the critical perspective in the first place. What it does conflicts with what it says; it can say this, too, but only in a permanently corrigible allegorical fashion. The reading is an allegory of the undoing of the symbol because 'trope as such' is available only, but very persistently, as the negative undoing of totalized tropological meanings; allegory narrates the impossibility of reading, turning on itself. It cannot come to rest in a final reading, some completed demystification. For it speaks as well of falling back into monumental or theological illusion, with which it is easily confusable.

V

The religious meaning is not peeled away to reveal sheer text. Such a purified language becomes apparent only in exposing the error of poetic language's perceived affinity with religion. By moving towards the devices, any hope of such a pure language is lost. There is no pure poetics (cf. p. 88). Benjamin says that where a work takes part in 'true language', it is directly translatable; de Man notes the French translation saying the apparent opposite ('*intraduisible*') (pp. 79–80).[49] But, ironically, he says they are the same.[50] This allegorizes the removal of the divine from view in the very indifference of language to a meaning that the divine seeks to name: language's indifference to meaning.

When a *temple* (Baudelaire's '*Correspondances*' opens with: '*La Nature est un temple ...*') can serve de Man as the icon of pure syntax, the threat of the more prosaic reading returning to the monumental and divine is pretty apparent.[51] This is especially so since the temple was also a figure for the tropological ascent from earth to heaven. The temple is static, unmovable; it is not a vehicle, and because metaphors enable one to change only from vehicle to vehicle, metaphor cannot reach it. Language cannot switch from 'being like a vehicle to being like a temple, or a ground'.[52] As blank inscription, the temple is not a figure; it stands apart from those semantic transfers it also makes possible. When de Man sees in Kant a similarly material vision of sea and heavens as a building, he needs to admonish the reader that this is 'not a trope'.[53] But it is not really literal, either, any more than is Heidegger's 'language is the house of being' (although he too points out that this is no glibly assimilable image, he does so in order to emphasize how the sentence opens a thinking of what both language and dwelling are in the first place).[54] De Man implies that temple and house are inscribed, a linguistic act, for a meaning to follow; they are not heaps of stones. That they are an uncomfortable dwelling for familiar meanings in de Man is not just a nihilistic upshot of a disillusioned world. Such a nihilism has its positive side (pp. 103–4). De Man is reading allegorically, and this is how his literalism, like his metaphors, needs to be read. In the Baudelaire essay this is foregrounded in de Man's talking, problematically, of language's being '*like* a temple'.[55] The reading demands that its provisionality be acknowledged, its movements weighed and explored, so that its event is not buried once more.

De Man links the perpetual wandering, *errance*, of the de-canonized original language, an exile without a homeland, with history (p. 92). History is this disruption of secluded dwelling – *contra* Heidegger. It is nihilistic, inhuman, but translation can begin to glimpse that unsecured, changeable, human grounds underlie this pathos of critique (p. 92, pp. 103–4). The agonistic language of the 'death' of the original, the 'pathos of uncertain agency', as

Neil Hertz dubs it, which attaches to translation as well as discussions of it (did it kill the original or find it dead? (cf. p. 84)) – obtrudes human significance at a point where some antiseptic 'linguistics of literariness' might have been expected.[56] But it is such expectations and solid determinations that translation disturbs. It reveals a play of the letter that defamiliarizes the world and language with it. By revealing life as an afterlife (p. 85), translation grasps an error, although it may have not have the efficacy of a talking cure. Translation occurs, because in it inscription fractures any sense of a totalized, transcendentally grounded system of categories.[57] De Man argues elsewhere that Keats's 'forlorn' – the 'very word', its mere sound, in the 'Ode to a Nightingale' – which is to 'toll' him back to his 'sole self', to the alienated man, marks, 'textually [not thematically] speaking [...] the very moment at which [the subject] starts to dream – for as we also all know since Freud, such plays of the letter are also the work of the dream, accessible to us only within a system in which the difference between waking and dreaming cannot be decided'.[58] Such effects may not wake us from the dream of history, but they motivate a fragile allegory, strung between the knowledge it narrates and its inscription, to wake us to the dream of language.[59]

Notes

1   Robert Moynihan, 'Interview with Paul de Man', *The Yale Review* 73: 4 (Summer 1984), pp. 576–602, p. 586.
2   Immanuel Kant, *Critique of Pure Reason*, trans. Werner S. Pluhar (Indianapolis and Cambridge: Hackett, 1996), B xxx. Cf. de Man in 1981: 'What is at stake [...] is [...] whether or not the teaching of literature, in the university, should be a substitution for or a complement to the teaching of religion or, a little less pragmatically put, whether we can say that the language of poetry and of literature have an affinity with the language of religion. This has, of course, nothing to do with the intrinsic quality of religious belief or with the philosophical value of theology. Nor is the question settled by historical perspectives that see literature as a secularization of religious experience; the concept of secularity is itself a deeply religious concept that could never reach critical insight into the complex relationship between poetic and religious discourse.' See 'Blocking the Road: A Response to Frank Kermode', in de Man, *Romanticism and Contemporary Criticism: The Gauss Seminar and Other Papers*, ed. E.S. Burt, Kevin Newmark and Andrzej Warminski (Baltimore: Johns Hopkins University Press, 1993), pp. 188–93; pp. 190–91.
3   See, for example, de Man's response to Stanley Corngold, 'A Letter from Paul de Man', *Critical Inquiry* 8:3 (Spring 1982), pp. 509–13. Extended readings of Kant are collected in de Man, *Aesthetic Ideology*, ed. Andrzej Warminski (Minneapolis: University of Minnesota Press, 1996).
4   G.W.F. Hegel, *Science of Logic*, trans. A.V. Miller (London: Allen & Unwin, 1969), pp. 131–7.

5 See Theodor W. Adorno, *Negative Dialectics*, trans. E.B. Ashton (London: Routledge & Kegan Paul, 1973), pp. 361–408.

6 On Adorno's argumentation in the final sections of *Negative Dialectics*, see Simon Jarvis, *Adorno: A Critical Introduction* (Cambridge: Polity Press, 1998), esp. pp. 207–11; and on the link of such passages to Adorno's view of aesthetic semblance, see J.M. Bernstein, 'Why Rescue Semblance? Metaphysical Experience and the Possibility of Ethics', in Tom Huhn and Lambert Zuidervaart (eds), *The Semblance of Subjectivity: Essays in Adorno's Aesthetic Theory* (Cambridge, Mass. and London: MIT Press, 1997), pp. 177–212.

7 See, for example, Walter Benjamin, 'On the Program of the Coming Philosophy', in *Selected Writings: Volume 1, 1913–1926*, ed. Marcus Bullock and Michael W. Jennings, trans. Mark Ritter (Cambridge, Mass.: Harvard University Press, 1996), pp. 100–10. The essay was written in 1918. For an exploration of the relation of speculative to transcendental thought in Benjamin, see Howard Caygill, *Walter Benjamin: The Colour of Experience* (London: Routledge, 1998). Caygill argues that Benjamin's 'concept of experience is not exclusively linguistic; indeed his "transcendental but speculative philosophy" is above all an account of experience characterised by an immanent totality. Language offers but one transcendental surface for the exploration of the properties of this totality' (p. 13).

8 See especially the title-essay of de Man, *The Resistance to Theory*, Foreword Wlad Godzich (Minneapolis: University of Minnesota Press, 1986), p. 11. De Man persistently examined the religious dimensions of reading, from the early readings of Hölderlin through to the second part of *Allegories of Reading* and beyond.

9 Karl Marx and Friedrich Engels, *The German Ideology* (Amherst: Prometheus Books, 1998), pp. 35–6.

10 Cf. Theodor W. Adorno and Max Horkheimer, *Dialectic of Enlightenment*, trans. John Cumming (London: Verso, 1979).

11 A point made clearly – and developed very intriguingly – in Slavoj Žižek, *The Sublime Object of Ideology* (London: Verso, 1989), pp. 28ff., for example.

12 Marx and Engels, *The German Ideology*, p. 49: 'The "mind" is from the outset afflicted with the curse of being "burdened" with matter, which here makes its appearance in the form of agitated layers of air, sounds, in short, of language. Language is as old as consciousness, language *is* practical, real consciousness that exists for other men as well, and only therefore does it also exist for me.' Here I am indebted, as at other points in my analysis, to Andrzej Warminski's suggestive 'Ending Up/Taking Back (with Two Postscripts on Paul de Man's Historical Materialism)', in Cathy Caruth and Deborah Esch (eds), *Critical Encounters: Reference and Responsibility in Deconstructive Writing* (New Brunswick: Rutgers University Press, 1995), pp. 11–41.

13 For the characterization of a (crucially oxymoronic) formal materialism, see, for example, 'Kant's Materialism' (1981) in de Man, *Aesthetic Ideology*, pp. 119–28. (For instance: '[this] radical formalism [...] is what is called materialism' (p. 128).)

14 A formulation Adorno levels at Lukács's attitude towards apparently 'autonomous' art: Theodor W. Adorno, *Notes to Literature*, 1, trans. Shierry Weber Nicholsen (New York: Columbia University Press, 1991), p. 225. For the locution 'critical-linguistic analysis' (an analysis he says he hopes to bring to bear on Kierkegaard and Marx), and for formulations of de Man's view of the relations of the linguistic, the ideological and the theological, see Stefano Rosso, 'An Interview with Paul de Man' (1983) in de Man, *The Resistance to Theory*, pp. 115–21, p. 121.

15 See, for example, de Man, 'The Return to Philology', in *The Resistance to Theory*, pp. 21–6, p. 24, and de Man, 'The Resistance to Theory', in *The Resistance to Theory*, pp. 3–20, p. 8.

16 Cf. the discussion of de Man's referential imperative in Werner Hamacher's very rich essay '"LECTIO": de Man's Imperative' in Hamacher, *Premises: Essays on Philosophy and Literature from Kant to Celan*, trans. Peter Fenves (Cambridge, Mass.: Harvard University Press, 1996), pp. 181–221.

17 On the religious and aesthetic humanism of literary teaching, see de Man, 'Return to Philology', *The Resistance to Theory*, p. 26.

18 De Man, 'The Resistance to Theory', in *The Resistance to Theory*, p. 11.

19 Ibid. Cf. Andrzej Warminski, 'Introduction: Allegories of Reference', in de Man, *Aesthetic Ideology*, pp. 1–33, p. 8.

20 See Jacques Derrida, *Glas*, trans. John P. Leavey, Jr and Richard Rand (Lincoln: University of Nebraska Press, 1986), p. 244a.

21 De Man, 'Semiology and Rhetoric', reprinted in de Man, *Allegories of Reading: Figural Language in Rousseau, Nietzsche, Rilke, and Proust* (New Haven: Yale University Press, 1979), pp. 3–19, p. 5.

22 Cf. Warminski, 'Ending Up/Taking Back', pp. 16–20, p. 26.

23 De Man, 'Anthropomorphism and Trope in the Lyric', in de Man, *The Rhetoric of Romanticism* (New York: Columbia University Press, 1984), pp. 239–62.

24 Charles Baudelaire, *Les Fleurs du mal*, ed. Jacques Dupont (Paris: Flammarion, 1991), p. 63.

25 See de Man, 'Anthropomorphism and Trope in the Lyric', pp. 249–51. For a detailed and insightful reading of this essay to which my quick comments are indebted, see Kevin Newmark, 'Beyond Movement: Paul de Man's History', in his *Beyond Symbolism: Textual History and the Future of Reading* (Ithaca: Cornell University Press, 1991), pp. 195–230.

26 De Man, 'Anthropomorphism and Trope in the Lyric', p. 251.

27 Fredric Jameson, *Late Marxism: Adorno, or, The Persistence of the Dialectic* (London: Verso, 1990), p. 46.

28 De Man, 'Anthropomorphism and Trope in the Lyric', p. 249.

29 De Man, 'Anthropomorphism and Trope in the Lyric', p. 251.

30 Newmark, 'Beyond Movement', p. 218.

31 De Man, 'Semiology and Rhetoric', *passim*.

32 See Warminski, 'Ending Up/Taking Back', pp. 17–20, for a good discussion of this issue.

33 Warminski, 'Ending Up/Taking Back', pp. 19–20.

34 De Man, 'Conclusions: Walter Benjamin's "The Task of the Translator"', in *The Resistance to Theory*, pp. 73–105, pp. 74–6. Page numbers will hereafter be given in the text. The piece is an edited transcript of the last of de Man's six Messenger Lectures delivered at Cornell University, and is based on tape recordings and what the editor, William Jewett, describes as 'eight pages of rough manuscript notes' (see his comments, p. 73n.). It is reproduced with an interesting question and answer session. The essay first appeared in *Yale French Studies*, 69 (1985), pp. 25–46, with a fuller editorial note (pp. 25–6), no discussion section, and the title punctuated differently ('Conclusions' appears in inverted commas). Wlad Godzich says that 'from the outset' *The Resistance to Theory*, which de Man left unfinished, was meant to include the essay on Benjamin, for which the lecture is a preparatory version (see his 'Foreword: The Tiger on the Paper Mat', in *The Resistance to Theory*, pp. ix–xviii, p. xi). De Man's 'tentative' plans for *The Resistance to Theory* and *Aesthetics, Rhetoric, Ideology* are recorded in a letter to Lindsay Waters of 11 August 1983 (which does not, however, mention the Benjamin lecture): see Lindsay Waters, 'Introduction. Paul de Man: Life and Works', in de Man, *Critical Writings, 1953–1978*, ed. Lindsay Waters (Minneapolis: University of Minnesota Press, 1989), pp. ix–lxxiv, pp. lxix–lxxn.

35 Cf. de Man, 'Blocking the Road', *Romanticism and Contemporary Criticism*, p. 191. This piece contains a brisk reading of Benjamin's essay on translation. It is in some respects a useful synoptic anticipation of the later lecture.

36 Ibid.

37 A phrase explored by Neil Hertz – most relevantly in his 'More Lurid Figures', *Diacritics* 20: 3 (Fall 1990), pp. 2–27, p. 3.

38 Walter Benjamin, 'Die Aufgabe des Übersetzers', in Benjamin, *Gesammelte Schriften*, ed. Rolf Tiedemann and Hermann Schweppenhäuser, vol. 4.1, ed. Tillman Rexroth (Frankfurt am Main: Suhrkamp, 1972), pp. 9–21; 'The Task of the Translator', trans. Harry Zohn, in Benjamin, *Selected Writings*, pp. 253–63. The essay was written in 1921 and published in 1923 as the foreword to Benjamin's translation of Baudelaire's *Tableaux parisiens*.

39 Benjamin, 'The Coming Philosophy', *Selected Writings*, p. 108.

40 Cf. Benjamin, *The Origin of German Tragic Drama*, trans. John Osborne (London: NLB, 1977), p. 36: 'The [I]dea is something linguistic, it is that element of the symbolic in the essence of any word. In empirical perception, in which words have become fragmented, they possess, in addition to their more or less hidden, symbolic aspect, an obvious, profane meaning. It is the task of the philosopher to restore, by representation, the primacy of the symbolic character of the word, in which the [I]dea is given self-consciousness, and that is the opposite of all outwardly-directed communication.'

41 On de Manian pathos, see Neil Hertz, 'More Lurid Figures', and his earlier 'Lurid Figures', in Lindsay Waters and Wlad Godzich (eds), *Reading de Man Reading* (Minneapolis: University of Minnesota Press, 1989), pp. 82–104.

42 Benjamin, 'Die Aufgabe des Übersetzers', pp. 13–14; 'The Task of the Translator', *Selected Writings*, p. 257.

43 Carol Jacobs, 'The Monstrosity of Translation: "The Task of the Translator"', now reprinted in Jacobs, *In the Language of Walter Benjamin* (Baltimore: Johns Hopkins University Press, 1999), pp. 75–90, p. 82.

44 Cf. Benjamin, 'Die Aufgabe des Übersetzers', p. 18: 'Die Forderung der Wörtlichkeit [ist] unableitbar [underivable] aus dem Interesse der Erhaltung des Sinnes'. This is Jacobs's revealing translation ('The Monstrosity of Translation', p. 83): 'The demand for literality is no *offspring* of an interest in maintaining meaning' (my emphasis). Cf. 'The Task of the Translator', *Selected Writings*, p. 260.

45 Benjamin, 'Die Aufgabe des Übersetzers', p. 21. Cf. Jacobs, 'The Monstrosity of Translation', p. 88.

46 De Man quotes Zohn's unrevised translation, as I do here ('The Task of the Translator' in Benjamin, *Illuminations*, trans. Harry Zohn [New York: Schocken Books, 1969], pp. 69–82, p. 78). I have removed a comma introduced, I presume, by de Man's editor. Zohn revised his translation: cf. Benjamin, *Selected Writings*, p. 260, though the new version still presents the same target: 'glueing' and 'matching' appear again, and the fragments are still not *broken* parts.

47 Benjamin, 'Die Aufgabe des Übersetzers', p. 18.

48 Cf. Jacobs, 'The Monstrosity of Translation', p. 84.

49 Benjamin, 'The Task of the Translator', *Selected Writings*, p. 262.

50 Cf. de Man's discussion of the indifference of the terms '*Angemessenheit*' and '*Unangemessenheit*' in Kant's third *Critique*: 'Phenomenality and Materiality in Kant', in *Aesthetic Ideology*, pp. 70–90, pp. 89–90. (Perhaps de Man recalled that the 1799 edition managed accidentally to mix these words up anyway.)

51   Baudelaire, *Les Fleurs du mal*, p. 62; de Man, 'Anthropomorphism and Trope in the Lyric', pp. 251–2.
52   De Man, 'Anthropomorphism and Trope in the Lyric', p. 252.
53   See de Man, 'Kant's Materialism', *Aesthetic Ideology*, p. 127.
54   Martin Heidegger, 'Letter on Humanism', in Heidegger, *Basic Writings*, rev. edn, ed. David Farrell Krell (London: Routledge, 1993), pp. 217–65, p. 260.
55   Newmark, 'Beyond Movement', p. 220.
56   Hertz, 'Lurid Figures', p. 86.
57   Benjamin's ideas concerning transcendental surfaces of inscription – from whose distortions a speculative possibility of an infinity of other surfaces is legible – is worth comparison here; see Caygill, *Walter Benjamin*, p. 4.
58   This is from a brief conference reply (1981): de Man, 'Murray Krieger: A Commentary', *Romanticism and Contemporary Criticism*, pp. 181–7, p. 186. The appearance of the word starts de Man musing about his own rather individual confusion of 'forlorn' with 'foghorn'.
59   For their help and inspiration I would like to record here my thanks to Julie Bishop, Katherine Cross, Simon Jarvis, Michael Rossington, and Richard Salmon.

3 Freud and the Force of History: *The Project for a Scientific Psychology*

CLARE CONNORS

In a review article entitled 'History and Psychoanalysis', Antony Easthope recalls Freud's Ratman moving a stone from his lover's path and then putting it back again. This story serves Easthope as an analogy for the relationship between 'history' and 'psychoanalysis':

> The question of the relation between history and the process of the unconscious, between ideology and phantasy, like Ratman's obsessive stone, is something we seem unable either to resolve or forget. There are two approaches to the issue, one from the side of history, the other from the side of psychoanalysis.[1]

What Easthope is describing is a kind of 'differend'.[2] To presume to arbitrate between an historical account of the psyche and a psychoanalytical account of history suggests that one has found a position from which to speak which is itself neither unconsciously inflected nor historically determined, or which manages to offer an unskewed account of the 'totality' of the historical and the psychic. Since, as it seems, no such position is available to us, all that remains is Sisyphean or Ratmaniacal stone-shifting.

What follows works at some remove from the discourses of 'history' and 'psychoanalysis' to which Easthope refers in what itself seems a rather 'totalizing' way. Instead of something which could confidently be called 'psychoanalysis' I examine what might be dubbed a mechanical psychoneurology, as it is propounded in an essay of Freud's entitled by his editor the *Project for a Scientific Psychology* (1895). And instead of 'history', I examine periodicity and, more grandly perhaps, temporality, as it relates to this mechanical/neurological account of the psyche. What I seek to show, however, is something that perhaps needs to be considered in any discussion of 'history and psychoanalysis' – namely that the stone-shifting manoeuvres which in Easthope's account seem to belong to the metadiscursive jockeying for explanatory primacy between 'history' and 'psychoanalysis', in fact turn out to be what comes 'first'.

First Things First: Positioning the *Project*

Within the history of psychoanalysis, Freud's *Project for a Scientific Psychology* has a dubious position. In many ways it has to be thought of as prehistorical, since, whilst indubitably signed by psychoanalysis's founding father, it cannot be said to belong to the body of psychoanalysis 'proper'. It is a work of neurology and biophysics – neat science rather than psychoanalytic interpretation. Elizabeth Wilson has summed up this rather dismissive opinion succinctly in her survey of scholarly attempts to place the *Project,* citing David Farrell Krell's description of it as 'this duckbilled platypus of a scientific psychology' in order to argue that for most critics the *Project*'s interest 'has been primarily a developmental or chronological one' since its neurological substratum leads it to be considered a 'prepsychoanalytic document'.[3] But other, more complex, textual histories have also been sketched for the *Project*. Both James Strachey and Jacques Derrida feel impelled to employ an 'uncanny' vocabulary to describe the text's relationship to the rest of the Freudian corpus; the former writes that 'the *Project*, or rather its invisible ghost, haunts the whole series of Freud's theoretical writings to the very end'[4] and the latter describes the trajectory 'from the *Project* (1895) to the "Note on the Mystic Writing Pad" (1925)' as 'a strange progression'.[5] From both these distinct perspectives then, it seems that Freud's early attempt to formalize a neurology and economics of the psyche cannot be related to his later writings in terms of a simple teleology, or a language of precedence or subsequence. The *Project* is not a first thing or position, but 'haunts' the later work in such a way that any notion of 'progression' from it becomes 'strange'.

I dwell on these troubled textual histories, because it seems to me that their temporal and historical problems are also those of the *Project*'s own *theoretical* preoccupations. What proves so baffling to attempts to situate it simply as a first thing in a developmental schema or oeuvre is partly the fact that it is itself disturbed by questions as to what *is* primal or primordial. What the *Project* attempts to do is to establish the 'first principles' of the psyche in terms of an interplay between neuronal substance and incoming 'force'. Because force is always presented as irrupting into the material, neuronal substratum of the psyche from an 'outside', in terms of a history of the psyche the earliest, most primordial thing in Freud's narrative ought to be neuronal substance. However, as I shall show, Freud's thinking is mobilized throughout the *Project* by a basic paradox: force is at once anathema to the psyche, causing it pain and unpleasure and driving it to all sorts of stratagems of avoidance and management, but at the same time force is absolutely fundamental to the operation of the psyche and determines it in its being. What this radically contradictory logic leads to in the *Project* is Freud's tenacious adherence to the idea of the primordial and untouched nature of neuronal substance – an idea which, however, cannot be sustained in the course of the essay's theoretical manoeuvres. This has important consequences, both for the trajectory of a developmental history *of* the psyche, and for the relationship posited within such an account between the psyche and time. As I demonstrate, the psyche emerges within this problematic as that which both mediates and fails to mediate the logico-temporal impossibilities arising from the substance/force dialectic.

First Principles

So what *are* the first principles of this text? What the *Project* ostensibly offers us is an encounter between two different branches of the natural sciences – neurology and mechanics. Freud glosses his aims in the *Project* in a letter to Wilhelm Fliess, dated 25 May 1895, thus:

> I am vexed by two intentions: to discover what form the theory of psychical functioning will take if a quantitative line of approach, a kind of economics of nervous force, is introduced into it, and, secondly, to extract from psychopathology a yield for normal psychology.[6]

Freud intends 'to represent psychical processes as quantitatively determinate states of specifiable material particles'.[7] These material particles are neurones, which are understood as the basic unit of the nervous system – the bottom line, in terms of a material science of the psyche.[8] Quantity ('Q') is glossed as 'what distinguishes activity from rest [...] subject to the general laws of motion'.[9] Whilst the character of 'Q' is somewhat elusive – Freud frequently asserts that the 'characteristics of neuronal motion [are] still quite unknown to us'[10] – we can think of it as force, as the 'nervous force' he refers to in the letter to Fliess cited above, in that it has an impact upon the neurones and produces an alteration in their state.[11] The first state of the neurones is presented as being one of *inertia*. This notion of inertia needs to be distinguished immediately from inertia as it is understood in physics, and more particularly in Newtonian mechanics. There inertia is a property of both mobile and immobile bodies, and refers to a zero level of acceleration, not of movement. Force (contra the Aristotelian model) is not necessary to maintain motion itself. If no force acts upon a moving body, its acceleration is zero, and in physical terms it is therefore inert. For Freud, on the other hand, inertia means the *immobility* of substance, and a constant level of movement or excitation (as we will later see posited in the constancy principle) can no longer be thought of in terms of inertia. So, the 'first things' in the *Project* are, on the one hand, inert neuronal matter, and on the other hand incoming, infracting force or 'Q'. And Freud's initial postulate is that these two things are originally distinct in their essence. The neurones do not 'have' any force of their own, and their aim is to remain in a force-free state.

The first guise in which we encounter 'Q' in the *Project* (and the 'first' way in which the psyche, Freud suggests, encounters 'Q') is as an influx into the nervous system from outside in the world – that is to say as an external stimulus. The operation of the neurones is to be understood at this point as being governed by the inertia principle, the principle 'that neurones tend to divest themselves of Q. On this basis the structure and development as well as the functions [of neurones] are to be understood'.[12] It is particularly interesting to note the casual elision of atemporal structure and historical development here, an elision which seems to fudge the historical issue. A structural propensity on the part of the neurones to boot force out suggests an initial spatial separateness of force, but implies that force and substance are equi-primordial. A developmental account, on the other hand, allows for the possibility that force comes later in time than substance. Its spatial status as structurally exterior slips into a temporal status as historically second. According to either narrative, however, neurones are initially 'inert', and exogenous force arrives late on the scene, whence it departs again almost immediately, since the neurones' main inclination is to return once more to an untroubled state of inertia ('neurones tend to divest themselves of Q'). So one fundamental condition pertains in these theorizations: hypothetically, if not actually, we are to think of neuronal substance as initially distinct from and innocent of force. In terms of the psyche's own history, its material substantial being is there *first*, before anything arrives to bother it.

This fantasy, or, to use a less psychoanalytically loaded word, hypothesis, of an originally forceless neuronal substratum leads to an odd situation. On the one hand the neurones must be pictured as jealously guarding their identity as distinct from incoming force, on the other this hostility to force takes the form of complete permeability *to* force, because only absolute unresistance could be deemed forceless. So only by completely giving themselves up to force can the neurones remain distinct from it.

But in fact the neurones never give themselves entirely over to force, even under the most simple and archaic laws of the inertia principle. The discharge of force under the auspices of this principle occurs through the 'axis cylinder' of the neurones to the body's muscular mechanisms, the 'Q' received being expended in the convulsive twitch of a reflex action.[13] Now, the fact that the neurone is already in possession of an 'axis cylinder' along which force is conducted, suggests that the neurone 'itself' is not undifferentiated substance, but consists of bits which resist force, in order that force be conducted along the proper unresisting route. So, the neurones *do*, always, counter force as *reflex* – as an angled reflection or deflection of force.

But what happens in the *Project* is that this possibility – that the neuronal substance is *itself* constructed out of an 'internally' differentiated force-field – cannot be acknowledged all at once, but only through a lengthy theoretical narrative of ever greater complexity and differentiation. To start with, Freud introduces this possibility as a *developmental* modification that still remains within the remit of the inertia principle:

> Here is room for the development of a secondary function. For among the paths of discharge those are preferred and retained which involve a cessation of the stimulus: *flight from the stimulus*. Here in general there is a proportion between the Q of excitation and the effort necessary for the flight from the stimulus, so that the principle of *inertia* is not upset by this.[14]

So the theme of preference of route is introduced as a secondary modification, when in fact the *existence* of routes or paths of discharge actually suggests that a differentiation of forces already exists within the neurone from the start. Freud's story of first things and second things holds off the notion that the neurones 'possess' force, thereby preserving the ostensible primacy of the inertia principle.

The physical untenability of the inertia principle adduced here can also be deduced in a more 'metaphysical' way. That is to say it is not merely an impossibility in terms of the structure of the neurones as Freud describes them, but also in terms of the theoretical possibility of the inertia principle itself. Inertia, as we have said, refers to an hypothesized original inert state of the neurones. But what is interesting is that inertia for Freud is not just a *state* of the neurones, but is also the *principle* of their operation and their *goal*. The immediate discharge of force is described as the '*primary function* of the nervous system'.[15] The neurones are therefore figured as having a drive *to* inertia, and this fact modifies what initially appeared as the simple logical and temporal precedence of inert neuronal substance over the activity and mobility of even exogenous force. This modification can be understood in two ways. First, it can be said that since the *raison d'être* of the neurones is to deal with force, then they will always have had to take force into account, prior to any actual instance of its manifestation. They must always – it is their 'primary function' – be geared up for force, precisely because, although its appearance is temporally subsequent, force can always overtake them. To this extent, force has a logical priority over the neurones, and determines them in their being, in a classically dialectical fashion, as the hostile 'other' against which they both define and guard themselves. In their anxiety to master force, they are enslaved by it. But secondly, if the neurones are thought of as constantly striving for inertia, then this striving is not, in itself, inert and could thus be thought of *as* a force. The very principle which strives to sustain the absolute irenic substantiality and unvitiated integrity of (neuronal) substance has to tip over into, or mimic, its obverse, for force turns out to be too strong for management and calculation by anything other than another force. This 'force' of inertia is never going to fulfil itself, because it is ruined in its very principle by its paradoxical or tautological status as an activity that aims for the cessation of all activity, a force that aims for the expulsion of all force. Its own action cancels its ends, serving and postponing them simultaneously. The 'inertia drive' (if we can thus designate it) is caught up in the attempt to catch its own shadow, Freud's accounts positing as something *simply* exterior and inimical to it what is in fact the very mode of its own operation or presentation.

If we were reading all this from what Easthope calls the 'side of psycho-analysis' we might refer to Freud's manoeuvres in terms of displacement and disavowal. But what starts to emerge is that something like 'displacement' already has to be 'happening' before what is being posited as the 'psyche' could be said to be *in* place. Whether we are talking about the 'internal' construction of the individual neurone, or the distinction between the neurones *qua* substance and exogenous force, what has to come 'first' is a differentiating conflict of forces. But in terms of Freud's theorizations, this differentiation has to be separated out – or deferred – into a sequential narrative. So first we have the inertia principle, and then we have its secondary modifications whereby certain paths of discharge are preferred, and then we have the constancy principle.

The Constancy Principle

The constancy principle arises because of the nervous system's corporeality or embodiment, which means it is not just prey to external forces that it can escape through the *use* of its body, but is also subject to forces (such as the needs of hunger, respiration and sexuality) which *come* from that body, and which can only be mitigated through a recourse to the outside world which will require greater force to enact than these stimulating demands themselves supply. That is to say that hunger pangs, for example, do not in themselves supply enough force to propel the body in a quest for food. These endogenous forces seem to be presented as a later *phylogenetic* development than that of the exogenous forces:

> With an [increasing] complexity of the interior [of the organism], the nervous system receives stimuli from the somatic element itself – endogenous stimuli – which have equally to be discharged.[16]

Because one cannot run away from oneself, it is necessary to store a certain amount of force, in order to deal with somatic exigencies as they arise. Freud also refers to this as the 'secondary function' of the nervous system, a designation which seems still to be in keeping with the assumption of the primordiality of the neurones and their concomitant 'primary function' of the maintenance of inertia. He writes that

> the nervous system is obliged to *abandon* its *original trend* to inertia. [...] It must put up with [maintaining] a store of Qη sufficient to meet the demand for a specific action. Nevertheless, the manner in which it does this shows that the *same trend* persists, *modified* into an endeavour at least to keep the Qη as low as possible and to guard against any increase of it – that is to keep it constant [my italics].[17]

So the initial, primary, original trend of the neurones to get rid of force as quickly as possible, since it has nothing, fundamentally, to do with them, gives way under the 'exigencies of life' to a subsequent, secondary, belated trend. The tendency of Freud's rhetoric is to suggest that the constancy principle arrives late on the scene, adopted as the least bad option; it is the *Realpolitik* of the nervous system – a policy of the possible, rather than the ideal origin and telos of unvitiated original substance. And yet, introducing the constancy principle, Freud acknowledges that it has, in fact, been there all along: 'The principle of inertia is, however, *broken through from the first* owing to another circumstance' [my italics].[18]

The very phrase 'broken through from the first' is expressive of a kind of temporal impossibility, for we have to think of a rupture that has its full force *as* a rupture, whilst at the same time not being in any sequential sense subsequent to the integrity *which* it ruptures. So we have a primary principle (inertia) and then a secondary principle (constancy) which operate simultaneously. The *Project*'s subsequent theorizations then separate this impossible simultaneity out again in spatial terms, in the positing of different 'classes' of neurones, which will allow for the elaboration of a structure of memory. What this seems to do is to displace the force/inertia or force/substance distinction, which is also to say the conflict between force and force. Force can no longer be cast as something simply exterior to the inert neurones, and so instead the exterior position of force is relocated to an exteriority within the psyche. This spatial division into permeable and impermeable neurones also has a concomitant temporal displacement, into forces experienced as periodic, and forces experienced as without period.

Memory, Force and Time: Introducing the Permeable and Impermeable Neurones

The theorizations of memory get the *Project* into another temporal tangle. As one of the principal features of the psyche, memory has to be accounted for. And memory understood at its broadest refers to any alteration in the neuronal substratum brought about by the passage of force. It can thus even be seen in the 'primary process' in the preferred paths for force, which determine the passage which force takes. The problem of memory, for which 'a psychological theory deserving any consideration must furnish an explanation',[19] turns out to be another way of working out the simultaneity of 'broken through from the first', or the paradox of a drive to inertia. For there to be memory, there has to be a way for the incursions of force to be recorded, but at the same time the psychic system has to be permanently free to receive new (i.e. future) forces, which in their turn can be remembered. The psyche has to be capable at once of guarding its identity through time, and simultaneously of allowing it to alter with time. Neither a simple notion of resistance and impermeability, nor one of unresistance and permeability, will do. If force made its mark solely through breaking down resistances, then once these were broken through, nothing more could be recorded. If, on the other hand, the neurones operated as first hypothesized, and were completely permeable and unresistant then not only would nothing be recorded at all, but, as we have already suggested, the neurones would themselves be untenable – they quite simply could not have an existence. So, Freud needs to postulate a structure capable at once of laying down memories and of receiving new ones, and he is thus led to posit 'two classes of neurones':

> (1) those which allow $Q\eta$ to pass through as though they had no contact-barriers and which, accordingly, after each passage of excitation are in the same state as before and (2) those whose contact-barriers make themselves felt, so that they only allow $Q\eta$ to pass through with difficulty or partially. The latter class may, after each excitation, be in a different state from before and they thus afford a *possibility of representing memory*.[20]

The 'two classes' of neurones, permeable and impermeable, are dubbed ϕ [phi] and the ψ [psi] respectively. Because of the relative 'impermeability' of the latter, force has to put up a fight as it goes through. In this strife the contact-barriers are 'breached', some of their resistance being overcome. This 'over-coming' can have a permanent effect, thus fulfilling the criterion of the permanent alteration to neuronal substance necessary for memory to be recorded, and Freud calls this process 'Bahnung', which literally means 'path-breaking'. Strachey translates this as 'facilitation', a word which aptly suggests the communicative link between neurones, but omits any sense of resistance, thereby abrogating the sense of forceful conflict which is at the heart of Freud's descriptions. Derrida's 'frayage', which his translator Alan Bass gives as 'breaching', renders this better, maintaining 'the sense of the *force* that breaks open a pathway, and the *space* opened by this force'.[21] Here, in Derrida's glossing of Freud's 'Bahnung', we can see how force and violence intersect:

> Breaching, the tracing of a trail, opens up a conducting path. Which presupposes a certain violence and a certain resistance to effraction. The path is broken, cracked, *fracta*, breached.[22]

Violence, understood as the violation of an integrity, occurs as a force breaks a path through a neurone, and as that neurone provides resistance to it. The very origin of memory, and hence of the psyche as such, would seem then to lie in force's violence.

But there are still problems with our account as it stands. For a start, it might seem here that having established, at the level of the single neurone, that difference and deferral of force has a certain precedence over the neurone's 'substance', we now have to insert a difference between two 'classes' of (pre-existing) neuronal substance, thereby reasserting the temporal (as well as transcendental) precedence of substance, and reinstating all the theoretical problems that we have seen this entails for an adequate description of the operation of the psyche. In fact, this newly-won precedence must again be ceded. For, to re-cap a little, the recalcitrance of impermeable neurones to force must still be thought of as force*ful* and the promiscuous availability of permeable neurones to force just as quickly sullies the purity of the force/substance distinction. Thus, considering the matter from 'the biological standpoint' Freud rejects the 'arbitrariness' of the assumption that there is an 'ultimate difference between the valence of the contact-barriers of ϕ and of ψ' (p. 303). He argues that the degree of neurone facilitation is a direct result of the amount of force passing through the neurones, and that the ψ [psi] neurones are more resistant to force because, dealing with endogenous force, they have less of it to deal with. He writes

> Let us therefore attribute the differences not to the neurones but to the quantities with which they have to deal. [...] A difference in their essence is replaced by a difference in the environment to which they are destined.[23]

So, once again, differences of force here linked with differences of *place,* are the determining factor in the differentiation of the neurones, and, as we have already seen, it is only through its difference from other neurones that the single neurone can exist. But, and this is the second problem that we need to deal with here, a simple monolithic bifurcation between permeable and impermeable neurones would not be sufficient to account for memory, for, Freud says, memory is one of the factors which direct the pathway of a force and, were resistance equal throughout the ψ neurones, it would be impossible to explain why one pathway is preferred over another. So, Freud concludes, *'memory is represented by the differences in the facilitations between the ψ neurones'*.[24] Memory does not arise through a discrete occurrence of breaching, as a simple trauma or wound suffered by a neurone, but through the difference between breaches. It should be emphasized that we are not simply talking about the difference between an opposing and a resisting force, but between the different encounters of forces. And in order for these 'encounters' to 'occur' and not to flood and explode the system from the start, there 'already' has to be difference – the possibility for the relaying, deferral and repetition of forces in the neuronal system. This is no longer simply to figure neurones dialectically as a counter-force, but to suggest that force's 'initial' deferral, differentiation and repetition is what enables a distinction between neurones (as substance, substrate and form) and force (as quantity and intensity), to operate.

This is the (uncomfortable) 'position' to which Derrida's account of the *Project* in 'Freud and the Scene of Writing' leads us. Arising out of an 'original' difference, memory's origin cannot be located at a self-identical geographical or temporal point. As Derrida says

> Trace as memory is not a pure breaching that might be reappropriated at any time as simple presence; it is rather the ungraspable and invisible difference between breaches. We thus already know that psychic life is neither the transparency of meaning nor the opacity of force but the difference within the exertion of forces.[25]

The Psyche and Time

So, tracking Freud's developmental account of the psyche as original substance subsequently and belatedly subject to the slings and arrows of an outrageous and forceful fortune, we come up instead with the less narratively comprehensible logic of a violent postponement, of something 'broken through from the first'. Having followed the temporal/historical problems this introduces into Freud's own theoretical narrative, we shall now look at how that narrative itself describes the relationship between the psyche and time.

In the hypothetical 'state' of neuronal inertia it is difficult to imagine anything like time. Inertia is not a state that exists 'in time'. For a start, as I have shown, it does not exist at all. And for seconds, surely even the temporal 'movement' of existence would spell the ruin of this superlatively lethargic state.[26] What effect then does the effraction of force have? Operating under the auspices of the inertia/constancy principles, the neurones have, in a sense, to take the future into account if they are to persist at all.[27] The neurones' survival is determined by their capacity to delay force in anticipation of future threat. But since this 'capacity' is the very condition of the possibility of the neurones' existence (in time), then that existence is predicated upon the deferral and delaying of force, and deferral must, in a sense, be 'first'.[28] So, the 'entry' of force into the psychic system is simultaneous with the psyche's 'entry' 'into' time, the psyche being strung out in time through force's deferral.

Oddly, however, this notion of being strung out in time suggests a kind of rectilinear temporality that is at odds with the notion of the sidestepping vicissitudinous processes of the deferral and displacement of force, and also with the punctual, evanescent periodicity that Freud now goes on to attribute to consciousness. In order to account for consciousness, Freud makes another neuronal innovation, inventing the ω [omega] neurones. Nothing is retained in these neurones, which are the province of consciousness, yet, transitorily, they register qualities. They take everything in and retain nothing. Freud's notion of consciousness here resembles nothing so much as the features of pure sense perception, the punctuality of the 'here' and the 'now' in the first stage of Hegel's *Phenomenology of Spirit*.[29] Freud accounts for this pure qualitative perception and absolute punctuality through a temporal differentiation of the concept of force, and a spatial differentiation of the neurones. Force is now thought in terms of *periodicity*. In the *Project,* the sequence of neurones is said to be φ-ψ-ω; force enters through the sense-organs, which like all nerve-endings act as Q-screens, but which also 'sieve' force, only allowing through forces with certain periods. These differences of period, function as differences of quantity in their transference to φ and thence to ψ and in being passed from there to ω are almost devoid of quantity, and thus 'generate conscious sensations of qualities'. The ψ neurones 'too have their period, of course; but it is without quality or, more correctly, monotonous'.[30] The reference to the neurones 'having' period must refer to the way in which the periodicity of force is 'experienced'.

All this terminology is in danger of being alienating, but in fact, in the temporal characterizations of the ω neurones and the ψ neurones, we have the two-sides of a classical notion of time as on the one hand a series of punctual intermittent moments, and on the other a momentless ongoing perdurance. So what the movement of force through the psyche seems to offer us is again a separating out of two paradoxical, mutually incompatible necessities. The paradox, in this case, would be Zeno's. In one set of neurones, there is periodicity, in the other, there is monotony. And what allows for these two possibilities is, once again, deferral and differentiation of force.

In Conclusion: History and the Psyche

What I have been suggesting, is that the displacement and deferral of force is key in two ways. First, it is the means by which the psyche is constructed, and by which it perdures. The psyche routes forces through itself, and is constructed by this routing. Second, it is also the theoretical mode of the *Project* itself. An initially intolerable and untenable opposition substance/force, is displaced into other oppositions – primary and secondary principles, permeable and impermeable neurones, periodic and monotonous forces – all of which seem to be a way of separating out an 'inaugural' clash of necessary and mutually antagonistic propositions into a temporal and topographical model expressed through a developmental theoretical narrative. The *Project*'s projections operate in the same way as force's deferral, as a repetition/alteration/ postponement of its founding propositions. And so, to think of the *Project* as a simple description of the psyche becomes problematic. Perhaps we could say that it is a kind of 'displacement' of it.

The psyche 'itself', then, appears in the *Project* on the one hand as what allows a linear and progressive model of history to maintain a certain currency, by separating out intolerable logico-temporal oppositions, and on the other, inasmuch as it operates as such a filter, as something which must always also appear as radically inassimilable to this kind of a history. The 'psyche' *at once* enables history, and simultaneously disables it. And, with an equally convoluted logic, both 'force' and 'time' are *at once* necessary to the psyche and yet its ruin. The obsessive stone-shifting that Antony Easthope describes vis-à-vis 'history and psychoanalysis' is not just a metadiscursive impasse, but has to be thought as the condition of (im)possibility of both terms, in their interrelation and their radical non-relation. This enabling/disabling condition of (im)possibility obeys the wild logic of an integrity that is 'broken through from the first'.

Notes

1   *Textual Practice* 9:2 (Summer 1995), p. 349.
2   See Jean-François Lyotard, *The Differend: Phrases in Dispute*, trans. Georges Van Den Abbeele (Manchester: Manchester University Press, 1988). A 'differend' is a point of intersection and conflict between two discourses that cannot justly be resolved, since any resolution would entail either the unjust appeal to one set of discursive terms over the other, or the violent imposition of a meta-language.
3   Elizabeth Wilson, *Neural Geographies: Feminism and the Microstructure of Cognition* (London: Routledge, 1998), pp. 134–6.
4   James Strachey, 'Introduction' in Sigmund Freud, *The Project for a Scientific Psychology* (1895), in *The Standard Edition of the Complete Psychological Works of Sigmund Freud*, trans. and ed. James Strachey, vol. 1 (London: The Hogarth Press, 1966), pp. 283–398, p. 290.
5   Jacques Derrida, *Writing and Difference*, trans. Alan Bass (London: Routledge, 1978), p. 200.
6   Quoted in Freud, *Project*, p. 283.
7   *Project*, p. 285.

8   Strachey tells us in a footnote, *Project*, p. 295, that the term 'neurone' referring to the ultimate unit of the nervous system, was introduced by W. Waldeyer in 1891. (Neuron, without the final 'e', is the more usual spelling.)

9   *Project*, p. 295.

10   *Project*, p. 372. See also p. 379, where Freud refers to 'the unknown neuronal motion'.

11   Strachey, 'Appendix C', ibid., points out that Q is similar to electricity in the two ways in which it can be measured – both as the level of the cathexis of the neurone, which corresponds to the measure of amperage in electrical terms, and as the flow between cathexes, which corresponds to voltage. This would suggest that Q is to be understood as energy. On the 'scientific' question as to whether either of these terms from the physical sciences should be imported into psychoanalysis, see J. Laplanche and J.-B. Pontalis, *The Language of Psycho-analysis*, trans. Donald Nicholson-Smith (London: The Hogarth Press, 1973), p. 129. Here they offer a pragmatic 'defence' of Freud's use of concepts from mechanics, arguing that 'natural science itself does not pronounce upon the ultimate nature of the quantities whose variations, transformations and equivalences it studies. It is content to define them by their effects (for example, force is that which effects a certain work) and to make comparisons between them (one force is measured by another, or rather, their effects are compared between themselves)'.

12   *Project*, p. 296.

13   Freud writes that 'a primary nervous system makes use of th[e] Qη which it has [...] acquired, by giving it off through a connecting path to the muscular mechanisms, and in that way keeps itself free from stimulus. This discharge represents the primary function of the nervous system' (ibid.).

14   Ibid.

15   Ibid.

16   *Project*, pp. 296–7.

17   *Project*, p. 297. Note that Qη tends to refer to quantity once it is inside the psychic mechanism. Strachey discusses this in his Introduction, *Project*, p. 289.

18   Ibid.

19   *Project*, p. 299.

20   Ibid.

21   Derrida, *Writing and Difference*, p. 329.

22   Ibid., p. 200.

23   *Project*, p. 304. Elizabeth Wilson draws on this feature of Freud's neurology to argue that the *Project* still has validity for the neurocognitive sciences, in that it prefigures various connectionist theories of cognition, in which 'a memory is not a property of the unit or a group of units (i.e. a store), but the effect of relational differences in the activation between units and across a network' (p. 161).

24   *Project*, p. 300.

25   Derrida, *Writing and Difference*, p. 201.

26   I have been trying, perhaps to the point of perversity, to refrain from suggesting ways in which these arguments 'prefigure' or even 'haunt' later *psychoanalytic* texts, but the time has come. The incompatibility between total inertia and temporal existence is dealt with more fully by Freud in *Beyond the Pleasure Principle*, in *The Standard Edition of The Complete Psychological Works of Sigmund Freud*, trans. and ed. James Strachey, vol. 18 (London: The Hogarth Press, 1955), pp. 3–64, where total inertia is seen as no different from death.

27 See Malcolm Bowie, *Psychoanalysis and the Future of Theory* (Oxford: Blackwell, 1993). Bowie gives an excellent account of psychoanalytic time, but one with which I disagree in specifics. He argues that whilst Freud made some concessions to anticipation and prophylaxis, in the practice of psychoanalysis 'the past always had a logical as well as a chronological priority over the present and the future; and it always had more explanatory force' (p. 19). For Bowie it is Lacan's paper on the 'mirror phase' which 'replaces a unilinear time-scale, generated from the relation 'earlier than', by a temporal dialectic, a backwards and forwards scansion' (p. 25). I am arguing that this unsettling 'dialectic' can already be glimpsed in Freud's *Project*.

28 See Derrida, *Writing and Difference*, p. 203: 'No doubt life protects itself by repetition, trace, *différance* (deferral). But we must be wary of this formulation: there is no life present *at first* which would *then* come to protect, postpone, or reserve itself in *différance*. The latter constitutes the essence of life'.

29 G.W.F. Hegel, *Phenomenology of Spirit*, trans. A.V. Miller (Oxford: Oxford University Press, 1977).

30 Freud, *Project*, p. 310.

PART II
TRAUMATIC HISTORIES

4 Parting Words: Trauma, Silence and Survival

CATHY CARUTH

For Elaine G. Caruth, PhD[1]

Freud begins his groundbreaking work, *Beyond the Pleasure Principle*, with his astonished encounter with the veterans of World War I, whose dreams of the battlefield bring them back, repeatedly, to the horrifying scenes of death that they have witnessed. Like the victims of accident neuroses, these dreams seem to bring the soldiers back to a moment of fright or surprise that constituted their original encounter with death:

> Now dreams occurring in traumatic neuroses have the characteristic of repeatedly bringing the patient back into the situation of his accident, a situation from which he wakes up in another fright. This astonishes people far too little.[2]

The repetition of battlefield horrors in the dreams astonishes Freud, because dreams, in psychoanalytic theory, had always served the function of fulfilling wishes: of allowing the unconscious, conflictual desires of childhood to find expression through the symbolic world of the dream. In the dreams of the returning veterans, however, the encounter with death and horror cannot be assimilated to the fulfilment of desire: rather than turning death into a symbol or vehicle of psychic meaning, these traumatic dreams seem to turn the psyche itself into the vehicle for expressing the terrifying literality of a history it does not completely own. But the peculiarity of this returning, literal history also strikes Freud because it does not only bring back the reality of death, but the fright or unpreparedness for it: the dreams not only show the scenes of battle but wake the dreamer up in another fright. Freud's surprised encounter with the repetitive dreams of the war – the beginning of the theory of trauma, and of history, that has become so central to our contemporary thinking about history and memory – thus raises the urgent and unavoidable questions: *what does it mean for the reality of war to appear in the fiction of the dream? What does it mean for life to bear witness to death? And what is the surprise that is encountered in this witness?*

Immediately after discussing the disturbing dreams of the war, however, Freud proposes to 'leave the dark and dismal subject of the traumatic neurosis' and to pass on to the 'normal' activity of child's play. Freud embarks here upon a story of his encounter with another repetitive behaviour, the 'puzzling activity' of a 'good little boy' of one-and-a-half, just beginning to speak. Freud says he observed the strange game of this child who repeatedly threw a wooden spool on a string into his cot, uttering the sound 'o-o-o-o', then retrieved it, uttering 'a-a-a-a'. With the help of the mother, Freud first interprets these sounds as meaning *fort*, gone, and *da*, here, and ultimately suggests that the child is re-enacting the departure and return of his mother, which he had just recently been forced to confront. The repetitive game, as a story, thus seems to represent the inner symbolic world of the child: as a story of departure and return, the game seems not only symbolically to fulfil a wish by telling the story of the mother's departure as the story of her return, but also to substitute, for the pain of loss, the very pleasure of creation itself.[3] But Freud himself unexpectedly proceeds to challenge his own first interpretation:

> Our interest is directed to another point. The child cannot possibly have felt his mother's departure as something agreeable or even indifferent ... It may perhaps be said in reply that her departure had to be enacted as a necessary preliminary to her joyful return, and that it was in the latter that lay the true purpose of the game. But against this must be counted the observed fact that the first act, that of departure, was staged as a game in itself and far more frequently than the episode in its entirety, with its pleasurable ending (pp. 15–16).

The creative activity of the child's game, Freud recognizes with surprise, does not ultimately involve a symbolic representation of the mother's pleasurable return, but repeats, in a kind of stammer that interrupts its story, the painful memory of her departure. Like the soldiers' dreams, the game thus re-enacts the very memory of a painful reality. What is most surprising in the child's game, however, is that this re-enactment of reality in the game places repetition at the very heart of childhood, and links the repetition to a creative act of invention. In the introduction of the child's game Freud's original question, *how does life bear witness to death?* is linked to another question, *what kind of witness is a creative act?*

I will propose in what follows that Freud's insight into trauma in *Beyond the Pleasure Principle*, his new understanding of personal and of collective history in the face of war, lies precisely in the striking and enigmatic leap that juxtaposes the nightmares of war to the child's game. This juxtaposition is not ordinarily taken into account in the critical reception of Freud's text – the study of trauma in contemporary fields tends to focus on a theory of history and memory derived ultimately from the example of the nightmare and the theory that grows out of it, and the writing on the child's game is not part of the tradition of trauma theory[4] – but it is crucial, I will suggest, for understanding the insight of Freud. My own understanding of this insight did not emerge, however, simply through a reading of Freud's text but began, in fact, in my encounter with a real child in Atlanta, a child whose best friend was murdered in the street and who is interviewed by the friend's mother. By reading together the language of the nightmare and the language of the child in Freud's text – two very distinct kinds of language whose intertwining strands are at the heart of Freud's theory – and in then understanding how Freud's text and the language of the real child shed light upon each other, we can begin to understand Freud's enigmatic move in the theory of trauma from the drive for death to the drive for life, from the reformulating of life around the witness to death, to the possibility of witnessing and making history in creative acts of life.

Death and Awakening

Freud's analysis of repetition compulsion in the origins of consciousness indeed attempts to explain the significance and surprise of the traumatic encounter with death in terms of a new relation between consciousness and life.[5] Consciousness first arose, Freud speculates, as an attempt to protect the life of the organism from the imposing stimuli of a hostile world, by bringing to its attention the nature and direction of external stimuli. The protective function of consciousness as taking in bits of the world, however, was less important, Freud suggests, than its more profound function of keeping the world out, a function it accomplished by placing stimuli in an ordered experience of time. What causes trauma, then, is an encounter that is not directly perceived as a threat to the life of the organism but that occurs, rather, as a break in the mind's experience of time:

> We may, I think, tentatively venture to regard the common traumatic neurosis as a consequence of an extensive breach being made in the protective shield against stimuli .... We still attribute importance to the element of fright. It is caused by lack of any preparedness for anxiety (p. 31).

The breach in the mind – the psyche's awareness of the threat to life – is not caused by a direct threat or injury, but by fright, the lack of preparedness to take in a stimulus that comes too quickly. It is not the direct perception of danger, that is, that constitutes the threat for the psyche, but the fact that the danger is recognized as such one moment too late. It is this lack of direct experience that thus becomes the basis of the repetition of the traumatic nightmare: 'These dreams are endeavoring to master the stimulus retrospectively, by developing the anxiety whose omission was the cause of the traumatic neurosis' (p. 32). The return of the traumatic experience is not the direct witness of a threat to life but rather the attempt to overcome the fact that it was not direct, to master what was never fully grasped in the first place. And since consciousness cannot bear witness to death, the life of the survivor becomes the repetition of the reality that consciousness cannot grasp. In the traumatic encounter with death, life itself attempts to serve as the witness that consciousness cannot provide.

The repetition exemplified by the nightmare, indeed, does not only concern (as I have analysed elsewhere)[6] the repetition of the image in the dream, but the repetition of waking from it:

> Dreams occurring in traumatic neuroses have the characteristic of repeatedly bringing the patient back into the situation of his accident, a situation from which he *wakes up in another fright* (p. 13, my emphasis).

If 'fright' is the term by which Freud defines the traumatic effect of not having been prepared in time, then the trauma of the nightmare does not simply consist in the experience within the dream, but in the experience of waking from it. It is the surprise of waking that repeats the unexpectedness of the trauma. And as such the trauma is not only the repetition of the missed encounter with death, but the missed encounter with one's own survival. It is the incomprehensible act of surviving – of waking into life – that repeats and bears witness to what remains ungrasped within the encounter with death. The repetition of trauma, therefore, is not only an attempt or an imperative to know what cannot be grasped that is repeated unconsciously in the survivor's life: it is also an imperative to live that still remains not fully understood. And it is this incomprehensible imperative to live that Freud ultimately places at the very origin of life, when he suggests that life itself began as the drive to death:

> The attributes of life were at some time awoken in inanimate matter by the action of a force of whose nature we can form no conception ... The tension which then arose in what had hitherto been an inanimate substance endeavored to cancel itself out. In this way the first drive came into being: the drive to return to the inanimate state (p. 38, translation modified).

Life itself originates, Freud here suggests, as an awakening from 'death' for which there was no preparation. Life itself, that is, is an imperative to awaken that precedes any understanding or consciousness and any possible desire or wish.[7] The witness of survival itself – the awakening that constitutes life – lies not only in the incomprehensible repetition of the past, that is, but in the incomprehensibility of a future that is not yet owned. Freud's central question raised by the war nightmare, *what does it mean for life to bear witness to death?* thus ultimately leads to another, more urgent and enigmatic question: *in what way is the experience of trauma also the experience of an imperative to live? What is the nature of a life that continues beyond trauma?*

The Child's Game

It might appear that with this analysis Freud had replaced the notion of the child, and its central place in psychoanalytic theory, with the theory of trauma. The child's repetition of its mother's departure could be explained as the unknowing reliving of its mother's (anticipated) death, and the child's life as the unconscious reliving of what is not yet grasped within the mother's departure. From the perspective of Freud's rethinking of life around its traumatic significance, the child's game thus peculiarly re-enacts the incomprehensible moment of the mother's act of leaving and reshapes the very life of the child as the unconscious witness to the death he has survived. Repeating the *fort* that is not his own, but his mother's act of leaving, the child's own life story – his departure into life – becomes inextricable from his mother's silent departure into death. In this incomprehensible departure, the child's life – like the origin of the drive – thus silently enacts a larger history he does not completely own.[8]

Freud's analysis indeed suggests that the encounter with traumatic repetition requires a rethinking of psychoanalysis itself, which had previously focused its model of the mind on the notion of childhood as the site of the pleasure principle. By modelling the mind on the encounter with war trauma, Freud thus appears to shift the centre of psychoanalytic thinking from the individual struggle with internal Oedipal conflicts of childhood to the external, collective activities of history, and to make of childhood itself a reflection of a more obscure painful encounter. Thus Robert Jay Lifton writes that the reversal of adult and child trauma as a model for the human mind was at the centre of *Beyond*, and produced the 'image-model of the human being as a perpetual survivor'.[9] The questions raised by war trauma concerning the nature of life thus require a new model for psychoanalytic thinking and, in particular, for the relation between psychoanalysis and history.

Beginning Again

Yet the game of the child playing *fort* and *da*, there and here, with his spool, seems to become not less, but more enigmatic when it is understood in relation to traumatic repetition. If the child's re-enactment of his mother's departure repeats, ultimately, her loss and her death, the game remains, still, an act of creation that, unlike the dream of the war veterans, does not simply compulsively repeat a history it does not own but creates, in its repetition, something new.[10] This very movement from the example of traumatic repetition in the war nightmare to the example of the child will, moreover, reappear surprisingly in Freud's text, and will reappear precisely at the moment that Freud has explained the notion of trauma in the very origins of life. For shortly after introducing the origin of life as an awakening out of death, Freud pauses abruptly and starts again:

> But let us pause for a moment and reflect. It cannot be so. The sexual instincts, to which the theory of the neuroses gives a quite special place, appear under a very different aspect ....
>
> The whole path of development to natural death is not trodden by all the elementary entities which compose the complicated body of one of the higher organisms. Some of them, the germ cells, probably retain the original structure of living matter and, after a certain time ... separate themselves from the organism as a whole. Under favourable conditions, they begin to develop – that is, to repeat the performance [*das Spiel wiederholen*] to which they owe their existence; and in the end once again one portion of their substance pursues its development to a finish, while another portion harks back once again as a fresh residual germ to the beginning of the process of development .... They are the true life drives (pp. 39–40, translation modified).

The origin of life as the death drive – as the beginning of the repetition compulsion, and as an awakening – is itself repeated, Freud audaciously suggests, and is repeated, moreover, precisely in the form of a game (*Spiel*). After disappearing for most of his text since his original introduction of the child – and disappearing in particular from the theory of trauma, which is entirely governed by the language of consciousness and awakening[11] – the language of the game reappears, and reappears to describe a different form of repetition: a repeating of the origin of life in another kind of beginning.[12] This repetition brings back, moreover, for the very first time the explicit language of the child's game, the language Freud uses at the moment he recognizes the game as a game of departure:

> But against this must be counted the observed fact that the first act, that of departure, was staged as a game in itself and far more frequently than the episode in its entirety, with its pleasurable ending [daß der erste Akt, das Fortgehen, für sich allein als Spiel inszeniert wurde, und zwar ungleich häufiger als das zum lustvollen Ende fortgeführte Ganze] (p. 16).

This game and the event of departure that it re-enacts is now repeated as the very action of the life drive:

> Under favourable conditions, they begin to develop – that is, to repeat the performance to which they owe their existence; and in the end once again one portion of their substance pursues its development to a finish [Unter günstige Bedingungen gebracht, beginnen sie sich zu entwickeln, daß heißt das Spiel, dem sie ihre Entstehung verdanken, zu wiederholen, und dies endet damit, daß wieder ein Anteil ihrer Substanz die Entwicklung bis zum Ende fortführt] ... (p. 40).

Freud thus reintroduces the language of departure not as the origin of the death drive, but as the way it repeats itself, differently, as the drive for life.[13] The departure into life is not simply the awakening that repeats an original death, but an act of parting that distinguishes, precisely, between death and life.[14] The repetition of this game, then, as an origin, is the beginning of life as a surprising repetition that both bears witness to and breaks from the death drive, that bears witness and repeats by precisely breaking away. It is a language of departure, that is, that does not repeat the unconscious origin of life as death, but creates a history by precisely departing toward survival.

This creative act takes place, moreover, not only in the child's game, but in Freud's own text, as well, through the very transformation undergone by the language of trauma: from the departure – the *fort* – that appears to be the repetition of the mother's anticipated death in the child's game, to the *fortführen* of the drive that is the pressure toward life.[15] This transformation also differentiates or parts the traumatized subject, the soldiers of war repeating death, from the individual testimony of Freud's own text, the creative act of language that becomes not only the story of departures but also the language of play, a language that would, in fact, become a new language for psychoanalysis in the future. In the life drive, then, life itself, and the language of creativity, begin as an act that bears witness to the past even by turning from it; that bears witness to death by bearing witness to the possibility of origination in life. History, here, is reclaimed and generated not in reliving unconsciously the death of the past but by an act that bears witness by parting from it. The language of the life drive does not simply point backward, that is, but bears witness to the past by pointing to the future. The return of the child's language in *Beyond the Pleasure Principle* thus transforms the original questions of trauma – *what does it mean for life to bear witness to death?* and *what is the nature of a life that continues beyond trauma?* into an ultimately more fundamental and elusive concern: *what is the language of the life drive?*

Mementos

The significance of this question arose, for me, not from within Freud's theoretical text, nor in the history of World War I, but in my own encounter with a child in Atlanta, within the contemporary history of urban violence in America. I encountered this child shortly after leaving New Haven and arriving in Atlanta, when I became familiar with a group established in Atlanta to help traumatized children who had witnessed violence, a group called 'Kids Alive and Loved'. This group was established by a woman named Bernadette Leite, whose oldest son, Khalil, was shot in the back one night when he was out with friends, shortly before graduating from high school. The impulse for the group came specifically, as she tells us, not only from witnessing the symptoms of anger and the violent re-enactment of trauma in the kids' responses to the death at the funeral and afterward, but when the mother of the dead boy, Bernadette, overheard the peculiar language of children:

> After his death I noticed that his friends were coming over every afternoon and hanging out in his room. And I began to listen, and I heard them speaking to him. They would come over every afternoon and hang out in his room and speak to him. And I realized that they needed someone to talk to.[16]

Hearing the language of the children addressed only to her dead son, Bernadette recognized the unresolved trauma of many of his friends in their inability to speak about their feelings to the living. She thus decided to found a group to allow the children to talk about their feelings to each other concerning the violence they had experienced, in weekly Wednesday night meetings and through video-taped interviews she has made for the Kids Alive and Loved Oral History Archive. Giving the group the name 'Kids Alive and Loved', whose initials – KAL – reproduce the initials of her child, Khalil Aseem Leite, Bernadette hoped to make the group not only a way of both helping the living children to get over their trauma by talking about Khalil (as well as other murders they had experienced), but also of providing a kind of living memorial to her dead son through the living children's words and lives.

The complexity of this process was most movingly portrayed for me, however, through the words of a single child, in the recorded interview of Bernadette with Gregory, Khalil's best friend. Gregory was 17 at the time of his friend's death. He had received a call from Khalil that morning to go out that evening, but argued about being called so early, and then was not at home when he was called again.[17] Gregory speaks, throughout the interview, in a language that tries to convey the difficulty of grasping Khalil's death: when asked to say something about Khalil's life he answers, 'He lived for everything. He died for nothing'. This inability to grasp the meaning of his friend's death resonates in his own difficulty in extricating a description of Khalil's life from his own survival of Khalil's death:

B: What do you want people to know about his life?
G: He had a good heart.

B: What does [the experience of Khalil's death] feel like?
G: It's like when somebody is actually pulling your heart out, or just repeatedly stabbing it.

The dead Khalil's life and Greg's survival of it are tied around a heart that they share and that has now been removed. Greg's heart, it would appear, being removed and stabbed, tells the story of Khalil's death. In the exchange between Bernadette and Greg, we see Bernadette's attempt to help Greg memorialize Khalil in a kind of language of memory, and we witness Greg's own transformation of her language of memory into a parting that allows for both a memorialization of his friend and a recognition of his own life.

Parting Words

This possibility opens up, strikingly, in a moment of surprise, in a remarkable moment of his interview with her, just at the place, moreover, when the interview turns to the topic of memorialization. Bernadette has been asking about Gregory's feelings concerning Khalil's death, and the interview has become very sombre and at times filled with sorrow. Then Greg makes the interview take a sudden turn:

> B: Do you have any mementos of Khalil?
> G: Let's see ...
> B: Do you have personal belongings of his?
> G: (suddenly smiling): He has something of mine!
> B: (laughing): I know he has something of yours ... a couple of things!
> G: He had ... That's what also made me feel good, because he was buried in my shirt that I loved, and my watch. At first that shirt bothered me because I loved that shirt –
> B: And I didn't know at the time ... Mark picked it out and I only found out later. It's too bad – I wanted to get him a Tommy Hilfiger shirt he'd seen downtown but I didn't have time to get it and get to the funeral parlor. It's too bad – but then maybe he wouldn't have been buried in your favorite shirt.
> G: That's OK, because it was my favorite shirt and my favorite friend.

Greg's first response to Bernadette's question – 'do you have any personal belongings of his?' – comes as a surprise because it reverses the order by which the living Greg would memorialize his dead friend and suggests that it is the dead friend that is keeping mementos of him: 'He has something of mine!', Greg says. This is also, in its irony and humour, a kind of maintenance of the playful relationship that Greg had with the living Khalil: the implicit joke that Khalil got away with his favorite shirt seems to recreate the very humorous relationship they had when Khalil was alive. Greg thus, in effect, says 'gone!' to his shirt and, in so doing, establishes a relationship with Khalil that recognizes, even within the fiction of personification, the ineradicable difference between his life and Khalil's death.

Bernadette's response, likewise, turns both to the dead and to the living at once, although in a somewhat different fashion. On the one hand she tells, very movingly, of a mother who wants to get one last gift for her dead son, to buy him the shirt that he had seen and wanted. But the telling of this story is simultaneously, and equally movingly, a kind of playful mothering of the living boy in front of her, because she empathizes with him that it is too bad that he could not have had his favorite shirt back. To Gregory's *'fort!'* or 'gone!' Bernadette thus says, in effect, *'da!'* or 'here!' and, in this way, makes her act of mothering the living boy a continuation of her mothering of the dead one, and makes of Greg the living memory of the dead Khalil.

It is thus particularly striking that Greg's final words, which are the true climax of the exchange for me, once again give up the shirt to Khalil: 'That's OK … it was my favorite shirt and my favorite friend'. If his first response brought Khalil to life as a youthful friend – and reanimated Greg too as he was before he had the horrible knowledge of Kahlil's death – this final response, in giving the gift to Khalil, gives up that former innocence and recreates Greg through his ability to give to and thus memorialize his dead friend. By once again saying 'gone!', Greg indeed departs from his former self and turns the memento – and the language of the memento – into an act, not of a symbolic return or wish for possession, but of an ability to give to the dead something that can never, now, be returned.

This double act is repeated, a few minutes later, in the next exchange, an exchange that now, significantly, concerns a game:

> B: So it made you feel good that your favorite friend was buried in your favorite shirt and your watch.
> G: (smiling again): And he has my – it's not really a hat, it's a cap. It's a little like a stocking cap, that colorful thing on his wall. Yeah, him and me and Maurice would play this game, 'left hand', where you call out what's in the person's left hand and you get to keep it. And he called that and he got it.
> B: I should give that back to you, you could take it with you as a memento.
> G: Uhuh, I would feel better if it would stay in his household. Because it's a memento of him but it's a memento of me too.

The game with his friend, Greg tells us, had been a game of naming and possessing; by calling out the other's clothing it could become yours, just as the friendship was perhaps a kind of reciprocal possession of each boy by the other. But when Bernadette offers, once again, to give the possession back – 'I should give it back to you, you could take it with you as a memento' – Greg once again repeats his *fort*: 'I would feel better if it would stay in his household. Because it is a memento of him but it's a memento of me too'. Naming the cap as a memento not only of Khalil but of himself, Greg not only gives up the part of himself that existed before Khalil's death, he also ties his life with Khalil's death: the cap is not only a memento of him for me, he says, but of me for him. This bond, however, does not confuse the living child with the dead one, nor does it symbolize the dead one in the living one, but precisely separates Greg, whose younger self is buried in the coffin, from the dead child who will not grow past this moment. Indeed, this refusal of Bernadette's offer to give the cap back is also (as my own mother pointed out to me), a way of saying 'I will not be your dead child'. In giving up the language of memorialization offered by Bernadette, however, he creatively transforms the language of the memento and achieves another language and another memorialization: a memorialization that takes place precisely through his separation and his own act of creation.[18] It is in this reclaiming of the meaning of the memento, even while giving it up, that Greg's *fort*, I would suggest, does not simply re-enact his friend's departure or attempt to return to his life, but bears witness, creatively, in the very act of parting from his dead friend.

This language, I would suggest, is the language of the life drive. It is this drive for life that is at work in Greg's description of how the death of his friend is also motivating him to achieve goals in his life, achievements that will also incorporate Khalil's name:

> B: How has his death changed your life?
> G: I am more determined to make it in the music business somehow and I know it will be because of him. We used to talk about it all the time. He did rap ... [W]e were to go to Clark Atlanta, him for business management and me for communication, music, and combine our talents. But now he can't do that ... But that's OK, because when I do it I'll bring all the people jobs, Mike, Maurice ... When we get that studio [Khalil's] name is going to be the name of it. And I have to have a son and his name will be in there.

In this language we can see the drive for life, a language of parting that itself moves the speaker forward to a life that is not simply possessed, but given, in some sense, and received, as a gift from the dead. In the memento, as Greg teaches us, the two children take leave from each other: as Greg gives Khalil back to death, Khalil, in a sense, gives Greg back to life. This is a creative act, an act that bears witness to the dead precisely in the process of turning away. It is indeed a new language of departure, parting words[19] that bind the living child to the dead one even as he takes leave from him, binds him to his dead friend even in the very act of letting go.

Freud's Game

In Greg's words, we see the insight of Freud's text as it touches on and resonates with our contemporary crises and with the actual struggles of children in contemporary culture. But Greg's words also shed light on the way in which the language of the child itself re-emerges at the very heart of Freud's own theoretical writing.[20] For Freud's elaborate staging of the game of the *fort/da* can be understood not only as a description of the puzzling game of the child staging the departure and return of the mother, but as Freud's own oscillation in his understanding of the child's game. This oscillation takes the form, moreover, of the alternation between a *fort* and a *da*:

> I eventually realized that it was a game and that the only use he made of any of his toys was to play 'gone' with them (p. 15).

> This, then, was the complete game – disappearance and return. As a rule one witnessed only its first act, which was repeated untiringly as a game in itself, though there is no doubt that the greater pleasure was attached to the second act (p. 15).

> It may perhaps be said ... that [the mother's] departure had to be enacted as a necessary preliminary to her joyful return, and that it was in the latter that lay the true purpose of the game. But against this must be counted the observed fact that the first act, that of departure, was staged as a game in itself and far more frequently than the episode in its entirety, with its pleasurable ending (pp. 15–16).

As Freud's interpretation passes from the *fort* to the narrative of *fort* and *da*, and back again to the *fort*, Freud shows himself as struggling in the face of a child whose language, in its shifting meaning for Freud, first brings him nearer and then distances him in Freud's understanding.[21] What is striking in Freud's example, that is, is not simply the child's struggle and re-enactment of the distance of its mother, but Freud's struggle with and re-enactment of the distance of the child. Freud's text, it would appear, repeats the story of the child he has encountered, and does so, moreover, in the very act of distancing. Paradoxically, then, it will be in his repetition of the child's distance, in his own distancing of the child at the moment of his failed comprehension of the game, that Freud's own text will connect with, and transmit, the story the child cannot quite tell. Freud's text, that is, itself repeats the child's traumatized *fort* – the stammering word that marks the very loss of the child's own story – but does so as the very creation of its own new language, a language that does not return to the pleasurable compensations of the narrative but speaks, precisely, from *beyond the story*. It is not necessarily on the level of the child's own game, that is, but on the level of Freud's repetition of it that the creative act of the game, the new conceptual language of the life drive, will take place.[22]

We could, moreover, understand the entire theory of trauma in *Beyond* not as simply an explanation of trauma from the distance of theoretical speculation, but as the very passage of the story of the child in a theoretical act of transformation.[23] For what is the story of the mind's attempt to master the event retrospectively if not the story of a failed return: the attempt, and failure, of the mind to return to the moment of the event? The theory of repetition compulsion as the unexpected encounter with an event that the mind misses and then repeatedly attempts to grasp is the story of a failure of the mind to return to an experience it has never quite grasped, the repetition of an originary departure from the moment that constitutes the very experience of trauma. And this story appears again as the beginning of life in the death drive, as life's attempt to return to inanimate matter that ultimately fails and departs into a human history.[24] Freud's own theory, then, does not simply describe the death drive and its enigmatic move to the drive for life, but enacts this drive for life as the very language of the child that encounters, and attempts to grasp, the catastrophes of a traumatic history.

A Final Parting

The most striking appearance of Freud's own speaking as the child will occur, however, not within the theoretical language of the text, but in a footnote that refers, in fact, to the entrance of a real death into the life of the child as well as into his own life: 'When this child was five and three-quarters, his mother died. Now that she was really "gone" ("o-o-o"), the child showed no signs of grief.' In noting the real death of the child's mother, Freud first explicitly links the child to himself, since the child's mother was also, in reality, Freud's daughter Sophie, who died toward the end of the writing of *Beyond the Pleasure Principle*. But whereas the (already traumatized) child shows no signs of grief, Freud himself begins to repeat, not simply the language of the *fort*, but the inarticulate sounds of the 'o-o-o-o' that constituted the very origin of the game (and the only moment in which the living mother had appeared in the example, when she agreed with Freud as to the meaning of the 'o-o-o-o' as indicating the word *fort*). By reintroducing the lost 'o-o-o-o' of the original child's game in his words, and in this footnote that announces his daughter's and the mother's real death, Freud implicitly connects the origin of the child's game with the very significance of his own theoretical text, a significance that now, in its very inarticulate stammer, serves as a kind of memory of and parting from Freud's own dead child.[25] The language of the theory, much like the child's stammering language, articulates the very notions of the trauma and of the death drive as a creative act of parting: a parting from the real child, and a parting from the psychoanalytic child – or from the mere psychoanalysis of childhood – toward an analysis of the collective catastrophes of death encountered in war, and toward the pressing cultural imperative for a new kind of survival.[26]

* * *

I would propose that it is through the child's words – through this literary, not fully articulated language of theory – that Freud's text speaks, moreover, most powerfully, in its full historical relevance, to us. For it is through the child's own stammer – the stammer of Freud as he faces the encounter with World War I, the reduction of the theoretical mind to the stammering struggle of the child – that Freud will first tell us about the necessity of witnessing the effects of death in the century of trauma. But it is also through the creative transformation of this stammer into a new language of psychoanalysis – not only the language of departure, which will be his language of history in *Moses and Monotheism,* but the very future language of psychoanalysis itself, in the rethinking of psychoanalysis, for example, around the individual's capacity for play – that the possibilities of Freud's not yet articulated insight are handed over to us.[27] I would suggest that it is only in listening to this second and literarily creative element in Freud's own writing, that the theory of trauma, now so prevalent in numerous disciplines, can extend itself beyond the theory of repetition and catastrophe, beyond the insight of the death drive, into the insight enigmatically passed on in the new notion of the drive to life. As such the theory of trauma does not limit itself to a theoretical formulation of the centrality of death in culture, but constitutes – in Freud's, and our own, historical experience of modernity – an act of parting that itself creates and passes on a different history of survival.

Notes

1   My mother was a psychoanalyst who worked for many years with children and adolescents and later with adults. She had discussed an earlier version of this text with me a number of times before her death in March 1998.

2   *Beyond the Pleasure Principle*, in *The Standard Edition of the Complete Psychological Works of Sigmund Freud*, translated from the German under the general editorship of James Strachey in collaboration with Anna Freud, assisted by Alix Strachey and Jan Tyson, 24 vols (London: The Hogarth Press, 1953–74), xviii, ch. 2 (hereafter cited as SE), p. 13. German quotations are taken from Sigmund Freud, *Studienausgabe* (Frankfurt am Main: Fischer Verlag, 1969–79), Band III. Hereafter, page numbers are given in the text.

3   Freud describes the game as the child's 'first great cultural achievement', and suggests that the child rewarded himself for not expressing his distress by creating a game instead. Thus the game not only represents the mother's wished-for return, but by substituting itself for the mother the game becomes, itself, a kind of symbolic return.

4   The game has been read, for instance, as a game of mourning. Within the literary critical tradition see for example Eric L. Santner, *Stranded Objects: Mourning, Memory, and Film*

in Postwar Germany (New York: Cornell University Press, 1990). The received understanding of the game is that it represents a form of mastery and is thus, not strictly speaking, purely traumatic repetition – unless traumatic repetition is understood as already itself a form of mastering. Freud does suggest at one point in his analysis that the game may express a principle of mastery 'beyond the pleasure principle' but the peculiarity of such repetition is rarely explored within traditional analyses. Exceptions to this line of thought can be found in Jacques Derrida, 'To Speculate – on "Freud"' in *The Post Card: From Socrates to Freud and Beyond*, trans. Alan Bass (Chicago: University of Chicago Press, 1987). Jacques Lacan analyzes the game in the context of a reading of traumatic repetition in *The Four Fundamental Concepts of Psycho-Analysis*, trans. Alan Sheridan, ed. Jacques-Alain Miller (New York: Norton, 1978). See also Rodolphe Gasché, 'The Witch Metapsychology', in Todd Dufresne (ed.), *Returns of the French Freud: Freud, Lacan, and Beyond* (New York: Routledge, 1997). On the crucial structure of the game in relation to the speculative structure of *Beyond the Pleasure Principle* see Samuel Weber, *The Legend of Freud* (Minneapolis: University of Minnesota Press, 1982) and his *Return to Freud: Jacques Lacan's Dislocation of Psychoanalysis*, trans. Michael Levine (Cambridge: Cambridge University Press, 1991).

5   For a related analysis of this aspect of Freud's text with a slightly different emphasis see my *Unclaimed Experience: Trauma, Narrative and History* (Baltimore: Johns Hopkins University Press, 1996), ch. 3, 'Traumatic Departures: Survival and History in Freud', pp. 57–72.

6   Ibid.

7   Life is thereby separated from the desire to live; survival is no longer linked to the wish to live but to another imperative that appears to have ethical force (thus the survivor mission to tell) as well as a relation to knowing or witnessing (as an 'awakening').

8   Thus the theory of individual trauma in *Beyond the Pleasure Principle* will lead to the theory of historical (and collective) trauma in *Moses and Monotheism*. I have analysed this in terms of the story of departure in *Unclaimed Experience*, op. cit., chs 1 and 3. The notion of an attempt to return that becomes a departure is a pattern that originates in *Beyond the Pleasure Principle* in the description of individual trauma and ultimately the foundation of life; in *Moses and Monotheism*, Jewish history is itself structured by a trauma that turns Moses's attempt to return the Hebrews to Canaan into an endless departure into a Jewish history of survival.

9   Robert J. Lifton, 'Survivor Experience and Traumatic Syndrome', in his *The Broken Connection: Death and the Continuity of Life* (1979; New York: Basic Books, 1983).

10 Freud emphasizes the creative element of the game by remarking that it is the 'first self-invented game' of the child (*das erste selbst-erschaffene Spiel*), an emphasis we see again in his letter to Wilhelm Zweig concerning his insight behind *Moses and Monotheism*, that 'Moses created the Jews', which uses a related although slightly different verb form (*hat ... geschaffen*). Freud's use of the word 'create' in *Beyond the Pleasure Principle*, which I am echoing in my own use of the word 'creative', thus has a specific, foundational meaning and is also, in both *Beyond the Pleasure Principle* and *Moses and Monotheism*, ultimately linked to a traumatic history. The creative element in the *fort/da* game appears, moreover, to be associated specifically with the origins of language; Freud notes that the game begins when the child is just beginning to make articulate sounds. Jacques Lacan thus suggests that this game represents the origin of symbolic language as such in the differentiation of the phonemes *o* and *a* (see his 'Function and Field of Speech and Language', in *Écrits*, trans. Alan Sheridan [New York: Norton, 1977]). The game is not, that is, about symbolizing

the literal but about moving from silence to speech. The foundational nature of the game – or of the scene as Freud presents it – points toward its link to the foundational moment that traumatic repetition repeats, which is the ultimate concern of *Beyond the Pleasure Principle*.

11 One line of theoretical (or in Freud's terms, 'speculative') elaboration of the notion of trauma in *Beyond the Pleasure Principle* begins in chapter II with the example of the nightmares of battle – which are compared to the nightmares of an accident that wake the patient up from his sleep – continues with the explanation of trauma in chapter IV, which speculates on the origins of consciousness and proposes that trauma is a break in the stimulus barrier that consciousness provides for the living organism, and culminates in chapter V, in which Freud suggests that life itself was an awakening from inanimate matter for which there was no preparation. This line of speculation appears to have an independent logic and does not completely align itself with the language of play that accompanies it in an apparently separate line of argument. The *Spiel* appears first in the example of the child, is repeated in chapter III in regard to the re-enactment behaviour in transference, and thenceforth is mentioned only in regard to children's play and theatre, until the introduction of the notion of the life drive. (Interestingly, the discussion of analysis in chapter III suggests that the entire theory of the Oedipal origins of unconscious conflict in childhood needs to be rethought after the encounter with trauma; at this point in his argument, then, Freud appears to be incorporating the earlier theory of neurosis into a larger speculation concerning traumatic neurosis.)

It is notable that the distinction between the terminology of the nightmare – a terminology of seeing and awakening – and the terminology of the game – a language of play and speech – also appears in contemporary discussions of the problem of traumatic imagery as opposed to the resolution of trauma in (symbolic) language. See for example Bessel A. van der Kolk, 'Trauma and Memory', in Bessel A. van der Kolk, Alexander C. McFarlane and Lars Weisaeth (eds), *Traumatic Stress: The Effects of Overwhelming Experience on Mind, Body, and Society* (New York: The Guilford Press, 1996).

12 The movement from the death drive to the life drive seems, in fact, to carry out a possibility contained in Freud's double denomination of trauma in chapter II, as both fright (*Schreck*) and surprise (*Überraschung*): ('daß das Haputgewicht der Verursachung auf das Moment der Überraschung, auf den Schreck, zu fallen schien', 'Schreck aber benannt den Zustand, in den man gerät, wenn man in Gefahr kommt, ohne auf se vorbereitet zu sein, betont das Moment der Überraschung').

13 Interestingly, it is not until the introduction of the life drive that the *fort* makes its appearance again literally in the language of Freud's text. Here we might see a possibility of bringing together Jean Laplanche's insight into the shared single energy of the life drive and death drive and Harold Bloom's insistence that Freud is a dualist. See Jean Laplanche, 'Why the Death Drive?', in his *Life and Death in Psychoanalysis* (Baltimore: Johns Hopkins University Press, 1970) and Harold Bloom, 'Freud's Concept of Defense and the Poetic Will', in his *Agon: Towards a Theory of Revisionism* (New York: Oxford University Press, 1982).

14 The repetition of the origin as the new beginning of the life drive thus distinguishes itself from the confusion between death and life enacted in the death drive. One thinks of the repeated confrontation with death in life in traumatic repetition associated with the sense of being a living dead by survivors (cf. Robert Lifton's *Death in Life: Survivors of Hiroshima* [New York: Basic Books, 1967] or of the literary example of the woman in Duras' and Resnais' *Hiroshima mon amour*, having missed the moment of her lover's death, exclaiming,

'I could not find the least difference between his dead body and mine'. So too, in that piece, the slap that breaks the traumatic repetition in her encounter with the Japanese man can be understood as a new beginning that distinguishes death from life, not as understanding but as act. One might say that the event of trauma is repeated, in the moment of parting in the life drive, as the act of survival, an act that, in a sense, fulfils the imperative to live that begins life, but fulfils it differently (the imperative and its fulfilment are not continuous). This act, though, is not just any act; since it repeats the 'awakening' of the life drive, it is inextricable from questions of witnessing or knowing that govern traumatic repetition (which is life and is also awakening) and thus can be understood as a different form of witnessing. To this extent, the question of creativity – as a creativity arising in the context of trauma – is bound up with the question of truth. Rather than providing an affective response to trauma, the life drive can be understood as providing another means of bearing witness. In other words, the life drive (unlike, say, the pleasure principle) cannot be understood within the economy of pleasure (which is also the economy of symbolization, as we see in the *fort/da* game) but must engage the problems of truth and knowing introduced by the trauma.

15   It should be noted that the passage from chapter II is already fairly complex and appears to be somewhat playful in its own use of *fort* and *da*, in naming the never-achieved pleasurable end of the game (the hoped-for *da*) as 'das zum lustvollen Ende *fort*geführte Ganze' – i.e., in naming the longed-for *da* by means of a *fort*. The question of departure could also be thought as a meditation on the nature of the return (Derrida suggests something of the sort in 'To Speculate – on Freud'); here it would be interesting to examine the shift from the *da* of the child – seen as the marker of the pleasure principle – to the *zurück* of the drives beyond the pleasure principle.

The new meaning of *fortführen*, moreover, brings out a remarkable reversal that occurs in the movement from chapters II and IV (where trauma is an exception to ordinary experience, an encounter with death that disturbs consciousness) to chapter V (where the traumatic delay defines the very origin of life itself, and ultimately, in its repetition in the life drive, the possibility of a new beginning). For whereas consciousness was understood, originally, to protect life against death (chapter IV), we can see (from chapter V) that, since trauma ultimately re-enacts an origin that marked the beginning of life, consciousness ultimately serves to protect the organism not from death but from life – or more accurately, from the surprise of new beginnings.

16   Bernadette Leite, personal communication. She has spoken of this (and reiterated the importance of speaking) in *The Atlanta Journal-Constitution* (24 July and 15 August 1999, among other dates) and is honoured in the November 1999 edition of *Redbook*. She worked for several years in association with the Minority Health Institute at the Rollins School of Public Health at Emory University.

17   As Greg says, 'He called early, like 10 or 11 … But again, that was the night I went to my cousin's home, he called again, but I wasn't there'.

18   The tone of Greg's language here might be understood as being achieved through a giving up of a certain kind of pathos, although, even in its humour, it attains a different pathos, perhaps the pathos of giving up pathos. I would like to thank Elizabeth Rottenberg for her insights into questions of humour and tone in the exchange between Greg and Bernadette Leite.

19   It is interesting to note that the question of departure and parting arises at the end of the interview between Bernadette Leite and Greg: 'B: Any parting words? G: Departing words? B: Parting words … Words to say to others' (KAL Oral History Archive).

20 Thus the future of Freud's text could be understood as a 'beyond' in the strict sense, both inside and outside of Freud's text in the language of a child both inside (in the game) and outside (in the experience of the real child), already there but not yet there, just as, perhaps, the life drive is beyond the death drive.

21 On the self-reflexive dimension of the scene see for example Derrida, 'To Speculate – on "Freud"'; on the self-reflexivity of *Beyond the Pleasure Principle* see Harold Bloom, 'Freud and the Sublime: A Catastrophe Theory of Creativity', in *Agon*, where he suggests that Freud's citation of Tasso in chapter three is 'an allegory of Freud's own passage into the Sublime', and Perry Meisel, 'Freud's Reflexive Realism', *October* 28 (Spring 1984). Freud's argument, as we have outlined, thus first appears to replace the notion of childhood Oedipal conflict with a kind of trauma modelled on the adult (war trauma), but the self-reflexive level of Freud's writing reintroduces the child's centrality or priority not as a concept but as a kind of language. Likewise, the notion of beginning wrapped up in the awakening at the origin of life becomes associated with a kind of origination in language.

22 Thus Freud's own creative act could be said to arise (as in the interview of Greg by Bernadette) out of an encounter: his encounter with the child. The shift from death drive to life drive, which remains fairly enigmatic in its original speculative introduction in chapter V – Freud unexpectedly ends the description of the death drive and starts again with the life drive – could be said to take place on the level of the encounter rather than as something that could simply be an object of speculation or knowledge within the theory. In other words, if one were to ask, pragmatically or clinically, what would make possible the move from death drive to life drive in an individual – what makes possible, for example, the language of the life drive for Greg – the answer would have to be found, in this particular text by Freud, on the level of the encounter, that is, as taking place in the context of an encounter.

23 Not the distance of theoretical knowing, then, but the distance of the child's game.

24 On the *fort* at the origin see Samuel Weber, *The Legend of Freud* and my *Unclaimed Experience*, ch. 3.

25 As Freud insists in his own letters, *Beyond the Pleasure Principle* was mostly written before the death of Sophie and thus does not (in the strictest sense) refer directly to her death; by introducing her death in a footnote, however, Freud allows the resonances to take place and also sets up another parallel with the child, for whom the mother died after the game just as Sophie died after the writing of Freud's text. On the death of Sophie see for example Jacques Derrida, 'To Speculate – on "Freud"' and Elisabeth Bronfen, 'Eine Frau verschwindet: Sophie Freud und Jenseits des Lustprinzips', *Psyche* 47:6 (January 1993). Anne Whitehead also remarks on the important contribution of Luce Irigaray to the unread position of the mother in the *fort/da* game in 'Belief Itself', in her *Sexes and Genealogies*, trans. Gillian C. Gill (New York: Columbia University Press, 1987): see Anne Whitehead, '"A still, small voice": Letter-writing, testimony and the project of address in Etty Hillesum's *Letters from Westerbork*', *Cultural Values* 5:1 (2001).

26 The interweaving of language and history, once again, emerges in Freud's peculiar association of the death drive with something 'unobtrusive' and, in later texts, 'dumb', and the life drive with noise or 'clamour'. This distinction occurs first in *Beyond the Pleasure Principle* and is reiterated in *The Ego and the Id* and *Civilization and Its Discontents*. Reading the death drive in terms of its historical shape in *Beyond the Pleasure Principle* and *Moses and Monotheism*, we could say that what the language of the life drive bears witness to is precisely the silence of history (or, in the child's game, the silence of the mother's departure).

27 To the extent that the life drive moves us away from the direct line of argument that leads from *Beyond the Pleasure Principle* to *Moses and Monotheism*, or from individual to collective history, the imperative for survival could be understood here as taking place within acts (or within a language of the life drive) that is neither simply individual nor simply collective in the sense of those terms that preceded the death drive/life drive analysis. In a sense, the introduction of the life drive in my argument is also the reintroduction of the notion of individual acts on the other side of the collective analysis of historical catastrophe implied in the death drive argument that leads to *Moses and Monotheism*. Here, the 'individual' act (or the language of the life drive) might itself carry with it the force of a larger history.

On psychoanalysis and play see D.W. Winnicott, *Playing and Reality* (London: Tavistock Publications, 1971). Here we might recall the importance of the word 'create' for Freud discussed above in fn. 10, and its passage into Winnicott in the notion of living creatively. It is also interesting to note that this later thinker of play was also interested, in this context, in the notion of surprise.

5 Reading Trauma: Charlotte Delbo and the Struggle to Represent

VICTORIA STEWART

If the aim of the Holocaust was to remove the possibility of there being any survivors (and therefore any witnesses), those who did come through would seem to have the most powerful incitement to tell their version. To speak or write of Holocaust experiences is to demonstrate resistance to an attempt at radical silencing. Dori Laub has described how difficult this resistance can in fact prove in the face of the disturbance of subjectivity which resulted from the Holocaust:

> Survivors often claim that they belong to a 'secret order' that is sworn to silence. Because of their 'participation' in the Holocaust they have become the 'bearers of a secret' (*Geheimnisstraeger*) never to be divulged.[1]

For Laub, part of the answer can lie in the passage of time and in the provision of an opportunity for the survivor to give testimony about what has occurred. Laub refers in particular to video-testimony projects; the reader of a written account is in a rather different situation to one who interviews a survivor, not only because listening and reading are fundamentally different ways of engaging with the testimony of another individual but also because a further distance in space and time are introduced in the case of an account being published and later read. Yet for both survivors who tell and survivors who write, the notion of breaking the silence remains a crucial one. In what follows I will be exploring how one writer in particular attempted not only to articulate the experience of existing in the camps, but also explored how writing, and indeed living might be possible after such a trauma. How can an individual negotiate between 'before' and 'after' when 'after' was never supposed to happen?

Charlotte Delbo was a French theatre practitioner and writer who, together with her husband Georges Dudach, a resistance worker, was arrested by the

French police and handed over to the Gestapo in 1942.[2] They had been discovered producing anti-German leaflets. Dudach was shot soon after, but Delbo was sent to Auschwitz, via Drancy, in 1943, and later on to Ravensbrück. She wrote 'None of Us Will Return' in 1946, but it was not published until 1965; in explaining this delay she commented: 'I wanted to make sure it would withstand the test of time since it had to travel so far into the future.'[3] Two further volumes followed soon after and these three comprise the trilogy which was published in English as *Auschwitz and After*, and in 1985, the year she died, a further volume, *Days and Memory*, a series of reflections on both the Holocaust and other human rights issues, was published. Delbo's writing in these works is a mixture of prose and poetry. Parts of both are written as a series of short first-person narratives in which Delbo adopts the personae of various of her fellow prisoners, imagining or recreating from their own accounts, their arrivals home. The act of ventriloquizing other women's experiences not only underlines Delbo's desire to emphasize the collective nature of this experience, the lives of varied individuals converging at this particular historical moment, but also serves to detach Delbo's work from both history and autobiography. It should be noted that Delbo also produced a more formal biographical account, *Le Convoi du 24 janvier* (1965), in which the fates of each of the deportees on her transport are recounted, almost in the style of a memorial book.[4] The existence of this earlier volume re-emphasizes that *Auschwitz and After* is not intended as a formal history. This implicit interrogation of generic categories underlines the struggle to find an appropriate form in which to communicate her experience (and indeed her experience as one of a group of women), which is enacted throughout Delbo's work.[5]

I would suggest that what is described in Delbo's writing is an attempt at understanding trauma. In Cathy Caruth's definition, a trauma is an event 'experienced too soon, too unexpectedly to be fully known and [...] therefore not available to consciousness until it imposes itself again repeatedly in the nightmares and repetitive actions of the survivor'.[6] Trauma would here appear to be a sudden shocking event, such as the paradigmatic railway accident,[7] not consonant with the ongoing experience of incarceration. Delbo's experience could better be described as a series of traumatic moments. A less specifically clinical definition of trauma is available, however: Caruth goes on to ask whether trauma is 'the encounter with death, or the ongoing experience of having survived it'.[8] This notion of the death encounter, which appears in a more specifically psychoanalytic context in Robert J. Lifton's work, will be an important element in the analysis of Delbo's writing. For Lifton, there has to be an acknowledgement of what has been survived (that is, the encounter with death) and this requires, on the part of the therapist, engagement in a particular kind of dialogue: 'You [the therapist] must in some significant psychological way experience what they experience [...] it's being a survivor by proxy, and the proxy's important.'[9] For Delbo it is not a case of attempting to reintegrate the trauma or come to terms with the death encounter. She attempts to anatomize the workings of memory, but not only as a means of recording an accurate account of what occurred during her imprisonment and making this part of her life story. Delbo wishes both to be accurate, and to be true to the exigencies of memory, and she is therefore at pains to describe how memory functioned, and failed to function, when she was in Auschwitz. This is by no means a self-regarding exercise, however. Whilst reintegrating her Holocaust experience into her life, she is also broadening the reader's conception of what the category 'experience' might constitute, even when what is communicated is the near impossibility of communication.

Delbo often finds that what she wishes to remember about her life in the camp is precisely that which is inaccessible. In 'Useless Knowledge', the second part of the trilogy, she relates an incident in which she and other women on a work detail were allowed to stop and wash in a stream, the first time they had been able to bathe since their arrival some months previously:

> All my thoughts were focused on what I had to do to wash myself, to remove the dirt as fast and thoroughly as possible [...] I rubbed, rubbed to the point of scratching myself [...] My skin was getting lighter [...] Yes, it really looked lighter [...] I grabbed my jacket and scarf to get into ranks. It must have happened like this, but I have no memory of it. I only recall the stream.[10]

Delbo knows that this must have been a moment of respite, and that it is therefore something she wishes to both recall and record: failing to recall, however, she must improvise. In a similar incident Delbo is unable to remember an occasion attested to by fellow ex-prisoners, when they managed to obtain some tomatoes:

> What should we remember and what must we forget in order to keep clear-headed? Stupid to forget those tomatoes. Tomatoes don't constitute a weighty memory. Why not rather forget the smell and color of smoke [...] twisted by the wind, sending the stench in our direction?[11]

Such moments, at which the lack of ability to control what is selected by memory and what is not, serve again to underline the very difficulty of representing anything at all. The measured, almost brutal tone of Delbo's writing is fractured by moments of crisis such as this. At other points the gulf between past and present experiences is emphasized with a comment appended to a story, such as, 'And now I am sitting in a café, writing this text'.[12] Such interjections jolt the reader into an awareness of an uncomfortable separation between the teller and the tale, a separation exemplified at the end of 'Useless Knowledge'. Delbo initially tells of attempting, when in the camp, to keep in touch with her former life by exercising her memory, trying to remember poems, or the sequence of stops on the metro, only to become disillusioned with this: memory becomes a burden, a cause of pain and sorrow at moments when the future itself seems an impossibility. Writing in the present tense, Delbo describes springtime in the camp, and the experience, then, of frustratingly useless memories:

> None of us will return [...]
> Far beyond the barbed wire, spring is flitting, spring is rustling, spring is singing. Within my memory. Why did I keep my memory? [...] None of us will return [...] My memory is more bloodless than an autumn leaf [...] None of us will return.[13]

Turning to the final page of this part of the trilogy, the reader is faced with the statement, 'None of us was meant to return'.[14]

This simple play with tenses, slipping from a fear, then, that 'none of us will return', to the knowledge, now, that as survivors they are an anomaly, contributes to the sense that Delbo refuses to allow any redemptive meaning to be drawn from the events she has witnessed. The conviction at the time of the events described that 'none of us will return' is countered by the very existence of the narrative. This seems to provide a sense of hope beyond the immediate dreadful occurrences because the reader knows that this fear proved false. To cap this, however, with, 'None of us was meant to return' undercuts any sense that this hope might be unalloyed. The fact of survival is a positive one, but it is also where the very problems of having faced a death encounter begin:

> I have returned
> From a world beyond knowledge
> And now must unlearn
> For otherwise I clearly see
> I can no longer live.[15]

Primo Levi emphasizes more strongly the guilt which can underlie such a sentiment:

we, the survivors, are not the true witnesses [...] We survivors are not only an exiguous but also an anomalous minority: we are those who by their prevarications or abilities or good luck did not touch bottom. Those who did so [...] have not returned to tell about it ...[16]

Such 'survivor guilt' is another manifestation of the urge to remain silent which Laub describes. To 'speak for' those who did not survive would seem to be an obscene imposition. It is noticeable in this respect that Delbo makes very little reference to the fate of Jewish women in the camp; she focuses instead on those with whom she was in immediate daily contact, and on her own troubling experiences. It has to be possible, therefore, to recognize the truth of Levi's statement, that there is no reason why some survived rather than others, whilst also acknowledging the value of attempting to represent this experience. Both Delbo and Levi realize that it is impossible to speak for those others, or to generalize and reduce 'camp experience' to a series of tropes. The testimony of individuals such as Delbo and Levi becomes more rather than less important, if only because its very existence implies the absence of those who, in Levi's words, did 'touch bottom'. Where there are survivors, there will also have been victims.

In her final work, *Days and Memory*, Delbo attempts to discuss memory in its most fundamental sense. Beginning with a comparison between 'shedding' her Auschwitz self and a snake shedding its skin, she develops the image and describes having grown a skin between her Auschwitz self and her present self.

No doubt I am very fortunate in not recognising myself in the self that was in Auschwitz. To return from there was so improbable that it seems to me I was never there at all [...] I live within a twofold being. The Auschwitz double doesn't bother me [...] Without this split I would not have been able to revive.[17]

Delbo goes on to describe a split she perceives in the process of memory, which seems to mark a development from her early autobiographical writings. *Auschwitz and After* necessarily bears the hallmarks of having been written in the immediate aftermath of the experiences described within it. By the time of writing *Days and Memory*, Delbo is at a temporal distance from those experiences, and her reflections thus become consciously analytical. The temporal distance notwithstanding, however, it is curious to observe how Delbo can step back from the process of her own memory and attempt to anatomize it; perhaps the peculiar nature of what her memory reveals serves to facilitate this process. She distinguishes between 'deep memory' and 'external memory'.

Memories of the camp, and by extension, accounts of her experiences there, issue from 'external memory [...] the memory connected with the thinking process. Deep memory preserves sensations, physical imprints [...] for it isn't words that are swollen with emotional charge.'[18] To illustrate this final comment she suggests that if this were not the case, a survivor would never be able to say 'I'm thirsty' without relating this sentiment to a memory of a much more dreadful thirst. If a memory of 'thirst' re-emerges in a dream, however, Delbo explains, 'I physically feel that real thirst'.[19] In this way, the rational and the physical become detached from each other: events can be recounted via the economy of external memory, or they can re-emerge unbidden from deep memory. This, together with the fact that deep memories can often manifest themselves in dreams, accounts for the fact that, as she remarks, 'while knowing perfectly well that it corresponds to the facts, I no longer know if it is real'.[20]

A parallel can be drawn here with Samuel Beckett's analysis of Proust's distinction between voluntary and involuntary memory, although the difference between these two categories is not only in how they manifest themselves but in the kind of material which they tend to represent or reproduce. Beckett suggests: '"voluntary memory" [...] is the uniform memory of intelligence, and it can be relied on to reproduce for our gratified inspection those impressions of the past that were consciously and intelligently formed'.[21] On the other hand, involuntary memory makes different kinds of connections, it is 'explosive [...] and in its brightness reveal[s] what the mock reality of experience can never reveal – the real [...] It chooses its own time and place for the performance of its miracle'.[22] Both involuntary memory and Delbo's deep memory share a quality of intrusiveness, or defamiliarization. In Proust's case, however, the moments at which involuntary memory intrudes can be productive in advancing his self-understanding, as in the moment when he realizes that 'for the first time since her death he knows that [his grandmother] is dead, he knows *who* is dead'.[23] Yet, if, as Beckett argues, the result of this is access to the 'real', the visceral experiences which return to Delbo in dreams serve in fact to stress the necessary distance between two realms of experience or kinds of memory. Delbo's real is in excess of reality. Returning to Auschwitz in dreams, Delbo explains, 'I feel death fasten on me, I feel that I am dying'.[24] For Delbo it is essential that such feelings be mastered in order that she can talk of her experiences 'without exhibiting or registering any anxiety or emotion',[25] and in this way communicate them to others. Whether one account can be said to be more 'authentic' than the other is probably not the point; this ambivalence is reflected by Delbo when she points to the potential gap between the factual and the real. It is not simply that she doubts the reliability of memory or is troubled by the gulf between dreams and reality; what is conveyed is a deeper questioning of how a remembered experience is constituted.

Delbo's suggestion of a split between intellectual and emotional memory can of course be viewed as a highly contrived mechanism for the greater preservation of sanity (or even, on the contrary, a symptom): it is a method she evidently developed during a period of struggle after her release, as these reflections were written some thirty years after the end of the war. There is clearly a tension between a desire to keep events dissociated, beneath the skin, and a desire, as in the incident at the river, to reintegrate, albeit in rewritten or altered form the events which have occurred. Questions of authenticity necessarily arise here, and an example of Dori Laub's can usefully be cited. He recounts how a woman survivor claimed to have seen four chimneys blown up during the uprising at Auschwitz, whilst historians who later watched her video testimony maintained that only one was destroyed and that the woman's memory was therefore at fault, and her testimony unreliable. For Laub, however, the reasons for the woman giving testimony were rather different to the historians' reasons for listening to it: 'She had come, indeed, to testify, not to the empirical number of chimneys, but to resistance, to the affirmation of survival, to the breakage of the frame of death.'[26] A similar example of the different inflections which can be placed on memory, and the reasons why this might occur, is cited by Deborah Dwork. She notes how particular myths or beliefs become woven into similar accounts of Holocaust experience, regardless of their relationship to external verification. Such recurrent beliefs, Dwork suggests, tell not so much about life in the camps as about the 'psychological circumstances of [the survivors'] daily lives'.[27] Dwork gives as an example the belief, common among female survivors, that they were given a drug to stop them menstruating, so that if they did survive they would be unable to have children. Dwork pointed out to those women she interviewed that amenorrhoea is a symptom of malnutrition, but the survivors would often revert to their original beliefs in later interviews. 'This construct rationalized their experience: the Germans wanted to annihilate the Jewish people, and everything they did to their victims lead to that end.'[28] Amenorrhoea could not be simply a contingent factor; it could be more easily dealt with if assimilated into a broader narrative.

These two examples are of 'spontaneous' or more or less unconscious forms of the reworking of memory. Equally relevant to the process Delbo describes are the approaches to trauma advocated by Pierre Janet, and discussed more recently by Bessel van der Kolk and Onno van der Hart, in which the traumatic memory is replaced by a more neutral or even comforting one as a means of reintegration: 'Memory is everything. Once flexibility is introduced the traumatic memory starts losing its power over current experience. By imagining [...] alternative scenarios, many patients are able to soften the intrusive power of the original unmitigated horror'.[29] Ruth Leys explains that Janet viewed traumatic memory as simply repetitive, and viewed the task of therapy as the transformation of traumatic memory into narrative memory, which narrates the past as having passed. The patient will no longer be constantly re-experiencing the initial traumatic shock but will have assimilated it as an event within a broader narrative of the past. However, as Leys points out, what is downplayed in an account such as van der Kolk's and van der Hart's, or indeed Judith Herman's, is 'that aspect of Janet's psychotherapy that seeks to make the patient forget'.[30] For Janet, Leys maintains, assimilation should be followed by the liquidation of the trauma, and the ethical and political ramifications of this have to be born in mind.

What this indicates in part is the difference between Delbo's experience of trauma and those of Janet's patients.[31] For Delbo, it is not simply a case of discovering the base level traumatic scenario and reintegrating or even dispelling it for, as I have shown, Delbo does have access to what happened to her, but experiences a split between the intellectual and more visceral aspects of it. That is to say, her attempt at narrativizing her trauma in *Auschwitz and After* cannot totally dispel her dreams, which still occur at the time of writing *Days and Memory*. Delbo does not repress or dissociate what occurred, or suffer symptoms, as Janet's patients did. There is no secret as such to be discovered here. Describing his experience of the torture he suffered at the hands of the Nazis, Jean Améry comments:

> It was over for a while. It is still not over. Twenty-two years later I am still dangling over the ground by dislocated arms, panting, and accusing myself. In such an instance there is no 'repression'. Does one repress an unsightly birthmark? One can have it removed by a plastic surgeon but the skin that is transplanted in its place is not the skin with which one feels naturally at ease.[32]

Like Améry, Delbo resolutely refuses to be a 'bearer of the secret'. One could suggest that Delbo's writing is her own form of therapeutic exercise (although its quality as literature should not thereby be downplayed, and Delbo was a writer before she was a prisoner). If this is the case, we should return to the question, raised earlier in relation to Robert J. Lifton's characterization of the therapeutic relationship: bearing witness necessarily involves bearing witness *to* another individual. As Caruth paraphrases Lifton: 'It's the meeting of [the survivor and the survivor by proxy] that constitutes the witness.'[33]

Such a formulation would seem appropriate for the kind of situation described by Lifton, and is also relevant to the case of video testimony. Geoffrey Hartman has suggested, in relation to the Yale Video Testimony Project that, 'It is our [the inquirers'] search for meaning that is disclosed',[34] indicating a shift in emphasis from the individual witness's search for self-knowledge to the investigator's quest for broader historical understanding. This is akin to the tyranny of the archive envisioned by Pierre Nora, in which memory is downgraded in favour of the historical: 'Memory has been wholly absorbed by its meticulous reconstitution. Its new vocation is to record; delegating to the archive the responsibility of remembering it sheds its signs upon depositing them there as a snake sheds its skin.'[35] What I think sets Delbo's work at a distance from Nora's vision is that she occupies the positions of both survivor and investigator, hence perhaps the need for the categorization of memory and the decision to leave her first writings unpublished for twenty years. Her later self is the proxy witness to the earlier testimony. If Delbo is requesting the reader to contribute to the working through of these events, it is as an acknowledgement that what she is investigating and experiencing is the trauma of *history*. As Caruth suggests, 'Freud's central insight, in *Moses and Monotheism* [is] that history, like trauma, is never simply one's own, that history is precisely the way we are implicated in each other's traumas'.[36] Nora's suggestion that 'Memory is absolute, while history can only conceive of the relative'[37] is broken down when memory confronts the absolute of history. The difficulty of having survived these events, of having to live after them becomes crucial, and what is asserted is not so much the positive fact of survival, but the problem of how to reclaim the uncertainty of the everyday. 'Today I am not sure that what I write is true. I am certain it is truthful.'[38]

Notes

1   Shoshana Felman and Dori Laub, *Testimony: Crises of Witnessing in Literature, Psychoanalysis and History* (New York: Routledge, 1992), p. 82.
2   After the war Delbo tracked down the individuals who had betrayed her and her husband to the police but discovered that as they had both later changed sides and begun working for the French cause they could not be prosecuted. See Lawrence Langer's introduction to Charlotte Delbo, *Auschwitz and After*, trans. Rosette Lamont (New Haven: Yale University Press, 1995), pp. ix–xviii.

3 Charlotte Delbo, *Days and Memory*, trans. Rosette Lamont (Vermont: Marlboro Press, 1990), p. x.

4 Charlotte Delbo, *Le Convoi du 24 janvier* (Paris: Editions de Minuit, 1965). Translated by Carol Cosman as, *Convoy to Auschwitz: Women of the French Resistance*, introd. John Felstiner (Boston: Northeastern University Press, 1997).

5 N. Bracher has discussed the use of figurative language in Delbo's work, in the light of debates over the propriety of literary representations of the Holocaust. R.A. Kincaid, in a different vein, discusses the effect of the collapse of the usual codes of signification in the camps. I will not here be discussing in detail the literary qualities of Delbo's work, but would acknowledge that literature is another genre which her work questions.

6 Cathy Caruth, *Unclaimed Experience: Trauma, Narrative and History* (Baltimore: Johns Hopkins Press, 1996), p. 4.

7 Freud uses the railway accident as an example in *Moses and Monotheism*, and compares the delay which can occur between such an event and the manifestation of symptoms to the delay in Jewish history before the emergence of monotheism. It is this common ground between the two examples, encapsulated in the notion of latency, which interests Caruth: 'The experience of trauma, the fact of latency, would [...] seem to consist, not in the forgetting of a reality [...] but in an inherent latency within the experience itself' (Caruth, *Unclaimed Experience*, p. 17).

8 *Unclaimed Experience*, p. 7.

9 Cathy Caruth, 'An Interview with Robert Jay Lifton' in Cathy Caruth (ed.), *Trauma: Explorations in Memory* (Baltimore: Johns Hopkins University Press, 1995), p. 145.

10 Delbo, *Auschwitz and After*, pp. 152–3.

11 Delbo, *Auschwitz and After*, p. 343.

12 Delbo, *Auschwitz and After*, p. 29.

13 Delbo, *Auschwitz and After*, pp. 111–12.

14 Delbo, *Auschwitz and After*, p. 113.

15 Delbo, *Auschwitz and After*, p. 230.

16 Primo Levi, 'Shame', in *The Drowned and the Saved*, trans. Raymond Rosenthal (London: Abacus, 1989), pp. 63–4.

17 Delbo, *Days and Memory*, p. 4.

18 Delbo, *Days and Memory*, p. 3.

19 Delbo, *Days and Memory*, p. 4.

20 Ibid.

21 Samuel Beckett, 'Proust', in *Proust and Three Dialogues* (London: John Calder, 1987), p. 32.

22 Beckett, pp. 33–4.

23 Beckett, p. 42.

24 Delbo, *Days and Memory*, p. 3.

25 Ibid.

26 Felman and Laub, *Testimony*, p. 62.

27 Deborah Dwork, *Children with a Star* (New Haven: Yale University Press, 1991), p. xxvi.

28 Ibid.

29 Bessel A. van der Kolk and Onno van der Hart, 'The Intrusive Past: The Flexibility of Memory and the Engraving of Trauma' in Caruth (ed.), *Trauma: Explorations in Memory*, p. 178.

30 Ruth Leys, 'Traumatic Cures: Shellshock, Janet and the Question of Memory', in Paul Antze and Michael Lambek (eds), *Tense Past: Cultural Essays in Trauma and Memory* (New York: Routledge, 1996), p. 121. Although van der Kolk and van der Hart do ask, in the conclusion of their essay, 'whether it is not sacrilege of the traumatic experience to play with the reality of the past?' (van der Kolk and van der Hart, p. 179) they answer this only by giving an example of how Janet's method appears to have alleviated the suffering of one of his patients, enabling her to live a fuller life, and by stressing the continuing usefulness of such methods in psychotherapy. Judith Lewis Herman's work, specifically *Trauma and Recovery* (New York: Basic Books, 1992) discusses not only war neurosis but also the treatment of survivors of sexual abuse, and what can broadly be termed the 'recovered memory' movement. What concerns Leys is not only that Herman appears to wish to retain Janet's concept of dissociation, whilst dismissing his apparent erasure of patients' memories, but also that 'what appears to motivate Herman's attitude [...] is a powerfully entrenched, if undertheorized commitment to the redemptive authority of history' (Leys, p. 123). Herman's belief in the therapeutic power of speaking out would, according to van der Kolk and van der Hart's model, appear to omit the next step, that of integration, but for Leys, none of these writers seem to fully address the difficulties in interpreting Janet's own position.

31 Interestingly, van der Kolk and van der Hart cite Delbo's description of the 'split' between her Auschwitz self and her present self as an example of dissociation, but they do not address the fact that the difference in Delbo's case is between the quality rather than the content of her memories.

32 Jean Améry, *At the Mind's Limits: contemplations by a survivor on Auschwitz and its realities*, trans. Sidney Rosenfeld (London: Granta, 1999), p. 36.

33 Caruth, 'An Interview with Robert Jay Lifton', in Caruth (ed.), *Trauma: Explorations in Memory*, p. 145.

34 Geoffrey H. Hartman, 'Learning from the Survivors: The Yale Testimony Project', *Holocaust and Genocide Studies* 9 (1995), p. 193.

35 Pierre Nora, 'Between Memory and History: *Les Lieux de Mémoire*', *Representations* 26 (1989), p. 13.

36 Caruth, *Unclaimed Experience*, p. 24.

37 Nora, 'Between Memory and History', p. 9.

38 Delbo, *Auschwitz and After*, p. 1.

6 Trauma, Testimony and the Survivor: Calling Forth the Ghosts of Bosnia-Herzegovina

STEPHENIE YOUNG

'Why have the Jews been killed?'[1]

I

Claude Lanzmann, the director of *Shoah* (1985), believes that there are tremendous risks in asking a question such as the one posed above, and perhaps even more in believing that a single answer exists. To ask such a question, to seek to place an historical moment such as the Holocaust into explanatory terms, is to take part in what Lanzmann calls an 'obscene' practice.[2] For Lanzmann, 'there is an absolute obscenity in the very project of understanding', and not seeking to understand was the philosophy by which he lived throughout the eleven-year process of filming *Shoah*.[3]

Setting new parameters about what testimony is, and how it should be recorded, relayed and studied, *Shoah* sets an historical precedent by repositioning the ways in which we have thought about testimony over the past 25 years or so. The film underscores an awareness of the responsibility that comes with listening to testimony, and the ethics involved in relaying or transmitting the traumas of others to an audience. Lanzmann's film also illustrates Shoshana Felman's assertion that in the transmission of testimony, the 'truth' relies heavily on the process of art for 'its realization in our consciousness as witnesses'.[4] As he became aware of his responsibility as a witness, and the role of his art in the transmission of testimony, Lanzmann realized that he must approach the subject of the Holocaust with as few presuppositions as possible about what is real and what is false, what is truth and what is fiction, what is moral and what is immoral.

The task of 'presuming not to know' led Lanzmann to practise 'blindness', which he understands to be the 'purest mode of looking'.[5] 'Blindness' is a way of conceptualizing how we bear witness to testimony by facing our subject with the admission that we may never understand his or her experience. We must be sensitive to our subjects, but also willing to confront the limits of our own understanding as we engage with the survivor's testimony. The process of making the film is a transmission, a creation of testimonial space, and Lanzmann insists that the '[...] act of transmitting alone is important and no intelligibility, that is, no true knowledge, preexists the transmission. It is the transmission that is knowledge itself.'[6] The transmission itself – the exchange between the survivor and the secondary witness, in this instance, through the medium of film – is the arbiter of the modern testimonial.

In his controversial essay 'Lanzmann's *Shoah*: "Here There Is No Why"', Dominick LaCapra makes the claim that Lanzmann's '[...] self-understanding and commentary give priority to his personal vision of the film as a work of art', bringing to the foreground the need for further examination and discussion of the ethics involved in translating testimony through an artistic medium.[7] I wish to take up these issues surrounding Lanzmann's concept of the 'obscene' and examine the relation between the filmmaker/witness and the survivor in *Calling the Ghosts* (1997), a film directed by Mandy Jacobson and Karmen Jelincic about two female survivors of rape in Bosnia.[8] I am concerned with the process of how we listen to testimony and I question whether we can place what we hear into a coherent narrative, while still avoiding the closure which comprises Lanzmann's notion of the 'obscene'. In other words, how does the film *Calling the Ghosts* function as a medium for witnessing? How does the film succeed or fail at sensitively translating both the language and the silence of the survivor, and placing them into a viable narrative without crossing into the 'obscene' or without 'presuming to know'? The film raises such questions as the nature of the importance of the relationship between the survivor and the filmmaker, and the process which is involved in first listening to and then transmitting the survivors' testimony, and seeks to uncover a new language not only for the translation of pain and violence into words, but also to articulate the wordless silences, breaths and gasps of the witnesses that accompany them. It is imperative for Jacobson and Jelincic that we listen to the survivor with an awareness that her testimony may further traumatize or violate a woman who has already suffered, and that she may suffer again each time she retells her story. As with Lanzmann's own philosophy regarding his creative process in relation to *Shoah*, Jacobson and Jelincic do not seek definitive explanations, nor do they question why the women have been raped in a direct manner – rather, they approach the survivor through a relation of ethical responsibility, by not presupposing that they know which questions to ask, or which answers to expect.

Beverley Allen, in her study *Rape Warfare: The Hidden Genocide in Bosnia-Herzegovina and Croatia* (1996) has argued that, during the war in Bosnia (1992–95), countless atrocities were committed and, among these crimes, thousands of women were raped and tortured under the auspices of 'ethnic-cleansing and genocide'.[9] Allen points out that, although there is nothing unusual about 'mass rape' in war, in Bosnia this mass rape had a rigidly systematic paradigm that coincided with a Serbian theory of ethnic genocide.[10] According to Allen, women were raped in great numbers, with the aim of causing pregnancy, in the desire to eventually abolish Muslim identity.[11] Many women were forcibly detained in 'detention centres' or 'camps' set up by the Serbs, and the first rumours of these rape/death camps in Bosnia reached Zagreb in late 1991.[12] As the women slowly emerged from the camps, stories circulated that in the 'detention centres' were nightly vigils of torture, which included seemingly indiscriminate rapes, beatings and murders.

Calling the Ghosts is a documentary that picks up the thread of the victims' memories and attempts to reconstruct a cohesive portrait of what life after 'rape' has been like for two Bosnian women. The film retraces the route by which two professional women, Jadranka Cigelj and Nusreta Sivac, were forced from their homes in Prijedor in April 1992 and taken to Omarska, one of the most notorious camps for human-rights abuses. In the film, the women describe how they survived with dirty drinking water and little food, while being raped and beaten over a four month period. The women also describe how they were deprived of a sense of identity, and were made to scrub blood from the walls and furniture of the offices, in which men were tortured during the day, and in which the women slept at night. The second, longer portion of the film, concentrates on life after the two women's release from Omarska, and the long walk back into their destroyed lives in Prijedor. The film portrays the women telling their own story of the brutal acts committed at Omarska, and sharing them with other women who were also raped and abused during the war. It retraces and documents the story of Jadranka and Nusreta through the process of them giving their testimony, taking action against their perpetrators, and seeing their accusations to the Hague, where they hope to find justice and restitution for themselves and the thousands of other women like them.[13]

II

In her moving essay, 'The Return of the Voice: Claude Lanzmann's *Shoah*', Shoshana Felman makes the vital statement that '[…] truth does not kill the possibility of art – on the contrary, it requires it for its transmission, for its realization in our consciousness as witnesses'.[14] *Calling the Ghosts* is a film which explores the notion of witnessing, and which maps the intimate relationship that exists between the survivor, her testimony and its reception. Seeking to elude the space of the 'obscene', or of understanding, Jacobson's and Jelincic's documentary gestures toward a new way of thinking about survival and victimhood, as the directors are cognizant of the problems for the survivor of reintegrating into society, and also of the dangers inherent in the testimonial project of re-traumatizing the survivor. The film explores the relation between testimony and transmission, both in terms of the transformation of trauma into language, and the transmission of testimony through film. It is both a study of the relation between the survivor and language, demonstrating how the filmmakers assist the two women to find the language that bears witness to their pain, and an exploration of trauma and victimhood.

The role of the witness and her importance in the transmission of testimony is evident from the beginning of the film, as the directors struggle to transmit the thoughts and feelings of the survivor.[15] *Calling the Ghosts* opens with a staged shot of Jadranka in the shadows of her house, avoiding the camera as it enters her domestic space and plays her in slow motion. This opening moment is structured to begin our relation to Jadranka, by reminding us that we do not know this nameless woman. She is a stranger, a foreigner, someone with whom we have no connection and of whom we have no understanding, except in our relation to her anguished gestures. Slowly, the scene is transposed as Jadranka's face fades away, and in its place appears a blazing field, with houses in the background, obscured by smoke. As the camera gradually pulls back to encompass this scene in its entirety, we first hear Jadranka's unsteady voice as she says, 'In the beginning I had the reruns of my own film'.[16] All that Jadranka had was the imprint of her own traumatic memory, which left her without space to breathe, to clear her mind, or to move on and put the past behind her. Here, as the film opens, we are not faced with a re-enactment of Jadranka's time in Omarska, rather Jacobson and Jelincic bring us to a different space and setting. They have chosen the privacy of Jadranka's home to begin the transmission between the filmmaker and the survivor, although it is clear that the traumatic past still obtrudes upon this familiar space.

The film then cuts to a scene on an empty beach, and we see only the back of a pale woman in a red bathing suit, sitting on the sharp black rocks, staring out to sea. In this stark setting, the camera hesitatingly approaches the woman from behind, in the same slow motion that was used in the opening shot, and the mood is one of dreamy surrealism. Once again, we see the woman, but we do not know her intentions. As viewers, we cannot interpret the woman's action, and we are unable to discern whether the scene represents thoughts of suicide – an ending of life – or of the immersion of baptism – a renewal of life. The position of the woman also recalls our own stance as secondary witnesses to the testimony of the survivor. Comparable to Jadranka, seated on the edge of the rocks while contemplating the next move she will make, we too are seated precariously on the edge of our own knowledge and understanding, where we face our limits and reside in an ambiguous position.

The camera follows Jadranka as she tentatively moves towards the sea and asks herself some of the most difficult questions a survivor can formulate. Splashing her face as if preparing for the shock of bodily exposure, Jadranka immerses only half of her body in the water as she asks: 'To stay silent or to speak?'[17] Should she take further steps and immerse herself in her memories? Should she risk facing the reruns of her personal tragedy? Or should she remain only half immersed, stranded in the void between language and survival, unable to move on and to begin to heal? All of these are questions that the survivor must face before she begins to tell her story. In the next cut, we see Jadranka swimming in slow motion, completely immersed in the water, except for her head. It is at this point that Jadranka says, 'If I stay silent how moral would that be?'[18] In this potentially baptismal scene, we are watching Jadranka's struggle to come to a conscious decision to speak out, and to expose herself to the camera, to the viewer, to the dangers that coincide with the decision to confront her oppressors. At the same time that she is questioning her own morals and ethics, Jadranka is not only facing the physical dangers of possible retaliation by Serbs, but she is making the equally hazardous decision to confront a part of herself which she may never fully be able to articulate. If she confronts such hazy depths, she may find the horrifying reruns of her own film, the repetition of her trauma. If she does not confront her terror and chooses to remain silent, what might be the outcome for herself and other women who are suffering? As viewers, we watch as Jadranka swims through the heavy, cold water of the sea, and we view her solely from the outside, as spectators. We have no part in her movement – the position of the camera insists on our position as mere onlookers and reminds us that we are secondary and contingent to the testimonial process.

The camera then shifts to its second movement as Jadranka begins to speak out, to attempt to remember. As she articulates a fragmented phrase, 'When I remember the night I was taken out [...]', the camera's position swings around and attempts to bring us toward Jadranka, to 'become one' with her.[19] The camera position shifts as Jadranka treads water, struggling to make a decision as to whether she should keep her head above the water, where she can breathe, or enter into the darkness of the blurry depths. In this pivotal moment, the camera looks out in the direction of the coast and follows Jadranka's glance, so that the viewer enters into what we are led to believe must be Jadranka's vision. Echoing Jadranka's movement, the camera begins to go beneath the surface of the water. We follow the camera moving upwards to the crystal-clear view of the coastline and then back downwards to the opaque and shifting depths of traumatic memory. The camera is attempting to identify with Jadranka, to enter into her traumatic history through her vision. If only for a moment, the filmmaker seeks to locate herself in the space of Jadranka's indecision as to what step to take next. Jadranka's slow motion, moving up and down in the waves, becomes a metaphor for remembering and repressing.[20] The lucid moments where her testimony will come alive in the film are followed by dark spaces, in which she slips back beneath the surface, to find herself tumbling out of language. It is a suffocating space where there is no air available, except for that which she is holding in her lungs, not willing to let go for fear of death, and the camera attempts to follow the testimonial process. As Jadranka makes the decision to dive into her memory, to try to understand what has happened to her, it is to this dark and fluid space that she attempts to take us, down into the abyss that trauma represents. If Jadranka enters this space, she must return to nightmares of screams and brutal shouts and endeavour to order them, so that both she and the listener can begin to make some sense of what she suffered at the hands of her torturers. It is as if the camera, too, has been pulled into this dark space. It is a moment between the survivor and the witness that seems dangerously close to crossing a boundary, but at the same time, it also briefly explores the possibilities and the limits of identification, which are created in the process of testimony.

The camera's third and final movement, in this opening scene, positions the listener for the remainder of the film. The camera moves away from Jadranka as she looks at the coastline, and observes, 'My own broken bones begin to hurt [...]'.[21] After Jadranka has submerged herself in the water and in memory, and has made the decision to speak, the camera retreats from its attempt to position itself and the viewer within her perspective and watches her from a distance once again. As Jadranka utters the words, 'If I speak how good is that for me? I would have to expose myself', she swims towards the coast, as if having made the decision to speak, she seeks some protection and begins her return to dry land.[22] Now that she is going to expose herself, the camera retreats, as if the filmmakers now realize that a point of complete identification is impossible: the remainder of the film requires us to question the position in which we are located in relation to Jadranka's narrative, and to ask what our role will be in the transmission of her story. The film interrogates the role of the camera, and confronts the possibilities of identification available to the filmmaker, without understanding *too* much – without crossing over into the space of the 'obscene'.

The opening scene occurs between the credits and the title, as if the connection between the survivor and the listener must be explored before the film can properly begin, and both parties take the plunge and immerse themselves in language and relation. Encapsulated and isolated from the main body of the film, the first minutes provide a meaningful framework and question the position from which the audience will receive the painful, personal testimony of Jadranka. The filmmakers move to bring us closer to Jadranka, and with that move, to attempt to begin to see the world through her eyes. Stranded in the repetition of her own nightmare, the 'reruns' of her own film, Jadranka seeks to break out of the trajectory of the return, which characterizes trauma. It is at this moment, when Jadranka begins to articulate her trauma, that a central question of the film comes to the forefront of her concerns: 'When I speak, who will be there to listen to me?'[23] Now that Jadranka has begun to move out of silence, into the foreground, and to risk exposure, the film questions what kind of witness will receive her testimony. As a survivor, Jadranka shares her testimony with the filmmakers and the film's audience. The film also explores Jadranka's sharing of her testimony with Nusreta, and with a group of other female survivors, who share similar experiences. Testifying risks exposure and re-traumatization, but it also entails the hope of progression and a tentative movement forward.

In the opening minutes of *Calling the Ghosts*, the camera captures both Jadranka's struggle to speak out and to begin to name her trauma, and the filmmakers' attempt to follow her words, and enter her trauma, by making the camera's movements parallel her language. Beginning with the encounter on the edge of the water, the camera makes three movements during this scene on the beach. We move from not knowing Jadranka's intentions, to her contemplation of the future and the possibility for remembering, and finally to her determination to testify. Each of these stages is signalled by a shift in the camera position, from observing Jadranka on the rocks, to merging with her viewpoint as she swims, and to following her return towards the coast. Each of these camera movements explores the filmmakers' attempts to approach the survivor without doing violence to her. The camera performs a visual reading of Jadranka's emotions, attempting to transmit to the viewer the fragile space between knowing and not knowing. The directors attempt to communicate meaning, but do not presuppose understanding, as they translate the witness's language into visual imagery. The first minutes of exchange between Jadranka and the camera explore the hazardous nature of witnessing. Jacobson and Jelincic must be sensitive to the dangers of witnessing and question whether Jadranka's immersion in memory represents, at each moment of her testimony, a baptism or renewal of the self, or a suicidal act, which can only result in self-harm.

In translating testimony, the filmmaker inevitably superimposes his or her own experiences and desires onto the survivor; one desire which is particularly hazardous is the wish to 'understand' the survivor. For Lanzmann, a refusal to understand is the 'only possible ethical and at the same time the only possible operative attitude' that he could take, in relation to his own film direction.[24] Basing his knowledge on Primo Levi's phrase, 'Here there is no why', Lanzmann argues that the filmmaker can never understand trauma, particularly through a causal approach, which seeks to determine reasons why.[25] Lanzmann's views surrounding the notion of 'understanding', and asking the question 'why', come to the forefront in *Calling the Ghosts*. In the second movement of the camera, during the opening scene, there is one brief moment when the filmmakers, through the camera, attempt to put themselves in the place of the survivor, and to see the world through her eyes. However, this moment is also an illustration of an astute self-awareness by the directors, that they can never be in the position of the survivor. When Jadranka says, 'When I remember the night I was taken out', she is recounting her memories for the first time, and the camera slips carefully into position, as if now ready to travel with her to the depths of her memory and to share her trauma.[26] But in the very next shot, as if the filmmakers have become aware of the slippery space in which they are playing, the camera withdraws, and switches back to the view of the outside. Aware of the dangers of putting themselves in the place of the survivor, Jacobson and Jelincic quickly pull the camera back from Jadranka, and once again it is clearly placed in a position outside of the survivor's pain. For one instant, the camera position swings around to look at the world through the survivor's eyes, but then rapidly withdraws from the position. This gesture by the filmmakers suggests an intelligent self-examination, an introspective look at their own work, and reflects upon current debates that surround questions of history, testimony and aesthetics.

Having pulled back from the survivor, in order to give her space to breathe – not to suffocate her with the belief that they can take up her position as easily as they can change a film shot – *Calling the Ghosts* explores the connection between testimony and spatiality. Shoshana Felman has questioned this point of connection in relation to the testimonial project of *Shoah*: 'Is it possible to witness [...] from inside? [...] Or are we necessarily outside [...] and witnessing it from outside?'[27] The filmmakers of *Calling the Ghosts* face the same dilemma, because the story that Jadranka tells is always and inevitably a retelling of an original event, never the event itself, and it is difficult for the filmmakers to know from where Jadranka speaks, and from where the camera should take its position. The film questions whether it is ever possible to witness from the inside of another's trauma. For one brief moment, the camera takes up Jadranka's position, and goes below the surface to witness what she sees, but all that it films are the black depths of the sea. The filmmakers must withdraw the camera from darkness and film from a distance, marking an acceptance that they may be 'necessarily outside' of something unnameable and therefore unreachable. The film also acknowledges that Jadranka's narrative of her experience is consciously altered for those who are 'outside' of the experience, or have not encountered a similar trauma in their own lives. The filmmakers' highlighting of spatial, as well as temporal modes of thinking through trauma, enables the conceptualization of an ethical relation between testifier and witness, which is marked not only by identification, but also by a necessary recognition of otherness and difference.

The narrativization of trauma also involves an ethical dimension. Trauma calls out to be ordered into a comprehensible narrative which provides meaning both for the subject and for the listener, but the process of ordering also has its dangers, because 'the capacity to remember is also the capacity to elide or distort', and with this narrative transformation comes the loss of the 'essential incomprehensibility' of the original story.[28] The filmmaker is, in one sense, bound to this paradox of telling, and must confront the elisions and distortions which are inherent in the narrative process. However, even with mistranslations and missed encounters, the testimonial project can make a record of something that before that moment was 'non-existent' and still 'a record that has yet to be made'.[29] The filmmaker must engage with the complexities involved in bearing witness, and understand that the record that she helps to make is of a moment that has not yet occurred until the testimonial act – until the moment of transmission. In this way, the witness resembles an empty notebook, or in the case of *Calling the Ghosts*, the filmmaker represents the unexposed film, she is a 'blank screen' upon which the event will become inscribed.[30] The vicissitudes of witnessing are a central force in the transmission of testimony and mark the relation between the survivor and the filmmaker with an ethic of accountability and of presence.[31] The filmmaker must approach a testifier sensitively and intimately and have the patience to wait, to listen, to observe, and to know when to speak and when to remain silent, when to turn the camera on and when to turn it off. The filmmaker is a subject, an *other*, a being whose presence has an effect on the testifier, and her camera not only records, but also affects the testimony which is produced.

Listening, waiting and watching are all integral to the process and transmission of testimony throughout *Calling the Ghosts*. In the opening scenes, Jadranka makes motions without attaching words to them, leading the filmmaker and the viewer to watch her body closely and attempt to read her gestures. In this way, her silences are as important as her words, and demand a form of interpretive witnessing, based as much in the physical gesture as in verbal language. The camera films patiently and allows Jadranka to arrive at her own articulation. The camera emphasizes that 'what is important is the situation of *discovery* of knowledge – its evolution, and its very *happening*'.[32] Jacobson's and Jelincic's camera attempts to be present at each moment of this 'happening', each moment of discovery, and through this painful journey, the survivor and the filmmakers of *Calling the Ghosts* have become inextricably linked.

III

In the representation of trauma, the story may end, the film may run its course, but the trauma of the survivor persists. Even though we have finished watching their story on the screen, Jadranka and Nusreta must continue to confront what they may just be beginning to understand. *Calling the Ghosts* is not concerned with narrative resolutions, but rather with thresholds. The end of the film reveals the hazards of attempting to represent closure and finality, in relation to something which inevitably is still in progress. That is to say, the film suggests that there is always something more to convey, that we cannot reach a position of understanding or final resolution. *Calling the Ghosts* is a stark reminder that trauma represents a forever missed encounter and that no amount of text on the subject, no amount of film footage, will ever fill the void. Instead, testimony carries with it the potential to create new histories, and new ways of thinking about traumatic events. Jacobson and Jelincic have begun to redefine the testimonial genre in film, through self-examination and an awareness of their limitations. They have sought to give an account of trauma from the voice of those who have suffered. They have attempted to write the story of Jadranka and Nusreta not as a 'fiction of the real', but as a world where reality parallels fiction in one of its most horrifying moments. The filmmakers have used the film to explore and reflect on the nature of testimony, and to think through new modes of conceiving the relation between the testifier and the witness.

In their attempt to follow Felman's statement that 'truth' requires art for its transmission and 'for its realization in our consciousness as witnesses', the filmmakers of *Calling the Ghosts* have addressed the historical situation in Bosnia and the traumatic experiences of two women, in particular. However, the film also reflects on the nature of the testimony which it produces. Historically, women who are victims of rape, in war or in peacetime, have not been listened to, so that the role of the addressee assumes a particular importance in *Calling the Ghosts*.[33] The opening scene of the film demands that the viewer come forward and take the risk of putting herself in the terrifying space of the survivor of trauma. At the opening of the film, we view Jadranka at a safe distance, as someone entirely separate from our own body, our own experience. But through Jacobson's and Jelincic's camera, we elide with Jadranka – we dive with her into the water, and are forced (albeit momentarily) to look through the survivor's eyes. Finally, *Calling the Ghosts* functions as an important testimonial device for survivors of rape in Bosnia, and as a political intervention in transmitting trauma. The film ends by refusing the possibility of closure for the traumas of rape it has represented, partly because many of the men who committed these crimes against humanity are still at large.[34] The directors of *Calling the Ghosts* appear to suggest that the personal and the political are inextricably linked, and that there can be no closure on the level of personal trauma until the political level has achieved a more satisfactory resolution.[35] It seems that the 'ghosts' of Bosnia (and Kosovo) which the film has called up cannot be 'laid to rest', but may continue to live on without justice or repatriation.[36]

Notes

1   Claude Lanzmann, quoted in Cathy Caruth, 'Recapturing the Past: Introduction' in Cathy Caruth (ed.), *Trauma: Explorations in Memory* (Baltimore: Johns Hopkins University Press, 1995), p. 154.

2   Ibid.

3   Ibid.

4   Shoshana Felman, 'The Return of the Voice: Claude Lanzmann's *Shoah*', in Shoshana Felman and Dori Laub, *Testimony: Crises of Witnessing in Literature, Psychoanalysis and History* (New York : Routledge, 1992), p. 206.

5   Claude Lanzmann, 'The Obscenity of Understanding: An Evening with Claude Lanzmann', in Caruth (ed.), *Trauma: Explorations in Memory*, p. 204.
6   Claude Lanzmann, quoted in Dominick LaCapra, *History and Memory After Auschwitz* (Ithaca: Cornell University Press, 1998), p. 101.
7   LaCapra, *History and Memory*, p. 96.
8   *Calling the Ghosts*, directed by Mandy Jacobson and Karmen Jelincic (Bowery Productions, 1997). Hereafter abbreviated as *CTG*. The film is available through the New York distributor, 'Women Make Movies'.
9   Beverly Allen, *Rape Warfare: The Hidden Genocide in Bosnia-Herzegovina and Croatia* (Minneapolis: University of Minnesota Press, 1996), p. 76.
10   Allen, *Rape Warfare*, p. 88. For a detailed study on 'mass rape' in Bosnia, see Alexandra Stiglmayer (ed.), *Mass Rape: The War Against Women in Bosnia Herzegovina* (Lincoln: University of Nebraska Press, 1994).
11   Allen, *Rape Warfare*, 'Foreword'. For an interesting account of Omarska by one of its prisoners see Rezak Hukanovic, *The Tenth Circle of Hell: A Memoir of Life in the Death Camps of Bosnia* (New York: Basic Books, 1996).
12   Allen, *Rape Warfare*, p. 58.
13   It is important to emphasize that there are no actors in this film and no narratorial voice to tell their story for the survivors. The only people who speak in the film are Jadranka, Nusreta and other survivors, who are giving their own testimony of what happened to them in Bosnia.
14   Felman and Laub, p. 206.
15   Here I am referring to the filmmakers, who, as the witnesses, must attempt to transmit language and testimony to the viewer of the film.
16   *CTG*.
17   *CTG*.
18   *CTG*.
19   *CTG*.
20   This is in reference to Cathy Caruth's comment in response to a presentation of an earlier version of this essay at the conference *Refiguring History: Between the Psyche and the Polis* (University of Newcastle upon Tyne, May 1999).
21   *CTG*.
22   *CTG*.
23   Felman and Laub, p. 218. Jadranka does not ask this question, but I am arguing that the idea is present throughout the film *Calling the Ghosts*.
24   Lanzmann quoted by Felman in Caruth (ed.), *Trauma: Explorations in Memory*, p. 204.
25   Lanzmann quoted by Felman, ibid.
26   *CTG*.
27   Felman and Laub, p. 227.
28   Caruth, 'Recapturing the Past: Introduction', in Caruth (ed.), *Trauma: Explorations in Memory*, p. 154.
29   Dori Laub, 'Bearing Witness or the Vicissitudes of Listening', in Felman and Laub, p. 57.
30   Ibid.
31   Ibid., pp. 70–71.
32   Ibid., p. 62.
33   Mandy Jacobson, telephone interview, 21 April 1999.

34 The text which concludes the film notes: 'A full year after the signing of the Dayton Peace Accords, 50,000 NATO troops stationed in Bosnia and Herzegovina had not yet apprehended any of the Serb, Croat or Muslim individuals indicted for war crimes' (*CTG*).

35 The concluding text of the film records that on the political level: 'Prijedor remains under the administration of the same Bosnian Serb leadership which seized power on April 29 1992' (*CTG*). This lack of political change or transformation also hinders personal development: 'Jadranka and Nusreta believe that they will never return to live in Prijedor again' (*CTG*).

36 I would like to thank Tom Keenan for introducing me to *Calling the Ghosts* in his seminar on Bosnia and the Media in Autumn 1997. I would also like to thank Mandy Jacobson for her encouragement and willingness to discuss the work at length.

PART III
MEMORY AND CULTURAL HISTORY

7 In the Penal Colony

JOHN FROW

I

What are the periodicities of remembrance shared with others? Writing in the final volume of *Les Lieux de Mémoire*, Pierre Nora identifies two primary forms of commemorative time: that of the *centenary*, 'voluntary, deliberate, impossible either to avoid or to manage', and that of the *generation*, 'involuntary and even unconscious, uncontrollable'.[1] These are the interwoven times of the nation-state and of living collective memory. In this chapter I ask about the kinds of connection that are possible between the pain or joy of generational experience and the forms of identification invoked by that larger periodicity of the nation. But the generational experience that I posit is not necessarily a direct experience of events, for reasons that Nora explicates: if the past has lost its organic, peremptory, constraining character, he says, commemoration now tends to be made up of media events, tourism, promotions and entertainment; its medium is no longer the classroom or the public square but television, museums, expositions, colloquia, and it takes place not in official ceremonies but in television spectaculars.[2] This is to say that the experience of historical events is shared and collectively remembered – of course in very different ways – both by those who are closely involved in them and by those who encounter them in a mediated form. Those experiences of hurt that typically knit a generational cohort together – a war, a national catastrophe, an assassination, a massacre – are experiences of shared grief and shared inability to understand the import of what has happened. They are traumatic in the sense in which Cathy Caruth uses that word: they open up a history which arises 'where *immediate understanding* may not',[3] and which returns to haunt its survivors not because it is known but because it is not. Yet it is important to say as well that there is something glib about the attempt to apply the concept of trauma directly to historical events (indeed, there is already something problematic about its application to non-somatic hurt).[4] It is this discontinuity or lack of fit between the historical time of the generation and the historical time of the nation, as well as the continuity between them, that I explore in what follows.

My argument is built around a place, Port Arthur in Tasmania, and around a set of stories associated with it – although these stories are not just there waiting to be told, part of an inherent factuality. The first is the by-now generic narrative of a lone gunman (think of the layers of irony that phrase has acquired since the first of the Kennedy assassinations, as well as the narrative structure that now flows unhesitatingly from it) who, on 28 April 1996, gunned down and killed 35 people at the site. The point of this story is that it has no point. There is absolutely no commensuration between the massive injury of the event, with all its consequences of grief and personal damage, and the triviality of any available explanation in terms, say, of Martin Bryant's low intelligence or of the influence on him of violent videos. The lack of commensuration is exacerbated by the technology: a weak and callow young man is given immense powers of destruction by the semiautomatic rifles which translate an impulse, a movement of the finger, into the mass slaughter of strangers. It is because there is no sense, no cause or motive that could sufficiently fit the crime, that the inevitable consequences flow: a community which at first came together in its grief is now torn apart, there are law suits, recriminations, broken marriages, all the devastation of lives lived in the aftermath of an intensely violent act. It is perhaps not surprising, then, that the event comes increasingly to be spoken of as a kind of uncanny repetition in which reality imitates its prior simulation: the carnage around those who survive to give witness to it is repeatedly described as being 'like a scene out of a movie',[5] or 'like something I might have seen on television'.[6] A security officer at the site draws on the training scenarios he has worked through in a simulated emergency exercise; the ambulance driver who is called and told of a mass shooting at Port Arthur, replies 'Oh yeah. When's the exercise going to be finished?' – only to be told 'This is not an exercise. This is a definite situation.'[7] It is for this reason too that the question of an appropriate memorial for the dead becomes so contentious. There are arguments over whether the Broad Arrow Café, where 20 people died, should be left standing as a place of mourning or razed to the ground (in the event it has been left half-destroyed, bullet holes pocked into the bare walls, an instant ruin). Nobody uses Bryant's name, but his denied presence is everywhere. Nobody knows the forms which will lay the ghost. Nobody knows what kind of monument will insert this story into the other story for which this site is known, into that other past which is barely available for understanding.

For Port Arthur is itself a memorial, a *lieu de mémoire*, its ruined traces bearing ambiguous witness to a whole system of punishment, involuntary exile, and unfree labour which has come to represent the foundational moment of the Australian nation. Established in 1830 in the natural prison formed by a narrow-necked peninsula, an almost-island in the far southeast corner of this island to the far southeast of the Australian mainland, Port Arthur was a secondary penal settlement to which transported convicts offending elsewhere in what was then called Van Diemen's Land were sent for punishment in the chain gang, the treadmill, and the solitary confinement cells of the Model Prison. Never the most brutal of the secondary penal settlements, its harsh and unremitting regime was nevertheless designed to break the spirits of its inmates in one of the most isolated places on earth. Its instrument of last resort was the lash, a switch of nine knotted cords soaked in salt water and dried to the hardness of wire which cut the flesh to shreds. 'A lot of violence has happened there. It must be the most violent place in Australia. It seemed the right place', said Bryant in an explanation of his crime at once compelling and cynical in its displacement of blame.[8] For a variety of reasons, not the least of which is the paradoxical beauty of its setting and of its ruined buildings, Port Arthur has come to emblematize the Gulag created by imperial Britain for its exiled criminal population. But I want to approach it indirectly, by way of another penal settlement and another practice of inscription on the body.

II

An explorer (*der Forschungsreisende*) is made the reluctant witness of an execution carried out in the penal colony. The condemned man is a soldier sentenced for 'disobedience and insulting behaviour to a superior' (*Beleidigung des Vorgesetzten*), and he is accompanied to his death only by a guard and an officer. The instrument of his execution is an elaborate apparatus invented by the former Commandant of the colony, of whose regime the officer is a fanatical but isolated partisan, and the officer explains the workings of the apparatus to the explorer in some detail. The machine has three parts: a bed, covered in cotton wool, to which the naked condemned man is strapped; the designer, which, like the bed, looks like a dark wooden chest; and the harrow which shuttles on a steel ribbon between the bed and the designer. The apparatus is thus a sort of cross between a Jacquard loom and an ink-jet printer; its central component, the harrow, made of glass so that an onlooker can see through it the inscription taking place on the body, contains two sets of needles, the longer ones for writing and the shorter ones for spraying jets of water to wash away the blood. What it writes on the body is the sentence (*Urteil*) that the court has handed down; but because the script is so complicated, so full of flourishes, so much like an illegible scrawl (this indeed is all that the explorer can make of it), it is only after the sixth hour that the radiance of Enlightenment comes to the condemned man, who begins to decipher the script 'with his wounds' until the moment of his death.

During the regime of the Old Commandant, executions were festivals to which crowds flocked to see Justice being done; children were given a privileged place near the apparatus in order to witness at the sixth hour the transfigured face of the suffering man, 'the radiance of that justice achieved at last and fading so quickly'. Now, however, no one attends; the machine is run down and the officer can get no spare parts for it because the New Commandant disapproves of all that it represents. It becomes clear that the explorer has been positioned in a struggle between the old and the new orders: if he condemns the apparatus as barbaric, the New Commandant will take advantage of this verdict (*Urteil*) to abolish its use; but if, as the officer implores him to, he approves of it, then the officer believes that his fantasy of a restoration of the old days will be realized. As for the explorer, although he is constrained by his position as a guest, a mere disinterested observer, from intervening to try to stop the execution, he is a liberal and humanitarian soul – a man of his progressive times – and he indicates that he does indeed disapprove of the apparatus. This is the end for the officer, who then frees the condemned man and takes his place. For him, however, there is no moment of enlightenment. In a mechanical frenzy the disintegrating machine tears the officer to pieces, the needles jabbing rather than writing: 'This was no exquisite torture such as the officer desired, this was plain murder.' In a coda after the officer's ugly death spitted to the needles, the explorer is shown the grave of the Old Commandant, marked by a low stone lying beneath a table in unconsecrated ground; an inscription prophesies his return. Fleeing the colony, the explorer has to shake off the guard and the condemned soldier, threatening them with a heavy knotted rope in order to keep them away.[9]

Let me make a number of brief comments on this text. The first is a question: why are there no convicts in this penal colony? The condemned man is a soldier who has broken a regulation; the story gives us no sight of anyone who is actually serving a sentence. But if we think of some of Kafka's other closed, pointless, and self-perpetuating hierarchies, it is perhaps no accident that it is a guard rather than a prisoner who undergoes punishment. There is no outside of such systems, and in this the penal colony resembles rather closely the hierarchy of surveillance envisaged in Bentham's *Panopticon*, in which it is not only the prisoners in their cells but the warders at every level of the apparatus of inspection who are held under constant scrutiny.

The second comment concerns the nature of the regulation that the soldier infringes. The man is a servant assigned to a captain; he sleeps outside the captain's door, and 'it is his duty ... to get up every time the hour strikes and salute the captain's door'; it is for failing to perform this duty that he will be executed. I shall have more to say shortly about the place of pointless obedience in carceral systems.

The third observation concerns the extraordinary elaborateness and prescriptive detail of the Old Commandant's machinery of inscription. What kind of rationality is at work here? It is a reason informed by what Robert Hughes calls 'a passion for bureaucratic exactitude about pain',[10] for the calculation of a precisely proportionate justice. Its philosophical counterpart is perhaps the Bentham of *The Rationale of Punishment* who, addressing the problem that whipping is administered with variable force and by means of instruments which are not standardized, suggests that

> a machine might be made, which should put in motion certain elastic rods of cane or whalebone, the number and size of which might be determined by the law; the body of the delinquent might be subjected to the strokes of these rods, and the force and rapidity with which they should be applied, might be prescribed by the judge: thus everything which is arbitrary might be removed. A public officer, of more responsible character than the common executioner, might preside over the infliction of the punishment; and when there were many delinquents to be punished, his time might be saved, and the terror of the scene heightened, without increasing the actual suffering, by increasing the number of the machines, and subjecting all the offenders to punishments at the same time.[11]

We recognize this officer, of course, as we do the desire that drives the rationale.

My fourth comment is that the needles inscribing a message on the bound body of the condemned man are the precise analogue of one of the central metaphors in European culture for memory, the stylus which inscribes a message on a wax tablet.[12]

Finally, let me note the formalism of the opposition of the old and the new regimes in the penal colony. Its point is of course to balance two moral perspectives, and thus to undermine our structural identification with the explorer and against the fanaticism of the officer. Against the brutal and authoritarian justice of the old regime are set the moral complicity and enlightened indecisiveness of the explorer; against the patriarchal authority of the Old Commandant the feminized world of the New Commandant, surrounded by his 'ladies' with their unhelpful pity for the condemned man;

against a religious fervour of belief in justice, a modern and tolerant absence of conviction.

III

While it would be wrong to read the story as a determinate allegory, I propose to use it as a template with which to read the two distinct regimes of punishment operative at Port Arthur. In the older mode, punishment is above all directed at the body in the form of the public spectacle of flogging, the chains worn in the work gangs, and physically arduous and dangerous labour in the settlement's various industries – farming, quarrying, shipbuilding, logging. The continuity between work and punishment is perhaps best exemplified by the treadwheel which operated in the flour mill and granary complex for several years from 1845: a form of work which was repetitive, wearing, and in which any cessation of movement on the treads would immediately cause injury. This was at least an economically productive mill: many of those in use in England at the time were nothing more than devices 'for equalizing, measuring, regulating and timing the performance of toil';[13] as they became more sophisticated, windsail masts were added to increase resistance to the rotation of the wheel, and subsequently even more precise brakes were devised to give precisely controlled and measured resistance. But this minute calculation of severity is characteristic of the Port Arthur regime as a whole. Hughes writes that

> To scrutinize into the punishment records of Port Arthur men is to look into a microcosm of bureaucratic tedium. Its horror comes not from unrestrained cruelty (as the Gothic legends and popular horror stories of the place insisted) but rather from its opposite, the mechanical apportioning of strictly metered punishments designed to wear each prisoner down into bovine acceptance – Arthur's criterion of moral reform. It is like looking into the memory of some dull god interminably counting fallen sparrows on his fingers.[14]

Public flogging declined at Port Arthur from the mid-1840s and ceased in 1848. While the more traditional form of incarceration was continued in the Penitentiary, constructed between 1854 and 1857 by conversion of the flour mill and granary, a radically different model of the ends of the prison was realized in another institution. Built in 1848–49, initially to accommodate convicts transferred from Norfolk Island, the Model (or Separate) Prison worked on the principles of solitude, silence, anonymity, and moral reflection. Designed as a cross enclosed by a circle, it consisted of three wings of single cells and, in the fourth wing, a chapel in which prisoners were enclosed in separate tiered stalls, cut off from sight of each other. Punishment was by confinement in the totally dark 'dumb cells' in which all sense of the passage of time, and indeed almost all sensory experience, were lost. The universal rule of silence meant that neither prisoners nor guards were allowed to speak, orders being given by the sounding of a bell or by hand signals, or, in the chapel, by a mechanical device displaying the number of the prisoner whose turn it was to enter or to leave. Prisoners, said the regulations, 'must never read aloud, sing, whistle, dance or make any other noise in their Cells, exercise yards, corridors or Chapel'.[15] Warders wore felt slippers in the corridors to muffle any sound they made as they patrolled. Meals were served to prisoners in their cells; in public spaces such as the corridors and the exercise yards they moved only with their faces covered by a 'beak' with eyeholes which extended as a flexible visor from their caps. Work, too – tailoring, shoemaking, the picking of oakum – was performed in solitude in the cells. In short, the Model Prison was so constructed as to destroy all social relations between prisoners and between prisoners and warders. It embodied a dream of total order, of a discipline so pervasive, so destructive of human contact, that each prisoner would have no alternative but to confront and wrestle with his moral state in penitential introspection. (Nothing, of course, guaranteed that any such thing would happen.)

This discipline is structured at once by a nobility of moral purpose and by the sort of nagging, petty meanness that required the guard in the penal colony to salute his superior officer's door on the stroke of every hour. The counterpart at Port Arthur – as at Pentonville Prison in London, on which the Port Arthur prison was closely modelled – was the telltale clock, an ingenious mechanical device standing in the Central Hall and monitoring the warders' attention to duty. As Ian Brand describes it,

> It resembled a standard grandfather clock except that it had no hands and the dial was surrounded by 48 brass pegs, one for each quarter of an hour. As the dial rotated, each peg came under a striker at the top. Operated by a wire, the striker could push the peg below it into the rim of the dial, but only exactly at the quarter hour. It was the job of the duty Officer at night to strike the clock every fifteen minutes, and if he was a little late, the brass peg would not go in and the Head-keeper on his morning round could see immediately that the officer had been negligent.[16]

Clockwork time, a strictly divided and repeated routine, and punishment: these are the elements of an all-embracing discipline that extends to prisoners and warders alike.

If the apparatus that the explorer witnesses in the penal colony belongs to the old regime of spectacular punishment written on the body, it also, paradoxically, partakes of the spirituality of the new, 'humane' regimes of moral inculcation which operate on the prisoner's soul. This is the crucial transition made by the 'reformed' prisons of the nineteenth century, and it comes to permeate every detail of prison architecture, prison administration, and prison discipline. Monika Fludernik gives a schematic outline of the opposition between ideal types of the 'old' and 'new' regimes in the following table:

old	*new*
prison as waiting room for trial and execution	prison as correctional and penal institution
darkness	light
closure (dungeon)	open to surveillance (bars)
filth	cleanliness
idleness	forced labour
dissolute behaviour	enforced discipline
association with others	solitary confinement
corporal constraint (chains)	freedom of movement
cruelty	humaneness
contact with outside (family)	complete isolation from outside
social stratification within prison	absolute standardization of treatment
corrupt prison administration	efficiency and professionalism
repentance before possible execution	repentance and disciplining supposed to result in production of a 'good citizen'
sentence as punishment	correction (privileges for good behaviour)
corporal punishment	behavioural disciplining (focus on prisoners' minds)

metaphors	
dungeon	cell (panopticon)
prison as world	world as prison
body as prison, freedom of mind	depersonalization, brainwashing (mind as carceral body)[17]

Such a dichotomized chart drastically simplifies the complexity of transitions and intermixtures between different conceptions of the prison (and, for Port Arthur, the fact that the Penitentiary and the Model Prison represent no more than different faces of the reformed, disciplinary prison); but it does convey a notion of the starkness of the historical transformation.

At the centre of the reforms initiated by Beccaria, Howard and others in the late eighteenth century and pursued through the first half of the nineteenth was a notion of moral reformation which depended on the infliction of a 'just and unvarying quantum of pain'.[18] Two things come together here: an operation effected upon the soul in accordance with religious conceptions of conscience and conversion from sin; and the development of forms of discipline which are equitable, non-arbitrary, mechanical, and thus independent of human will. Their object is a self conceived as 'at once isolated and transparent to view'.[19] In Foucault's account, this birth of the prison as a technology of moral conversion is a moment of a larger elaboration of a disciplinarity which, emerging from monastic and military organizations of life, comes to govern the school, the workshop, the hospital, the reformatory, indeed all of those systems which at once control and productively form the 'isolated and transparent' self, its habits and its moral consciousness, within the complex of power/knowledge. The unrealized prototype of disciplinarity is Bentham's Panopticon, a utopian model prison formed on the equation of power with visibility and using architecture as its major instrument of moral correction. The question that preoccupied Bentham, writes Robin Evans, is: 'How could human behaviour, and through behaviour the human condition as a whole, be controlled and made certain by design?'.[20] This question brings into play that mobilization of architecture in the service of virtue that Evans describes as underpinning the strategies of nineteenth-century prison reform, and which addressed two related sets of problems in existing regimes of punishment.

The first was the psychological problem that 'impalings, burnings, flayings and dismemberings could only serve to exacerbate the passions and increase the culprits' hatred of God. The problem was to describe a punishment that did not alienate in this way. The solution was to put mental anguish in the place of physical tortures.'[21] *Memory* thus becomes the instrument of moral conversion, and its effects are to be heightened through an enforced solitude which will necessarily promote introspection. The cellular prison comes to stand at the centre of a 'technology of salvation'[22] employed by the state rather than the church.

The second problem is the reproduction of a culture of crime through the association of criminals in a confined space, and especially the cultural (and, although this is rarely made explicit, sexual) contamination that results from mixing different categories of prisoner (the hardened with the novice, for example). Two major solutions are proposed in the early nineteenth century, conveniently symbolized for contemporaries by the 'associated' system in operation at Auburn in New York, and the 'separate' system at Cherry Hill in Philadelphia. At the former, after an initial failed experiment in total solitary confinement, the regime consisted of hard labour in 'silent association', with any communication between convicts being rigorously punished. As Mayhew explains, however, this system is open to subversion by the prisoners' use of codes and muttered words to remain in contact with each other.[23] The separate system, in which a rule of total silence is enforced by the almost continuous separation of prisoners in their cells, removes this possibility. It raises the classification system 'to the highest level of generality',[24] since each prisoner belongs to a category of his own, and is segregated accordingly; and its use of solitude depends upon three principles which had been central to the first wave of reform in the late eighteenth century: 'reformation through reflection, resistance to the spread of corruption through the prevention of communication, and deterrence through terror'.[25]

The logic of the reformed prison is that of an architecture which, working passively and continuously to shape and control experience, invests power in places rather than people. With the eventual triumph of the radial over the polygonal design of the prison, and thus of a logic of multiple, ramified classification and of an unlimited surveillance which comprehends the supervisors amongst the supervised,[26] it comes to function in a fully performative manner as 'an instrument for the imposition of the very authority it had set out to symbolize'.[27] Its most complete nineteenth-century expression is the prison at Pentonville, completed in 1848. This 'total institution',[28] which Mayhew compares both to the Crystal Palace and to 'a bunch of Burlington Arcades', contains 520 cells which are, for all intents and purposes, separate and self-sufficient buildings, each one carefully connected to but isolated from each other by a complicated machinery of thermo-ventilation.[29] Each prisoner is wrapped in anonymity; it is an offence for an officer to utter his name, and his face is covered, when he leaves his cell, in a cloth mask with slots for the eyes. As with the Model Prison at Port Arthur, the purpose of this machinery is 'to crush the will of its 450 inmates by means of absolutely inflexible routine, complete isolation and unvarying task-work, with each convict identically engaged in a twelve-hour day of cobbling or weaving'.[30] As at Port Arthur, the effect of a regime of silence and solitude is to produce high levels of neurosis and insanity. Mayhew carefully documents the fact that 'the discipline pursued at this prison yields *upwards of ten times more lunatics* than should be the case according to the normal rate'; these figures, he writes, 'tell awful tales of long suffering and deep mental affliction; for the breaking down of the weaker minds is merely evidence of the intense moral agony that must be suffered by all except the absolutely insensible'.[31] Ignatieff, finally, reports that

> those who observed prisoners upon their release noticed that many suffered from bouts of hysteria and crying. Others found the sounds of the street deafening and asked for cotton wool to stop up their ears. Still others frightened their families by a listless torpor that took weeks to shake off. Even those who thought they had got used to solitude found themselves dreaming about the prison long after.[32]

IV

If memory has so central and so institutionalized a place in the disciplinary systems to which we are heir, then it is surely wrong to oppose, as Nora does, the involuntary memory of lived, generational experience to the voluntary memory of national historical time. The former is always in some sense rehearsed and repeated; the latter is in some sense always beyond our control. Disciplinary memory, if I can call it that, continues to play an important role in the routine formation of moral selves, perhaps most particularly in its transformation into a memory-work understood as the therapeutic exorcism of repressed and traumatic material. This is not a matter of a historical evolution away from some lost premodern realm of spontaneous and natural memory – we know that memory has always had a technical foundation. It is a matter, rather, of the modalities of remembrance which are specific to our world, and of the pasts that they construct. My question, then, is: how has the lived violence of Port Arthur's past been folded into national historical time? To what extent has this making-past happened within a moral economy where memory still functions in a disciplinary way, as a duty of self-healing, as moral catharsis? And how – to pose this as an ethical task – *should* the violence of those events be remembered? How is it possible to keep alive the intensity of their wounding while at the same time turning it to productive use?

The dream of the prison continues to be dreamed in the many aftermaths of nineteenth-century penality and of the convict transportation system. At Port Arthur the vision of total order and an all-pervasive discipline declined as the settlement did. Transportation to Van Diemen's Land was finally abolished in 1853. Although Port Arthur was retained as a penal settlement well after the other stations were closed, the proportion of its inhabitants classified as paupers, invalids and lunatics – men who had known nothing but prison for most of their lives and were incapable of surviving outside it – grew steadily; a Paupers' Mess was erected in 1864, and a Lunatic Asylum in 1867. The penal settlement was closed in 1877, and although it survived as a town, its buildings were vandalized by tourists and then gutted by bushfires in the 1890s.

To this aftermath of physical and civil decline, however, which was to continue for a century after the closure of the settlement, was counterposed a different kind of aftermath as Port Arthur was slowly and unevenly integrated into an imaginary of national origins. The process was complex, and involved a forgetting as much as a remembering. And this was more generally true of the afterlife in memory of the convict system: Stanner speaks of two 'cults of disremembering' in Australia,[33] deep-rooted reticences about the dispossession of the indigenous peoples and about the convict beginnings of European settlement. Until well into the twentieth century, convict ancestry was 'that hated stain', a social and perhaps genetic taint which few, and perhaps especially few Tasmanians, were willing to acknowledge. This anxiety about origins was reflected in attitudes towards the physical remains of the Port Arthur settlement. An editorial in the Hobart *Mercury* of 1913 recommended that

> the large rambling ruin of the Penitentiary, a relic of that very worst style of British architecture which gave the Old Country the most hideous factories that Lancashire and Yorkshire ever possessed, should be razed and cleared away entirely and its site used for some edifice of more aesthetic appearance, and pleasanter associations ... We need memorials and reminders that are cheerful and inspiring, not depressing, humiliating, saddening ... Men rise on stepping-stones of their dead selves, and need not have those ugly corpses hung round their necks or sitting at their tables.[34]

And when fires gutted many of the buildings in 1897, 'the *Tasmanian Mail* observed that many people would "make no concealment of their satisfaction at the destruction of the penitentiary". Some thought the fire a manifestation of Divine vengeance; others saw it as symbolizing the final release from the spell of convictism'.[35]

The only way, it seems, in which Port Arthur and the convict system it represented could be appreciatively seen was through an aesthetics of ruin. Anthony Trollope, indeed, envisages the place as always already ruined: 'It seems hard to say of a new colony, not yet seventy years old', he wrote after his first visit to Australia in 1871–72, 'that it has seen the best of its days and that it is falling into decay, that its short period of importance in the world is already gone, and that for the future it must exist, – as many an old town and an old country do exist,- not exactly on the memory of the past, but on the relics which the past has left behind it'.[36] Later, with a self-consciously elegiac cadence, he adds that if, as it inevitably will be, Port Arthur is abandoned, 'there can hardly, I think, be any other fate for the buildings than that they shall stand till they fall. They will fall into the dust, and men will make unfrequent excursions to visit the strange ruins'.[37] His vision of what he calls 'probably the most picturesque prison establishment in the world'[38] inaugurates a tradition of convict tourism for which, as another early visitor puts it, 'it is easy to forget, wandering through this beautiful garden, that 700 fellow creatures, who have lost home and liberty through crime, are in chains so near you'.[39] But it is above all the ruins that capture the imagination and effect a reconciliation with a distanced past. 'The infamous penal colony of Port Arthur on the Tasman Peninsula is now a collection of picturesque ruins set in a spectacular landscape', writes one recent guide; 'the work of man there, wrought in the interests of British penal policy, joins harmoniously with nature in all her moods'.[40] The Port Arthur church, in particular, came to have iconic status; 'its ivy-covered walls made it seem like Australia's Tintern', that is, 'like a genuine (i.e., English) ruin'.[41] It is on this basis that successive regimes of site-conservation begin to come to terms with the ways in which its fabric bears witness to a past of which it is the direct indexical trace.

At the core of the aesthetics of the ruin is the sense that an edifice passes, with time and weathering, from its social function (punishment, for example) to a merging with the natural world. Gilpin wrote that 'It is time alone which meliorates the ruin; which gives it perfect beauty; and brings it, if I may so speak, to a state of nature ... Rooted for ages in the soil; assimilated to it; and become, as it were, part of it; we consider [the ruin] as a part of nature, rather than of art'.[42] We might at the same time suspect in this aesthetic a disavowed pleasure at the ratio between past devastation and present survival.[43] But in a *lieu de mémoire* like Port Arthur it is surely the softened glow that the ruin gives to a convict past now half-merged into the natural world that constitutes its appeal. Hence the paradox that, to the extent that the buildings of the Port Arthur penal colony are preserved at all, they are preserved precisely *as* ruins.

The fate of the site after 1877 is largely a history of accident and of government incompetence. Many of the major buildings were completely destroyed by the fires of 1895 and 1897–98; the rest survived numerous schemes for the management of the site which, while often seeking to restore or maintain the church, sought also to tear down the largest and least stable remaining structure, the Penitentiary; they were saved by bureaucratic hesitation and the failure of prosecution, rather than by any policy of preservation. Only the determined opposition of a few individuals prevailed over government indifference and widespread resentment towards the shameful past that the site represented. The Tasmanian Engineer-in-Chief, T.W. Fowler, recommended in 1913 against the demolition of the Penitentiary, arguing that the entire complex of ruined buildings was an asset in fostering tourism; and the Superintendent of Reserves at Launceston, W. McGowan, commissioned in 1944 to produce a graphic representation of the Minister's vision of a cleansed and prettified tourist park, instead successfully argued the case that

> the attraction of Port Arthur lay in its 'historical nature'. Consequently, 'to alter it by endeavouring to make modern improvements would have a tendency to loss of splendour'. Tourists, he argued, could see modern gardens and parks in almost any township, but historical buildings of such a nature were very rare. McGowan therefore proposed not to 'attempt to intermingle the "new with the old", but to preserve the old landmarks in such a way as to convey to those who visit them, the architectural nature of the times and its historical value'.[44]

It is important to be clear about what this appeal to the value of the past entails: it means that the past is entirely separate from the present, and that the traces of the past can represent it to the present. The ruin thus signifies in its very form the nonexistence of the past which it simulates. This historicist vision is spelled out with great clarity in the 1975 Port Arthur Management Plan, which states that 'The site and buildings must ... retain their romantic flavour.... To achieve this feeling, some structures will be maintained as ruins, stressing by their condition the fact that, whatever it was that happened there, it is gone and will not return'.[45] 'Whatever it was that happened there': euphemism connives in the abolition of that past which is here sealed off in its pastness. And because it is sealed off, because it is discontinuous with all other times, it exists as a kind of essence of the site. It is for this reason that the argument to historical value tends at the same time to call for the demolition of all of the accretions to the site that date from after the convict period, accretions which are seen as an inauthentic overlay on the authentic historical core.

We can see something of the tenacity of this historicist structure of thought in a critical account by Jim Allen of the federally funded archaeological restoration that began to take place in the 1970s. Restoration, in Tony Bennett's definition, is a 'fabrication of idealized pasts by stripping ancient buildings of their subsequent accretions so as to restore to them the architectural purity they were once thought to have had', or at least a purity thought to be 'essentially and spiritually theirs no matter what the historical record might say'.[46] The practice that Allen describes is one in which two contradictory tendencies operate: on the one hand, buildings are brought back as close as possible to the state they were in prior to 1877; on the other, highly sophisticated stabilization techniques are used to counter their decay. Thus some of the crumbling bricks in the Penitentiary, which were never fired at a sufficiently high temperature in the settlement's primitive kilns, are refired and the walls rebuilt; and damp courses are inserted into the fabric to counter the erosion from the reclaimed land on which the foundations stand. For Allen these practices represent a failure of historical imagination: the historical reality is the decay of the site and of the system it represents; this system 'should be *seen* to have failed and the ruined buildings are the most poignant testimony of its failure'. The technical deficiencies of the buildings, which render them vulnerable to decay, 'underline the inadequacies of the system – a lack of skills, a lack of understanding of the environment, and the imposition of an alien culture by force'. Thus, he concludes, 'to replace original building standards with modern ones of greater durability cannot be historical restoration but merely renovation – the creation of a grotesque silhouette which does violence to the past and defrauds the future'.[47] In writing this, however, Allen espouses precisely that criterion of fidelity to a single authentic past, an originary essence, which restoration sets as its aim and which leads it to exclude all other historicities from its purview.

Historicism is one major strand in the struggle for preservation of the site. The other is that of the repeated attempts to turn it into a theme park, with *son-et-lumière* shows, ghost tours, reconstructions of working life, craft production, and guides in period dress. Again, it is accident rather than good management that has prevented much, but not all, of this recurrently proposed theatricalization. In one sense these two strands are opposed, as the serious to the entertaining, the scholarly to the touristic. In another sense they are not. Each has as its goal the representation of a vanished past, and they converge in the notion of a 'heritage' which is to be preserved and enhanced for the sake of the rapidly expanding market in heritage tourism.

The approach to Port Arthur is now physically dominated by a Visitors' Centre which mediates access to and experience of the site. All visitors pass through it, and are encouraged before entering the site itself to induct themselves (bearing a historical identity randomly assigned to them with their entrance ticket) into the past as it is recreated in a series of displays on the Centre's lower floor. The displays attempt, with considerable ingenuity and on the basis of solid and detailed scholarship, to give a sense of the life lived in the settlement at its height. It follows the careers of various convicts, and it works hard to reconstruct the material ambience of the prisons and workplaces. Workshops – the smithy, the carpenter's shed, the cobbler's shop, the saw-pits, the commissariat store, the overseers' room, and so on – are fully recreated, as are the cells and watch-houses in which prisoners were incarcerated. Cardboard cutouts represent convicts, guards, officers, and the miscellaneous personnel of a penal colony. Maps and scale models construct in its entirety a living penal settlement of which, beyond the Centre, there are now only broken and scattered traces.

The contrast set up as one passes outside is that between the hermeneutic fullness of the simulation and the bare, scattered bones of the ruined township. The site itself then becomes a secondary appendage to this reconstruction – opaque, resistant to interpretation, puzzling. One barely needs to visit it when the reconstruction is so much richer, carries so much fuller a sense of the texture of lived experience. In this it conforms, of course, to that highly mediated structure of commemoration that Nora describes as its dominant contemporary mode. Everything is meaningful here, far too meaningful ....

V

Let me make a very particular criticism of the historicist vision as it is carried both by a certain form of archaeological restoration and by the three-dimensional reconstructions of the Visitors' Centre. It is that it conceives of the past as singular, cut off at the moment when the penal functions of the settlement ended, and thus discontinuous with the living growth of the township and with that present in which, among other things, a massacre took place. This process of continuing growth was one in which, for example, the Lunatic Asylum functioned as a civic centre comprising a dance hall, a gymnasium, a concert hall and a church, before being converted into a Town Hall in 1895–96, then into Council offices in the 1930s and finally a museum in 1990. Margaret Scott writes that

> some of those who went to school in the restored Asylum and went shopping at Gathercole's General Store and Bakery are still very much alive. They remember

playing in the ruins where some of their forebears had been held prisoner, reciting the pledge of loyalty on Empire Day and, when dances were held in the Asylum building, sliding up and down the floor between dances in a mixture of sawdust and candle grease.[48]

A different way of thinking about the complexly layered temporality of the site is to note that even at its height in the 1840s and 1850s it was made up of buildings of diverse and changing ages and functions; the granary was transformed into a Penitentiary; the wooden prisoners' barracks, which later became a temporary asylum for the insane and then a store, coexisted with the guard tower and the Commandant's house but, unlike them, did not survive the fires of the 1890s. And the rigid, totalitarian world of the Model Prison coexisted with the economically and socially diverse worlds of the settlement in which people worked as boat-builders, schoolteachers, loggers in a chain gang, market gardeners, book-keepers, lunatics, noncommissioned officers, and trusties.

To singularize the past and to isolate it in its pastness is to reduce this complexity to a single story, to sever a monumental time of national origins from the generational times which continuously modify it. This means in part the continuing institutionalized forgetting of that system of penal exile and civil death which has been rendered so bland, so quaint, so much a period costume drama in the national imaginary. It means forgetting the line that runs from the Model Prison to the coldly violent maximum-security institutions of today.[49] It means failing to understand how the violence of the past is both repeated in and is radically discontinuous with Martin Bryant's shooting spree in April 1996, which cannot be told as part of the 'same' story. 'Every attempt is made', writes Richard Flanagan, 'to quarantine Port Arthur in its convict past, to present it as an endpoint to the British Empire rather than as a series of beginnings for modern Australia'.[50] Commemoration is mourning, and it is not achieved when remembrance and meaning are so easily given.

VI

Before it was invaded and settled by Europeans, the Tasman Peninsula was the country of the Pydairrerme band of the Oyster Bay tribe. Rhys Jones estimates that bands numbered from 30 to 80 people. In Tasmania as a whole, he writes, under the onslaught of European invasion and the effects of pulmonary diseases, 'the aboriginal population collapsed until by 1830 there were only about 300 of them still living'.[51] In the few years between the 'war of extermination'[52] which culminated in 1830 with a line of over two thousand armed men seeking to drive the Aboriginal population of Tasmania into the 'natural prison' of the Tasman Peninsula, and George Robinson's philanthropic rescue which led to the effective extermination of the native population,[53] they vanish from sight. The comment of a visiting British officer summarizes their fate. Tasman's Peninsula, he writes, 'remained unnoticed for many years, and it was at last selected as a good place to confine the aborigines, who were doing much mischief'. The 'grand "Battue"' having failed, 'other plans were adopted, and they were all at last got together in Flinders Island, where they gradually became extinct.'[54]

Notes

1   Pierre Nora, 'L'Ère de la commémoration', *Les Lieux de Mémoire III: Les France, 3: De l'Archive à l'emblème*, ed. Pierre Nora (Paris: Gallimard, 1992), p. 979 (my translation).
2   Ibid., p. 985.
3   Cathy Caruth, *Unclaimed Experience: Trauma, Narrative, and History* (Baltimore: Johns Hopkins University Press, 1996), p. 11.
4   Ian Hacking, *Rewriting the Soul: Multiple Personality and the Sciences of Memory* (Princeton: Princeton University Press, 1995), p. 183.
5   Margaret Scott, *Port Arthur: A Story of Strength and Courage* (Milsons Point: Random House, 1997), p. 130.
6   Ibid., p. 108.
7   Ibid., p. 102.
8   *Hobart Mercury*, 25 Nov. 1996; quoted in Scott, p. 15.
9   Franz Kafka, 'In the Penal Colony', trans. Willa and Edwin Muir, *The Complete Stories*, ed. Nahum N. Glatzer (New York: Schocken Books, 1971).
10 Robert Hughes, *The Fatal Shore: A History of the Transportation of Convicts to Australia, 1787–1868* (London: Collins Harvill, 1987), p. 430.
11 Jeremy Bentham, 'Principles of Penal Law, Part II: Rationale of Punishment' [1830], *The Works of Jeremy Bentham, Vol. 1*, ed. John Bowring (Edinburgh: William Tait, 1843), p. 415.
12 Cf. John Frow, '*Toute la mémoire du monde*: Repetition and Forgetting', in *Time and Commodity Culture: Essays in Cultural Theory and Postmodernity* (Oxford: Clarendon Press, 1997), pp. 225–6.
13 Robin Evans, *The Fabrication of Virtue: English Prison Architecture, 1750–1840* (Cambridge: Cambridge University Press, 1982), p. 297.
14 Hughes, p. 404.
15 Ian Brand, *The 'Separate' or 'Model' Prison, Port Arthur* (Launceston: Regal Publications, n.d.), Appendix I, p. 48.
16 Ibid., pp. 13–14.
17 Monika Fludernik, 'Carceral topography: spatiality, liminality and corporality in the literary prison', *Textual Practice* 13:1 (1999), p. 44.

18 Michael Ignatieff, *A Just Measure of Pain: The Penitentiary in the Industrial Revolution 1750–1850* (1978; reprinted London: Penguin, 1989), p. 10.

19 John Bender, *Imagining the Penitentiary: Fiction and the Architecture of Mind in Eighteenth-Century England* (Chicago: University of Chicago Press, 1987), p. 201.

20 Evans, *The Fabrication of Virtue*, p. 196.

21 Ibid., p. 67.

22 Ignatieff, *A Just Measure of Pain*, p. 57.

23 Henry Mayhew and John Binny, *The Criminal Prisons of London, and Scenes of Prison Life* (1862; reprinted London: Frank Cass, 1968), p. 101.

24 Evans, *The Fabrication of Virtue*, p. 325.

25 Ibid., p. 326.

26 Michel Foucault, *Discipline and Punish: The Birth of the Prison*, trans. Alan Sheridan (Harmondsworth: Penguin, 1979), p. 177.

27 Evans, *The Fabrication of Virtue*, p. 294.

28 Ignatieff, *A Just Measure of Pain*, p. 11.

29 Evans, *The Fabrication of Virtue*, pp. 357, 360.

30 Hughes, *The Fatal Shore*, p. 649, n. 64.

31 Mayhew and Binny, p. 104.

32 Ignatieff, *A Just Measure of Pain*, p. 11.

33 Quoted in Tom Griffiths, 'Past Silences: Aborigines and Convicts in our History-Making', *Australian Cultural History* 6 (1987), p. 18.

34 Quoted in David Young, *Making Crime Pay: The Evolution of Convict Tourism in Tasmania* (Hobart: Tasmanian Historical Research Association, 1996), p. 82.

35 Henry Reynolds, '"That Hated Stain": The Aftermath of Transportation in Tasmania', *Historical Studies* 14:53 (October 1969), p. 23.

36 Anthony Trollope, *Australia*, ed. P.D. Edwards and R.B. Joyce (St Lucia: University of Queensland Press, 1967 [1873]), p. 487.

37 Ibid., p. 518.

38 Ibid., p. 501.

39 Captain H. Butler Stoney, *A Residence in Tasmania: With a Descriptive Tour through the Island from Macquarie Harbour to Circular Head* (London: Smith, Elder and Co., 1856), p. 48.

40 *The Heritage of Australia: The Illustrated Register of the National Estate* (Melbourne, 1981), quoted in Kay Daniels, 'Cults of Nature, Cults of History', *Island Magazine* 16 (Spring 1983), p. 4.

41 Jim Davidson, 'Port Arthur: A Tourist History', *Australian Historical Studies* 26:105 (October 1995), pp. 657, 658.

42 William Gilpin, *Observations on ... the Mountains and Lakes of Cumberland*, 3rd. edn (1792) I, p. 74; III, p. 183; cited in Charles Kostelnick, 'Wordsworth, Ruins, and the Aesthetics of Decay: From Surface to Noble Picturesque', *The Wordsworth Circle* 19:1 (1988), p. 23. Cf. Barbara Maria Stafford, *Voyage Into Substance: Art, Science, Nature, and the Illustrated Travel Account, 1760–1840* (Cambridge, Mass.: MIT Press, 1984), p. 10 and passim.

43 Cf. Laurence Goldstein, *Ruins and Empire: The Evolution of a Theme in Augustan and Romantic Literature* (Pittsburgh: University of Pittsburgh Press, 1977).

44 Young, *Making Crime Pay*, p. 129.

45 Cited in Davidson, p. 661.

46 Tony Bennett, 'History on the Rocks', in John Frow and Meaghan Morris (eds), *Australian Cultural Studies: A Reader* (Sydney: Allen and Unwin, 1993), p. 222.

47 Jim Allen, 'Port Arthur Site Museum, Australia: Its Preservation and Historical Perspectives', *Museum* 28:2 (1976), p. 105.

48 Scott, p. 31.

49 Daniels, p. 6.

50 Richard Flanagan, 'Crowbar History: Panel Games and Port Arthur', *Australian Society* 9:8 (1990), p. 38.

51 Rhys Jones, 'Appendix: Tasmanian Tribes', in Norman B. Tindale, *Aboriginal Tribes of Australia: Their Terrain, Environmental Controls, Distribution, Limits, and Proper Names* (Berkeley: University of California Press, 1974), p. 319.

52 Marcus Clarke, 'Port Arthur Nos. 1, 2, and 3' [1873], *Marcus Clarke*, ed. Michael Wilding (St Lucia: University of Queensland Press, 1976), p. 512.

53 The story is more complicated. There was no final solution, no 'last Tasmanian'; people of Aboriginal descent survived into the twentieth century, and were discriminated against as such. Cf. Lyndall Ryan, *The Aboriginal Tasmanians* (St Lucia: University of Queensland Press, 1981); Henry Reynolds, *Fate of a Free People: A Radical Re-Examination of the Tasmanian Wars* (Ringwood: Penguin, 1995).

54 Stoney, p. 43.

8 Séance Fiction: Confronting the Ghost(s) of the Mexican Revolution in *Madero, el otro* by Ignacio Solares

ROBIN FIDDIAN

An interest in historical themes has been a constant feature of the dramatic and fictional output of contemporary Mexican author, Ignacio Solares. Whilst *El jefe máximo* (1991) and *El gran Elector* (1993) can serve as outstanding examples of Solares's writing for the stage, *Madero, el otro* (*The Other Madero*) (1989) and *Columbus* (1996) illustrate the choice of subjects from the history of Mexico for treatment in the form of narrative fiction. Solares's choice of Francisco I. Madero as the subject of his novel of 1989 is readily explained. Madero played a crucial role in the process of the Mexican Revolution, inasmuch as it was he who opposed the re-election of Porfirio Díaz, the country's then ageing president, between 1908 and 1910. Welcomed by the dispossessed and the affluent liberal classes in equal measure, Madero immediately became a catalyst for the national revolution which completely changed the face and constitution of Mexican politics in the second decade of the twentieth century. His death, in February 1913, some 16 months after acceding to the presidency, conferred on him the undeniable aura of a martyr: Madero would subsequently be remembered as a sincere advocate of social justice and democracy, yet also criticised as a political naïf who underestimated the forces that he unleashed and that would eventually be deployed against him.

In the wider context of Mexican and Latin American culture, *The Other Madero* responds to three major impulses which have shaped contemporary work on historical subjects. The first of these is 'the new historical novel' – a continental literary phenomenon which flourished, according to its principal commentators, in the last quarter of the twentieth century, attaining the highest standards of artistic achievement in novels such as *Noticias del Imperio* (*News*

143

of the Empire) (1987) by Solares's fellow Mexican, Fernando del Paso, and *El general en su laberinto* (*The General in His Labyrinth*) (1989) by Colombian Nobel Prize winner, Gabriel García Márquez.[1]

The second source for works like *Noticias del Imperio* and *The Other Madero* is the ongoing reconsideration and revision of Mexican history, with an emphasis on the Revolution of 1910–17. *The Other Madero* takes its place, in the national arena, alongside fictional works such as *The Old Gringo* (1985) by Carlos Fuentes and *Mal de amores* (1996) by Angeles Mastretta, and paved the way for the publication, in 1999, of a massive new biography of the Mexican revolutionary figurehead, Pancho Villa, by North American historian, Friedrich Katz.[2] Reviewing *The Life and Times of Pancho Villa* in the pages of the *Los Angeles Times Book Review*, Carlos Fuentes hailed 'a masterpiece of contemporary historiography,' which he compared to the efforts of creative writers such as Fernando Benítez and, more pertinently, Ignacio Solares in his recuperation of the only partially understood figure of Madero.[3]

Finally, in seeking to fashion fictional representations of a national or continental past, Spanish American authors such as Solares, Del Paso, Fuentes, and García Márquez engage with postmodern theories of history and historiography that have circulated freely in the final decades of the twentieth century. Amongst these, the most significant are postcolonial theory, psychoanalysis (or psycho-history), and various theories of narrative.[4]

A clearly signalled concern with alterity identifies Solares's novel unmistakeably with currents of contemporary thought. The alterity of 'the other Madero' can be conceived partly in psychological and characterological terms; it also has an epistemological significance residing in the differences between an empirical and a mystical episteme. Additionally, alterity is defined in *The Other Madero*, and in a satellite text by Solares,[5] in relation to a certain orthodoxy regarding the theory and practice of history.

Against this backdrop of concerns, *The Other Madero* lends itself particularly well to a reading informed by the theoretical writings of French thinker, Michel de Certeau. *Heterologies: Discourse on the Other* and *The Writing of History* (originally entitled 'L'Écriture de l'histoire') explore the subject of history and alterity from a number of angles that have the potential to illuminate a study of *The Other Madero*. In the two books cited,[6] de Certeau articulates oppositions between the institutional discipline and practice of historiography and two other logics which he regards as its Others: namely, fiction and psychoanalysis. For de Certeau, historiography is associated with both a general and a specific referent; in general use, the term denotes the practice of constructing meaning about the past in written form; more specifically, 'historiography' connotes the institutional practices of the discipline of history, as they prevailed in the West after a certain point in the eighteenth century, when 'the religious or metaphysical aim of stating the truth of beings according to God's will was replaced by the ethical task of creating or making history [in the original, 'faire l'histoire']' (*Heterologies*, p. 199).

I

As a modern practice, historiography, and the discipline of history to which it is allied, seeks to produce the 'real' in discursive form. It pursues this 'ambition to speak the 'real'' (*Heterologies*, p. 202) by drawing on a number of technical practices which make up what de Certeau calls the 'historiographical operation' (*Writing*, pp. 56ff.). The major assumptions on which that operation rests can be summarised as follows.

First, historiography assumes a clean break between the past and the present.

> It is the product of relations of knowledge and power linking two supposedly distinct domains: on the one hand, there is the present (scientific, professional, social) place of work, the technical and conceptual apparatus of inquiry and interpretation, and the operation of describing and/or explaining; on the other hand, there are the places (museums, archives, libraries) where the materials forming the object of this research are kept and, secondarily, set off in time, there are the past systems or *events* to which these materials give analytic access (*Heterologies*, p. 4).

Secondly, historiography posits a difference between the subject, or agent of historical analysis, and the object of that analysis. This matter of principle is bound up with 'a will to objectivity' (*Heterologies*, p. 4) – a claim of disinterestedness which invests historiography with the properties of a rational and scientific discourse. The sifting of evidence contained in the archive, and use of the computer as a means of producing solid and extensive statistical data (*Heterologies*, p. 212), are just two symptoms of the supposed disinterestedness of the discipline of history and of the representations of historical realities that it provides.

Thirdly, the assumptions concerning the identities of time, place, subject, and object rehearsed above support the pretensions of historiography 'to furnish discourse with referentiality, to make it function as "expressive," [in other words] to legitimize it by means of the "real"' (*Heterologies*, p. 31). Modern historiography, according to de Certeau, lays a particular claim to represent the 'real'.

Together, this set of assumptions and claims unmasks historiography as an ideological project. In a splendid categorical assertion, de Certeau writes that 'modern French historiography is bourgeois and – not [surprisingly] – rationalist' (*Writing*, p. 10), a claim which he follows up by inviting his contemporary readers to acknowledge that 'History is probably our myth' (*Writing*, p. 21).

Given the demystifying thrust of his argument, the logical next step for de Certeau is to identify further strategies employed in historical discourse for the purpose of its self-legitimation. Principal amongst these is the 'rather sly' way in which historiography 'pass[es] itself off as the witness of what is or has been' (*Heterologies*, p. 203). Historiography pretends to represent past realities, and, in pursuing that aim, does all it can to conceal the means of its own operation. According to de Certeau,

> The discourse gives itself credibility in the name of the reality which it is supposed to represent, but this authorized appearance of the 'real' serves precisely to camouflage the practice which in fact determines it. Representation thus disguises the praxis that organizes it (*Heterologies*, p. 203).

A second strategy to which historiography resorts consists in invoking a distinction between itself and other categories of discourse which are based on error and falsehood, in a word, on fiction. 'Western historiography struggles against fiction,' to such an extent that its driving impulse is towards 'falsification' rather than verification (*Heterologies*, pp. 200–1). In de Certeau's characterisation of the historian, 'He spends his time in [pursuit of] the false rather than in the construction of the true, as though truth could be produced only by means of determining error [...]. The assumption is made that what is not held to be false must be real' (*Heterologies*, p. 201). Drawing an analogy with the use, made in the past, of arguments against 'false' gods to induce belief in a true God, de Certeau observes, 'The process repeats itself today in contemporary historiography: by demonstrating the presence of errors, discourse must pass off as "real" whatever is placed in opposition to the errors'. He then adds pointedly, 'Even though this is logically questionable, it works, and it fools people' (*Heterologies*, p. 201).

These last remarks are made in the penultimate chapter of *Heterologies*, entitled 'History: Science and Fiction'. There, de Certeau anchors his analysis of historiography 'in the context of a question too broad to be treated fully here, namely the antinomy between ethics and what, for lack of a better word, I will call dogmatism' (*Heterologies*, p. 199). Glossing ethics as 'defin[ing] a distance between what is and what ought to be,' and characterising dogmatism as a form of representation of reality and a system which imposes laws in the name of that reality, de Certeau comments that 'Historiography functions midway between [those] two poles; but whenever it attempts to break away from ethics, it returns toward dogmatism' (*Heterologies*, p. 199). His subsequent remarks are to be read in the light of his repudiation of dogmatism and his defence of the place of ethics on the agenda of history.

Essentially, 'History: Science and Fiction' challenges the discipline of history to cease regarding fiction as a separate category and to admit it as integral to its operations. As a framework for his argument, de Certeau reviews four possible ways in which fiction operates in the historian's discourse, and implicitly deflates that discourse's claims to internal coherence and respectability. In brief, de Certeau argues that historiography relies on procedural fictions and scenarios 'when it investigates the past, but applies hypotheses and scientific rules of the present' (*Heterologies*, p. 202); science and fiction are inseparable in the respect that 'the "real" produced by historiography is also the orthodox legend of the institution of history'; the scientific apparatus employed by some historians has a certain fictive quality in their work; and, finally, the relationship of historiography with a professional institution and its adoption of a scientific methodology lead de Certeau to view it as 'something of a mix of science and fiction or as a field of knowledge where questions of time and tense regain a central importance' (*Heterologies*, p. 203). Furthermore, viewed in a historical perspective, historiography has tended, since the seventeenth century, 'to camouflage its links, inadmissible to scientific thought, with what had been identified during the same period of time as "literature".' In order that the discipline should regain its integrity, de Certeau insists that 'we must first "recognize" the repressed, which takes the form of "literature", within the discourse that is legitimated as scientific' (*Heterologies*, p. 219).

II

This remark, made near the end of *Heterologies*, introduces the second main focus on alterity in de Certeau's work, which is psychoanalytical. Employing a contrastive strategy once more, de Certeau considers the ways that historiography and psychoanalysis remember and represent the past, and works his way towards the conclusion that history is haunted by 'the return of repressed alterity' (*Writing*, p. xxvi). For de Certeau, Western 'discourse about the past has the status of being the discourse of the dead' (*Writing*, p. 46): 'Death obsesses the West,' he writes, and history – along with ethnography, religion, and other cultural practices – provides a means for dealing with that obsession. On its own account, historiography

> takes for granted the fact that it has become impossible to believe in [the] presence of the dead that has organized (or organizes) the experience of entire civilizations; and the fact too that it is nonetheless impossible 'to get over it,' to accept the loss of a living solidarity with what is gone, or to confirm an irreducible limit (*Writing*, p. 5).

History and psychoanalysis confront the same human predicament, but adopt different strategies for dealing with it. De Certeau turns to Freud and his 'discovery' of the return of the repressed to point up those differences.

As his starting point, de Certeau invokes the Freudian orthodoxy that 'If the past [...] is *repressed*, it *returns* in the present from which it was excluded, but does so surreptitiously' (*Writing*, p. 3). Under the bold heading 'Two Strategies of Time,' de Certeau describes the approach of psychoanalysis to the problem of the past. 'There is,' he writes, 'an "uncanniness" about this past that a present occupant has expelled (or thinks it has) in an effort to take its place. The dead haunt the living. The past: it "re-bites" [il *re-mord*] (it is a secret and repeated biting).' In this dazzling showcase of concepts belonging to psycho-history, de Certeau pictures the dead and the past as deeply unsettling and as exercising a 'cannibalistic' effect on the living, who are the object of 'remorse' in the original Latin sense of 'a biting again'. In addition, although the past might appear to have slipped into oblivion, it actually remains in the form of a residue that 'turns the present's feeling of being "at home" into an illusion'. Elaborating on this image of domestic (in)security, de Certeau suggests that 'behind the back of the owner (the ego), or over its objections, [the residue of the past] inscribes there the law of the other' (*Heterologies*, p. 4) as an uncanny presence that threatens the imagined stability and identity of the subject.

De Certeau follows up his reformulation of Freud with some observations on how historiography relates to the past.

> Historiography is based on a clean break between the past and the present [...].
> Even though [it] postulates a continuity [...], a solidarity [...], and a complicity

(a sympathy) between its agents and its objects, it nevertheless distinguishes a difference between them (*Heterologies*, p. 4).

De Certeau contrasts this with the view of the past that is held by psychoanalysis:

> Psychoanalysis recognizes the past *in* the present; historiography places one *beside* the other. Psychoanalysis treats the relation as one of imbrication (one in the place of the other), of repetition (one reproduces the other in another form), of the equivocal and of the *quiproquo* [sic] [...]. Historiography conceives the relation as one of succession (one after the other), correlation (greater or lesser proximities), cause and effect (one follows from the other), and disjunction (either one or the other, but not both at the same time) (*Heterologies*, p. 4).

Positing an equivalence between 'the past, the real [and] the death of which the [historical] text speaks' (*Writing*, p. 99), de Certeau notes the particular way in which historiography deals imaginatively with death. On his account, '[Historical] writing places a population of the dead on stage', as it attempts to 'resuscitate' or 'revive' a past to which it has gained access via knowledge (*Writing*, p. 99). However, de Certeau disputes that the historical text has this capacity. He contends that 'Discourse is incessantly articulated over the death that it presupposes, but that the very practice of history constantly contradicts. [...] history does not resuscitate anything' (*Writing*, p. 47). In fact, de Certeau continues, there are strict limits to, and limitations on, the scope of historiography: 'Writing speaks of the past only in order to inter it. Writing is a tomb in the double sense of the word in that, in the very same text, it both honors and eliminates' (*Writing*, p. 101). In theory, the writing of history 'aims at calming the dead who still haunt the present and at offering them scriptural tombs', but it does so only conditionally, exacting a price in terms of the domestication and reduction to silence of the voices that haunt and otherwise disturb the present: 'the dear departed find a haven in the text *because* they can neither speak nor do harm anymore. These ghosts find access through *writing* on the condition that they remain ever silent' (*Writing*, p. 2).

Such are the methods and pretensions of historiography, according to Michel de Certeau. However, those methods and pretensions are subverted in the light of the principle of the return of the repressed. Praising Freud for reanimating the 'scientific system' of history at the end of the nineteenth century, and using Michelet as a benchmark, de Certeau notes 'A half century after Michelet, Freud observes that the dead are in fact "beginning to speak". But they are not speaking through the "medium" of the historian-wizard, as

Michelet believed: *it is speaking* [*ça parle*] in the work and in the silences of the historian, but without his knowledge.' De Certeau elaborates: 'These voices – whose disappearance every historian posits, which he replaces with his writing – 're-bite' [*re-mordent*] the space from which they were excluded; they continue to speak in the text/tomb that erudition erects in their place' (*Heterologies*, p. 8). Through this assessment and reinterpretation of Freud, de Certeau lays bare the Achilles heel of a hidebound history, which he claims is no less vulnerable to the return of repressed material than any other discourse that is concerned with the past. Against a horizon of institutional atrophy and deceit, de Certeau advocates 'the renewal of historiography ... by its encounter with psychoanalysis' (*Heterologies*, p. 5).

III

De Certeau's principle of the 'return of repressed alterity' (*Writing*, p. xxvi) stands in a close and illuminating relation to the treatment of the past in *The Other Madero*. Solares's novel sets out to rehabilitate an aspect, or set of aspects, of Francisco I. Madero which had been edited or censored out of conventional accounts of the statesman's private life and brief career as president of the nation. Madero's spiritualist leanings, his habit of communicating with the spirits of the dead, whom he would allow to influence decisions concerning matters of state, the military, and the security of his presidency, constitute the basis of a complex, not to say eccentric, personality which discredited him in the eyes both of his relatives and of those who wrote historical accounts about him. In the process, Madero '[came to be] converted into a hero of stone, unmoveable, and what is worse, mutilated' ('Madero en la historiografía', p. 181). Solares gives details of the family's embarrassment at the sight of the writing pads onto which Madero transcribed the messages that he received from beyond, and remarks on the zeal with which they concealed the 'shameful evidence'.[7] Family members and historians were united in the desire to construct and preserve the image of a one-dimensional man: 'a man stripped of contradictions, a monolithic figure,' while, as Solares notes, the truth all along was that Madero 'lived invariably in a state of permanent contradiction between the mystic and the man of action, the pacifist and the politician, the optimist who nevertheless "knew" exactly what end awaited him' ('Madero en la historiografía', p. 183). The depiction of a multiple and contradictory personality is a major aim of Solares's revisionist historiographic project, which seeks to recover the pacifist-cum-vegetarian-cum-mystic as integral to the man who came to be labelled, worshipped, and finally pigeonholed as the 'Apostle of Democracy' of early Revolutionary Mexico.

In their efforts to domesticate Madero, conventional historical representations have suppressed various elements of his character, which Solares wishes to resurrect. Amongst these is Madero-the-man-of-action who yielded to the thrill and the passion of violence. The narrative traces the roots of adult aggression back to an adolescent fight at school in Baltimore where it imagines Madero discovering 'the true enemy that you had to combat: the enemy within […]: violence, constant and irreducible, which showed you, as if in front of a mirror, a face that you had refused to recognise as your own' (p. 47). Focusing on a later phase of Madero's life, the narrative voice wonders 'Were you frightened by the *other* Madero that you had discovered in your fascination with action, in contrast to the Madero of mystical retreats, meditation and silence?' (p. 140; cf. p. 163).

Considerations of Madero's character aside, otherness impinges on several other aspects of the mimesis of *The Other Madero*. It manifests itself, for example, in relation to a category of beings referred to as 'them'/'*ellos*' (p. 23) who are identified with a space that is located elsewhere, in a distant 'there'. The transcendental realm of 'that other world' is differentiated from 'this world [with] its fragile constitution, its laws, its affectations, and its [political] ploys' (p. 16) – a world of political institutions and trickery that late twentieth-century readers have little difficulty in recognising as their own. Otherness, then, comes in many forms and guises in the realm of the mimesis of *The Other Madero*.

Arguably the most salient feature of Solares's narrative is the presence throughout of a voice in the second person which addresses the dead Madero's soul or spirit, calling him 'brother' and assuming the mantle of a double (pp. 13, 16, 90, etc.). Also addressed is the reader of Solares's novel, who naturalises its narrative operations by drawing on a competence derived from familiarity with other instances of second person narration, in *La muerte de Artemio Cruz* by Carlos Fuentes, for example.[8]

The opening lines of *The Other Madero* apostrophize Madero immediately, and read as follows:

> How noticeable is the last beat […], the pain – the final connection – which died with you and left only the echo of pain. And after? What name to give to this anguish which wells up, this desire to continue, to remain, to bear witness, in spite of being no longer attached to yourself? (p. 7).

In this excerpt, we sense the presence of a voiced entity that we assume inhabits our world, and, quite separately, a spirit, which yearns to continue and to transcend physical dissolution and which is located on a separate, and as will shortly be confirmed, higher plane. However, within the same paragraph, the notional dividing line between two points of reference is erased, as the narrative consciousness visualises the corpse of Madero, and focuses on the 'asymmetrical eyes, popping out of their sockets, which seem, from down there, to be searching, searching for you, searching for me, here' (p. 7). The earlier perspective on 'you, there' is now dismantled. The narrative consciousness is no longer grounded on earth. In fact, it has migrated to a higher plane and imagines being looked at from the perspective of the place where Madero's corpse has fallen.

In subsequent pages, the narrative viewpoint will alternate between one plane and the other, sometimes separated from the spirit of Madero, which it interpellates from afar, sometimes identifying with it and sharing the perspective of 'this other world of ours'. The psychology and aesthetics of this narrative device remind readers of *Pedro Páramo* by Juan Rulfo, a novel narrated from the grave. Yet, in Solares's novel, the bearings and the parameters of the narrative consciousness are indefinite, they resist any attempt at anchoring them in space. The voice in Solares's shifting narrative speaks now from a metaphysical beyond, now from a phenomenal world of terra firma which, amongst other things, is where the reader imagines himself or herself to be. On a more technical level: the narrative consciousness seeks to define, and at times attains, an intermediate position which it refers to as an 'interval', where mutually contradictory hypotheses are held in balance and not resolved in any synthesis (*The Other Madero*, pp. 249–51). In keeping with this conception, the narrative of *The Other Madero* conveys transcendental perceptions, as when it describes the scene of an incident involving Madero, which occurred in a private salon of the Plaza Hotel, Mexico City, and observes that the reflection of 'everything that happened [there] is still registered in the great mirror hanging on one of its walls' (p. 94).

Elsewhere, the narrative of the materialising of the spirit of Madero's brother, Raúl, in a session of spiritualism (pp. 62–3) held some four years after his death, is not differentiated at all from the narrative of historical events. Heuristically, the episode could be naturalised by accounting for it as a ghost story. But, then, so too could the narrative as a whole. It is therefore worth taking seriously the proposition that *The Other Madero*, as well as purporting to recreate the past like any other historical novel, actively models itself on a 'spiritualist event' ('Madero en la historiografía', p. 190). A significant passage

in this regard is one that relates and then glosses Madero's routine experience
of being visited by the spirit of Raúl:

> All you had to do was pick up the pen and summon him. Your hand would
> begin to move of its own accord, brother. What a marvellous sensation. Not to
> be yourself; or rather, not to be only yourself, because he was also present in the
> writing. His presence was felt in each and every word, with the result that, in
> the act of writing jointly, you were more fully yourself than ever. You and him,
> in the same way that you and I are talking at this moment. Me: you: him (p. 55).

Here, an analogy with events in the narrative present is signalled quite plainly
in the sustained reference to the physical act of writing. That analogy is then
confirmed in the penultimate statement and reiterated in the forceful assertion
of an equivalence between 'Me: you: [and] him.' On such a basis, the narrative
of *The Other Madero* would resemble nothing so much as a spiritualist event
involving communication with the beyond, in which the reader is invited to
act as sympathetic witness and participant in a session of 'séance fiction'.

The ghosts of the dead are the most immediately recognizable ciphers of
repressed alterity in Solares's novel. They acquire their fullest significance,
probably, in connection with the atmosphere of guilt, remorse and anguish
which suffuses the narrative, weighing heavily on Madero and affecting an
entire community which has yet to come to terms with his death. Madero's
feelings of personal responsibility for the destructive violence of the Mexican
Revolution are registered in the first pages of the novel, by a narrator who
tells him not to try to walk, like Christ on the road to Calvary, 'with this great
burden of guilt on your shoulders' (p. 9). In another expression of fraternal
solidarity, the narrator acknowledges how implacably 'guilt and doubt [...]
undermine the fragile constructs of reason and, before [we] realise what's
happened, have taken over our very beings' (p. 16). This is illustrated most
painfully in Madero's sense of having been ultimately responsible for the
death, by torture, of his brother Gustavo – a truly barbaric episode on which
the narrative lavishes prolonged and detailed attention mimicking Madero's
continuing susceptibility.

At the same time as it seeks to explore and represent Madero's inner
torment, Solares's novel fashions a conduit for the expression of collective
guilt, exemplified in the anguished address of Pancho Villa at the graveside
of Madero. On that solemn occasion, the 'Centaur of the North' (as Villa is
conventionally pictured) admits the inadequacies and collective responsibility
of Madero's friends and allies, referring to 'the insufficient help, or the

considerable blame that attaches to us all' (p. 247). The narrative itself is contaminated by this generalised remorse, returning again and again to the scene of Madero's execution and dwelling on the moment when Francisco Cárdenas delivered the coup de grace with a .38 Smith and Wesson (pp. 9, 80, etc.). Recurrent images of a 'red veil' ('un velo rojo') (pp. 47 and 234) and 'a red wave' ('una ola roja') (p. 59) both capture the dramatic moment of the shooting and convey Madero's bloodstained perception of the world at the final, liminal moment of his life.

Remembering de Certeau's picture of historical writing as deceitfully offering scriptural tombs for the ghosts of the dead, it is significant that Solares does not seek to effect a final laying to rest of the ghost of Madero: instead, his objective is to summon up that ghost and to maintain it in a state of permanent awareness which may satisfy its 'infinite desire to acquire bodily form time after time after time' (p. 247). The way is thus paved for the endless return of all that has been denied in the national consciousness with respect to the life and death of Francisco I. Madero, martyr of the Mexican Revolution.

Coincidentally, this strategy of resuscitation and permanent awakening matches exactly Carlos Fuentes's assessment of the achievement of Friedrich Katz in *The Life and Times of Pancho Villa*. In a telling comparison with fictional treatments of historical themes in Mexico, Fuentes praises Katz on the grounds that he 'presents Mexicans with our ghosts – alive' ('Centaur of the North', p. 2). This interpretation of the Villa biography provides a context for appreciating the significance of Solares's historical novel, at the same time as it confirms the deep-seated moral and psychological motivations of much historical writing produced in Mexico over the course of the final decade of the twentieth century.

IV

A note at the end of the text of *The Other Madero* underscores the extent of the novel's partial compliance with, and simultaneous subversion of, normal conventions of historical writing. As García Márquez also does at the end of *El general en su laberinto*, Solares identifies some of his primary sources and points to the existence of insoluble contradictions in those 'historical texts'. He then explains that his procedure when confronted with contradiction was to 'choose the version which best suits the purposes of the novel …' (p. 250). Interestingly, Solares's modal blueprint of historical writing openly accommodates the literary elements that for de Certeau are constitutive of all historical discourse, the difference being that, while the historian pretends to exclude the literary, the novelist owns up to his procedures. The novelist, of course, has the freedom to do just that. And it is a freedom that Solares exploits to an even greater extent, in the light of his admission that 'inevitably, there are scenes [in my novel] which I 'made up', drawing on available information' (p. 250). Detailing some of the liberties that he took with the historical record, Solares points to the essential violability of the boundaries that are conventionally held to separate the discourse of literature from that of historiography. Within the theoretical parameters of this study, his practice throughout *The Other Madero* provides a clear and instructive example of the restoration of the fictional, as understood by de Certeau, to the discourse of history.

One final observation concerns the imbrication of the unconscious in the historical process and in writing about the past. Solares takes for granted the pressure exerted by the unconscious, when he asks the rhetorical question, 'How can we understand history without the unconscious elements contained in it, elements that are contained in all human affairs?' (p. 251). He then refers to his own experience writing the novel, and reports that there were times when the character of Madero usurped some of the author's control and 'claimed a life of his own' (p. 251). As the examples of Cervantes, Unamuno, Pirandello, and Borges suffice to remind us, this is hardly an original observation. However, in the context of *The Other Madero*, it blends in perfectly well with the novel's overall concern with transcendence, the release of the spirit, and the defiance of death. Along with all the other aspects of the novel analysed in this study, it illustrates some of the possible mechanisms and salutary effects of the renewal of historiography by its encounter with psychoanalysis, as envisaged by Michel de Certeau in his imaginative and iconoclastic studies, *Heterologies: Discourse on the Other* and *The Writing of History*.

Notes

1   On the new historical novel, with some remarks on differences between it and the traditional, 'not so new' historical novel of Spanish America, see Seymour Menton, *Latin America's New Historical Novel* (Austin: University of Texas Press, 1993). A shorter and no less informative introduction to the genre is provided by Gustavo Pellón in 'The Spanish American Novel: Recent Developments, 1975–1990', in *The Cambridge History of Latin American Literature*, 3 vols, ed. Roberto González Echevarría and Enrique Pupo Walker (Cambridge: Cambridge University Press, 1996), ii, pp. 279–302.

2 Friedrich Katz, *The Life and Times of Pancho Villa* (Stanford: Stanford University Press, 1999).

3 Carlos Fuentes, 'Centaur of the North,' *Los Angeles Times Book Review*, Sunday 4 April 1999, p. 2.

4 See Richard J. Evans, *In Defence of History* (London: Granta, 1997) for a user-friendly and highly recommended introduction to the contentious subject of history and post-modernism. See also *The Postmodern History Reader*, ed. Keith Jenkins (London: Routledge, 1997), *passim*. Finally, *The Houses of History. A Critical Reader in Twentieth-Century History and Theory*, selected and introduced by Anna Green and Kathleen Troup (Manchester: Manchester University Press, 1999), contains the following chapters which are of relevance here: 'Freud and psychohistory,' pp. 59–86, 'The question of narrative,' pp. 204–29, and 'Postcolonial perspectives,' pp. 277–96.

5 Ignacio Solares, 'Madero en la historiografía de la Revolución mexicana', in Karl Kohut (ed.), *Literatura mexicana hoy. Del 68 al ocaso de la revolución* (Frankfurt am Main: Vervuert Verlag, 1991), pp. 180–90.

6 Michel de Certeau, *Heterologies: Discourse on the Other*, trans. Brian Massumi, Foreword Wlad Godzich (Manchester: Manchester University Press, 1986) (hereafter *Heterologies*); and *The Writing of History*, translated by Tom Conley (New York: Columbia University Press, 1988) (hereafter *Writing*).

7 Ignacio Solares, *Madero, el otro* (Mexico City: Joaquín Mortiz, 1989), p. 105. All page references included subsequently in parentheses are to this edition, and all translations of quoted material are my own.

8 The literary competence that I invoke here is discussed by Jonathan Culler in *The Pursuit of Signs. Semiotics, Literature, Deconstruction* (London: Routledge & Kegan Paul, 1981), ch. 3.

9 The Angel of Memory: 'Working Through' the History of the New South Africa

CHRISTOPHER J. COLVIN

> This is how one pictures the angel of history. His face is turned towards the past. Where we perceive a chain of events, he see one single catastrophe which keeps piling wreckage upon wreckage and hurls it in front of his feet.
>
> *Walter Benjamin*

Introduction

In February 1996, South Africa embarked on a now-famous experiment in conflict resolution and sociopolitical transformation when the Truth and Reconciliation Commission (TRC) first convened hearings on apartheid-era human rights violations. Its mission was to enable South Africans to 'come to terms' with the apartheid past by recording the testimony of victims of apartheid-era abuses and by offering amnesty to perpetrators in exchange for confessions that fully disclosed the details of these violations. In explaining and defending this ambitious and controversial agenda, the TRC drew upon multiple legal, moral and medical discourses. It stressed the legal, democratic and constitutional foundations of the commission. It spoke eloquently of the need for confession to be met with Christian forgiveness and compassion. In addition to these appeals to rational-legal and Christian principles, the commission also turned to a language and ethics of psychotherapy. Throughout the hearings, many commissioners, TRC staff members as well as the media commented on the 'psychotherapeutic' power of this process. They spoke of 'catharsis', 'working through' and 'closure', on both individual and national levels, as fundamental components of the TRC's effort to 'heal the nation's traumatic past'.

This chapter will begin by introducing the TRC and tracing the outlines of its particular therapeutic imagination. Then, by looking at attempts at TRC hearings by the African National Congress to begin writing its own history of the South African past, I trace the effects of this therapeutic imperative on what I identify as a new mode of South African historiography. Specifically, I explore how in this mode of historiography, the various strategies for understanding and representing the past are inspired by recent psychological models of trauma, memory and recovery. Finally, I briefly consider the question of why this therapeutic framework seems to be so effective a way for the TRC and the South African government to author(ize) a new history of the old South Africa. In the end, I suggest that the therapeutic ethic at the heart of the TRC provides a new avenue for memory's transformation into history. This therapeutic ethic casts traumatic memories in a way that authenticates those memories and allows them to become a principal, alternative source of memory for the work of a nationalist and therapeutic historiography.

The Truth and Reconciliation Commission (TRC)

Composed of a group of seventeen judges, lawyers, academics and mental health professionals of diverse racial, ethnic and class backgrounds, and chaired by Desmond Tutu, the TRC was empowered to '[grant] amnesty to persons making full disclosure of all the relevant facts associated with a political objective committed in the course of the conflicts of the past ..., [afford] victims an opportunity to relate the violations they suffered ..., [and take] measures aimed at ... the rehabilitation and the restoration of the human and civil dignity of victims'.[1] Designed to 'enable South Africans to come to terms with their past', its various committees held hearings in all of South Africa's major cities and in many of its smaller towns.[2]

The Commission was one of the compromises that developed out of the multiparty negotiations held over several years in South Africa that worked to find a peaceful way to end apartheid. The main political parties involved in the negotiation process were: the African National Congress (ANC), led by Nelson Mandela; the National Party (NP), the party that began instituting the original apartheid legislation in 1948; and, to some extent, the Inkatha Freedom Party (IFP). In addition to input from these political parties, there were two formal conferences held in which the Commission planners heard advice from academics, mental health care professionals, theologians, and politicians. In the end, the religious and mental health communities provided the bulk of the input, and the compromise reached reflects their contribution.[3]

The TRC's Therapeutic Ethic

TRC Chairman Desmond Tutu is perhaps the most ardent defender of both the Christian and the therapeutic facets of the TRC. On his appointment to the TRC, he remarked, 'I hope that the ... Commission, by opening wounds to cleanse them, will thereby stop them from festering. We cannot be facile and say, bygones will be bygones, because they will not be bygones and will return to haunt us'.[4] He later reiterated this sentiment, saying,

> We are a wounded people because of the conflicts of the past ... We all stand in need of healing ... We [the commissioners] are privileged ... to assist our land, our people to come to terms with our dark past once and for all. They say that those who suffer from amnesia, those who forget the past, are doomed to repeat it.[5]

Similarly, the TRC as a whole has spoken of its mission to 'open the wounds only in order to cleanse them, to deal with the past effectively, and close the door of that dark and horrendous past forever'.[6] It speaks of that past as a time of 'untold suffering'[7] and says that 'public acknowledgment' of that suffering is a prerequisite for reconciliation.[8] Further developing these themes, Lloyd Vogelman, with the Centre for the Study of Violence and Reconciliation, has written that only through the work of the TRC can the 'secrecy of evil [be] unlocked and society begin to come to terms with itself'. He argues that the 'undemocratic system' of apartheid was 'imprinted on the public conscience' and continues that only by the 'working through of victimisation' and through a process of 'cathartic vocalisation', can the victim 'begin to integrate the trauma into his or her personality'.[9]

Besides commissioners, therapists and those directly associated with the TRC's work, others speak as well of the psychological dimensions and demands of suffering and reconciliation. One South African theologian referred to the TRC commissioners as 'psychological archeologists'.[10] Robert Brand, a journalist remarked, 'if the primary purpose of the [TRC] is, as its members insist, to bring about catharsis and healing, the first weeks ... have been a resounding success'.[11] A man who signed the TRC's Register of Reconciliation, a guest register and comment book for the public at each of the TRC main offices, said that 'reconciliation is the struggle to accept the dark bits of ourselves'. He continued that his struggle was a struggle to reconcile the present condition of his life with a 'past that no longer makes sense'.[12]

For the TRC, the trope of therapy was not merely a popular *figurative* device for talking about reconciliation; the *practice* of therapy played a prominent role as well. The TRC itself made visible use of a small army of psychological counsellors before, during and after the hearings to deal with the entire range of TRC participants: the victims and their families and lawyers; the perpetrators, their families and lawyers; the TRC commissioners themselves; the TRC staff; the audience; the media; and even the data entry temps hired to transcribe victim testimonies. At the outset, Tutu warned that 'Our work is going to be harrowing and demanding. We will need counselling periodically to recoup'.[13] Counsellors (known both as 'briefers' and as the 'Cry People') were available to witnesses before, during and after hearings.[14] They ran 'closure programmes' for TRC staff members facing the prospect of ending their work with the TRC and reintegrating into 'everyday life'.[15] The TRC even extended this therapeutic ethic to those whom the TRC did not officially identify as victims of gross human rights violations since failing to qualify for victim status was understood in itself to be a traumatizing event.[16]

These references to the dangers of a haunted past destructively repeating itself, like a festering physical wound, until it is lanced and cleansed, draw, in part, from a set of therapeutic narratives and images of trauma grounded in twentieth-century psychological knowledge and practice. The prominence of psychological counselling services at the hearings further indicates the TRC's investment in a set of institutional, social and economic relationships centred around this kind of psychological knowledge and practice. The particular therapeutic ethic that seems to be emerging in the context of the TRC is inspired by certain aspects of Freudian psychology, but adds elements of a newer therapeutic discourse prominent in the United States, Canada and Europe. Paul Antze and Michael Lambek have argued, of the West broadly, that 'increasingly, memory worth talking about – worth remembering – is memory of trauma'.[17] In a similar vein, Kirby Farrell has identified the 1990s as a period of 'post-traumatic culture' wherein the trope of 'trauma' has become a dominant interpretive framework for making sense not only of specific past injuries, but of the past itself more generally.[18] All of these writers agree that one of the unique features of this recent emphasis on trauma, traumatic memory and the various therapeutic strategies for recovery is that the ground of the (new, healed) self – of the patient or of the nation – is understood to be constituted out of the *mastering of a painful past*.

The Therapeutic Process

I will sketch the basic outlines of the therapeutic model at work here, and will elaborate further when I consider the political party submissions.[19] The principal stages of the particular therapeutic model in South Africa follow a basic Freudian model, 'undoing the patient's resistance, bringing repressed material into consciousness, releasing energies that have been inhibited, [and] allowing them to find new aims'.[20] First, there must be a repressed trauma in the past that, because of its persistent repression, becomes 'pathological', damaging the patient's current mental health. The traumatic event becomes what Allan Young termed the 'pathogenic secret'.[21]

The job of the therapist is to search for the secret of the repressed trauma, bring it into the full light of awareness and allow the sufferer to understand the significance of the trauma for their current condition. In order to do this, the patient is required to 'relive' every detail of the traumatic experience. This step is usually accompanied or followed by a *catharsis*. The cathartic moment is identified as evidence that the traumatic event has been fully relived by the patient and is a sign that the violent effects of the trauma have finally been appreciated.[22]

'Closure' is finally obtained when the patient has been able to integrate the new-found significance of the traumatic secret into his or her own self-conception. Retelling the story of the trauma re-establishes the narrative framework that was torn apart by the traumatic secret. By putting the traumatic event back into its rightful place in the narrative (in the past), the ability of the past to further impact the present is removed.[23] '*The goal of therapy is to convert "traumatic memory" into "narrative memory"*'.[24]

For the rest of the chapter, I will use the term 'therapeutic ethic' to refer to the general kind of moral and medical discourses I have identified above. The therapeutic ethic at work in the TRC is not only comprised of a particular psychotherapeutic notion of the causes of illness and the processes and aims of recovery – it also incorporates the broader cultural configurations of trauma, memory and recovery that undergird and enable this particular conception of the therapeutic. Thus, in my analysis I include a consideration of the prominent place that memory, especially of trauma, and the notion of 'recovery' have taken up in recent years. In considering the social and political implications of this therapeutic ethic, I approach any cultural configuration of trauma, memory and recovery as an ideological construction of the proper relationships between self, other and past – a construction that must be continually reproduced, politically and culturally. This symbolic (re)production and legitimation of a therapeutic ethic is especially visible in the work of the TRC, and it is through this lens that I will read the submission made by the African National Congress to the TRC.

This is not an argument that psychotherapy has somehow definitively captured the South African imagination, or even that of the TRC. The Christian and rational-legal aspects of the TRC's self-presentation and justification are certainly as strong, if not stronger. Nor do I wish to argue that the tropes of trauma and therapy are necessarily misguided, inappropriate or any less real than any other kind of moral discourse coming from the TRC. I do want to make the case, however, that the use of a language of *individual* suffering and recovery to, on occasion at least, describe the *social and political* work of making sense of the nation's past is a significant innovation in South African political culture. Psychotherapy in South Africa has, until very recently, been the near-exclusive domain of a small portion of the white, English-speaking middle and upper classes. The widespread, though by no means total, embrace of this ethic apparent during the TRC hearings by a diverse cross-section of South Africans reflects an unexpected and, I argue, important moment of cultural innovation.

Therapy and History: the ANC Submission

Having sketched out the therapeutic ethic at work in the TRC and beyond, I now explore the ways 'history borrows from psychotherapy'[25] by considering how this therapeutic ethic is related to a new, therapeutically-inspired mode of historiography that seems to be developing in post-apartheid South Africa. To illustrate, I will look at the submission made by the African National Congress (ANC) to the TRC concerning its role during apartheid.

Each major political party in South Africa made a submission to the TRC detailing their involvement in the struggle against apartheid. The ANC submission is a document of over two hundred pages chronicling the political party's involvement in South Africa's past. The following passage from the preface of the submission illustrates the ANC's intentions for the submission as well as its acceptance of the therapeutic imperatives of the TRC:

> The ANC campaigned actively for the TRC ... because we believe that such a Commission can play an important role in ensuring the psychological, intellectual and political well-being of the new democracy. Only by unveiling and acknowledging as far as possible the truth, ... can the millions whose basic

human rights were legally trampled upon ... be accorded the kind of respect which they deserve ... Only by confronting the past can there be genuine reconciliation, nation-building and unity in our country. Creating an official record of what happened could help in a cathartic way to heal South Africans psychologically. By knowing what happened and why, South Africa will be better placed to ensure that the evil deeds of the past are never repeated.[26]

The passage above, through its invocation of a therapeutic ethic, reveals the ANC's broad allegiance to the TRC's therapeutic mission and frames its look at the apartheid past in terms of this mission. The rest of the submission presents a detailed look at the ANC's involvement in the apartheid struggle. It breaks the apartheid era into four different periods and provides a section on the overall historical context. The struggle against apartheid is represented as a national liberation struggle with full support from international governments and institutions and presents apartheid as a 'crime against humanity' of the same general order as the Holocaust. At the end of the submission is an exhaustive list of all of the ANC members known to have died in exile.

I argue that the way the ANC writes about the significance of the apartheid past for the present and the ways it analyses the mechanics of apartheid's peculiar 'pathology' reflect an historiographical genre structured in terms of a therapeutic ethic. The traces of this therapeutic inspiration can be grouped into several broad categories, all of which relate to the model of trauma and therapy outlined above: first, the identification and 'excavation' of the pathogenic event; second, an analysis of the mechanics of secrecy and repression surrounding this event; third, a presentist orientation towards a 'fully citable' past necessary for recovery; and, lastly, the eventual separation of the traumatic past from the recovered present.

The Pathogenic Event

The aspect of the ANC's history of apartheid that is most striking in its contrast to the National Party submission, is its portrayal of the historical period under consideration by the TRC as qualitatively different from the periods that come before and after it. The TRC could only grant amnesty for acts committed between 21 March 1960, the date of the Sharpeville Massacre, and 10 May 1994, the day of the inauguration of Nelson Mandela as State President.[27] These limits mark, for the TRC and the ANC, a qualitatively different period of the systematic repression of democratic practice. According to the ANC's submission, 'The Sharpeville Massacre ... and the subsequent banning of the

ANC signaled the beginning of a new era in South African history – an era in which repression and conflict were to reach their peak'.[28] This event in 1960 led to the decision by the ANC to reverse its previous policy of nonviolence in favour of a revolutionary, military approach.[29] It also led to the declaration of the first State of Emergency of apartheid.[30] These facts provide the foundation for the claim on the next page:

> [W]hen one compares the 1950s with what followed, it is clear that in the 1960s there was a *qualitative* shift towards more repressive policies and practices by the National Party government ... The specificity of the 1960s is important, for it was also in this decade that the ANC was proscribed by the government and consequently turned to underground forms of organisation, and adopted the armed struggle.[31]

The emphasis on the special nature of post-1960s apartheid is further emphasized by the fact that in the section on the general historical context in the ANC's submission, periods of time before 1960 are given relatively scant attention. For the ANC, apartheid is seen as an historical anomaly, an event that stood outside the flow of normal historical events (much the same way a 'trauma' is defined as an event outside the range of everyday experience) and had explicit connections with other famous genocides and crimes against humanity:

> Apartheid oppression and repression were therefore not an aberration of a well-intentioned undertaking that went horribly wrong. Neither were they, as we were later told, an attempt to stave off the 'evil of communism'. The ideological underpinning and the programme of apartheid constituted a deliberate and systematic mission of a ruling clique that saw itself as the champion of a 'super-race'.[32]

This passage highlights one of the rhetorical strategies the ANC uses to emphasize the extreme nature of apartheid-era policy and suffering – linking apartheid implicitly and explicitly to the Holocaust. Building on frequent citations of apartheid's status in the international community as a 'crime against humanity', the submission contains sections detailing the early mutual admiration between National Party ideologues and Nazi officials.[33] It later claims that 'the brute bureaucratic reality of the apartheid era – an unthinking, everyday denial to individuals of their basic human dignity – is directly analogous to Hannah Arendt's characterization of the 'banality of evil' in Nazi Germany'.[34] The ANC uses these references and others to the Holocaust and Nazism to code the experiences of apartheid as similarly traumatic and historically unique.

Here then we find the classic description of the traumatic event – what Allan Young calls the 'pathogenic secret' or what Isabel Allende calls the 'key to unlocking the labyrinth of history'.[35] An event of such extreme disruption that it acts as the central organizing principle for a relationship to the past or, as Carina Perelli has identified it, 'so pivotal an experience that it becomes the standard of evaluation against which every single situation – past, present and future – will be judged'.[36] For the ANC, apartheid, and specifically the period between the 1960s and the 1990s, supplies and organizes the key categories and symbols of South Africa's past. Apartheid then acts not only as an organizing principle for history but forms the ground out of which the 'new South Africa' will be able to rebuild a new identity. Just as the 'working through' of therapy locates both the secret of the present illness and the source of future recovery in the traumatic, pathogenic event, for the ANC, South Africa's new national identity must spring from a serious encounter with its apartheid past.

Secrecy and Repression

Another key feature of the traumatic narrative is the repression of the traumatic event. This repression works against healing, since it prevents the trauma *of the past* from being 'dealt with' by the self *of the present*. Like the mechanism of repression identified in the therapeutic model, the ANC submission codes the period of apartheid between 1960 and 1994 as increasingly repressive.

Political repression and psychological repression are not usually considered together. There are, however, useful parallels between the two terms. In the context of a traumatic secret identified as the apartheid state, the political repression during apartheid could be seen, partly, as an attempt to obscure, from the present *and* the future, the qualitatively different (and evil) nature of apartheid. Here, political repression, by silencing protest, attempts to deny the voices of the apartheid present (in a position to identify the pathogenic secret) to the future. Psychological repression of a particular kind does the same thing – by repressing the traumatic secret, it attempts to obscure the reality of the secret both for the present and the future self.

Political repression does, of course, include behaviour not intended on its surface to hide, but rather to terrorize. Michael Taussig's work on the 'culture of terror' is especially relevant here as he reflects on the ways states can engineer a perception of the omnipresent and arbitrary nature of terror in order to control its population.[37] However, if we look at the problem from the perspective of a present looking back on a past, the *effects* are still essentially the same – the full reality and significance of a trauma in the past is kept hidden from the present. In a culture of terror, the nature of the true crimes of the state (that is the actual incidents of torture, kidnapping and murder) is hidden behind the phantasm of 'state terror', an empty category full of dread and symbolic import but void of all detail of specific crimes. At the end of the repressive regime's rule, the *fact* of terror's presence – of the traumatic secret – is usually well-established. However, the *facts* of terror are not. Like the psychological self, the true nature of that secret, that is the 'actual facts' of the many past political traumas often remain unknown to the present.

Whether through a silencing of protest or the active fostering of a terrorized climate, the historical consequence is the same. Both psychological and political repression aim, in part, to keep the facts of the past concealed to the present. I do not want to claim below that the ANC makes an explicit connection between the two types of repression. However, the language they use and the rhetorical strategies employed in their submission point to an understanding of the effects of political repression remarkably similar to psychological repression.

The specific language of repression in the submission extends far beyond the going 'underground' of the ANC in 1961.[38] The submission speaks of the 'psychological armour' needed by apartheid's functionaries to 'be free of all restraint as they carry out their daily work'.[39] It considers apartheid to be so evidently evil that the 'self-delusion' of the majority of its supporters was required to make it practical.[40] The trauma of apartheid, then, becomes so evil on its face that even its proponents must be prevented from knowing the full extent of what they are committed to.

The chronology of apartheid the ANC offers in its text also develops this theme of repression. The four key periods identified are as follows: first, the 'bureaucratic terrorism' of the 1960s; second, the 'mass repression' of the 1970s; third, the 'total strategy' of the 1980s and, finally, the 'transition period' of the 1990s that was actually a period of 'far more elaborate, covert' methods, where 'the consequences of these campaigns were far worse than anything experienced in the emergency years'.[41] What this timeline traces are the attempts by the apartheid government to push the secret evil of apartheid further and further down, out of public view through increasingly strong and well concealed acts of repression. What began as a 'bureaucratic' (and thus more public) terrorism changed into a strategy of mass repression. The 'total strategy' of the 1980s marks a new level of comprehensiveness in repression, and the continued covert action, even under the aegis of transitional negotiations in the 1990s, signals the development of newly sinister and elusive agents of repression. This chronology follows one of the general outlines of psychological repression (as it is manifested in post-traumatic stress) which often consists of constant attempts to master the traumatic memory, keeping it out of view of the conscious, changing to new strategies of repression when old ones fail.[42] This accounting also parallels the familiar stories of traumatic events too horrible to be held in check by the mind (or the government) and which eventually 'come bursting forth'.

Presentist Orientation Towards a 'Fully Citable' Past

The historical posture of the ANC submission is one of the present looking back towards a past shrouded in secrecy. The intent of its submission is to begin the excavation of the past necessary for a full 'reliving' of its horrors. Given the special nature of the traumatic secret and the extraordinary effort put into its repression, the therapeutic ethic demands nothing less than a full accounting. In that spirit, a significant portion of the ANC submission consists of a list of all the names of ANC members it knows to have died in exile during apartheid. Using a similar memorial strategy as the Vietnam Veteran's Memorial and others, on which the name of every fallen soldier is written, the ANC attempts to make the past 'fully citable', by recovering for history the names of every person in the ANC that fell victim to apartheid.[43] In a follow-up submission to the TRC, prepared in response to a series of questions the first submission engendered, the ANC continues this approach, detailing numerous case studies of apartheid-era human rights violations and providing an exhaustive list of all of the ANC's military operations during apartheid.

The National Party submission provides an instructive contrast in this case. Their historiographical project is committed to a stridently broad and historicist perspective. Its representation of the past is concerned primarily with explaining what it calls the 'historical contexts' and circumstances surrounding apartheid-era violence which include but are not limited to the 'progressive enlightenment' of the National Party, the useful work of anti-apartheid forces who worked with the government, the threat and subsequent collapse of Communism, socioeconomic changes domestically and internationally and the pressures of the international community.[44] Their submission is also governed by a rhetoric of statistical knowledge wherein it seeks to summarize broad periods of history through this kind of mathematical condensation. The ANC submission, on the other hand, has very few statistics and concerns itself instead with the names, dates and specific numbers surrounding apartheid-era events. Its focus on the detailed mining of a tragic past interrupts a historicist perspective on history (an approach especially favoured by the NP), and forces a confrontation with the minutiae of history rather than its broad themes. In this approach, the reasons for events and the multiple, interpretive contexts that surround them are less important than the need in the present for their full and complete *recitation*. This approach is consistent with the therapeutic narrative's unique imperative that the remembering of the trauma be complete to the last detail.[45] From this perspective, a history of 'great men' or even of 'great revolutionary masses' will not do – in this account, every individual lost must be accounted for if history as therapy is to be effective. In this therapeutic history, then, there is less concern for the broad analysis of the 'forces of history' (grounded in the useful fictions of the 'market', the 'state', the 'people') and the historical 'contexts' that explain those forces; rather, a therapeutic history resists these condensations and interpretations and asks instead for a recitation, a full accounting, a making visible of the entire scope and depth of suffering before any such interpretive exercises can be undertaken.

Separating the Traumatic Past from the Recovering Present

The final connection between the contours of the therapeutic ethic and the ANC submission concerns the final therapeutic step of (re)establishing a separation between the past and the present. In the diagnosis of post-traumatic psychiatric disorders, one of the key symptoms of illness is an inability to recognize, on occasion, that the traumatic secret is a *past* event. Instead, the event intrudes on the present to such an extent that the patient can often not tell the difference between experiences in the past and in the present. The trauma continues to work on the present, interrupting it, violating it. The goal of therapy is to firmly resituate the traumatic event in the past where it belongs and to release the present from its grasp.

In a similar fashion, the ANC identifies its submission as an attempt to mark a clear break between the past of apartheid and the present of democracy:

> All these efforts will afford us the confidence to say: Never Again! We hope that at the end of this process, South Africans will be the wiser, and better able to march to the future with confidence in one another and in their capacity to create a prosperous, peaceful and just society in which any violation of human rights will be fading memories of a past gone by, never to return.[46]

Having identified the uniquely evil and traumatic nature of the apartheid era, the ANC is now determined to establish the present as a period of history wholly separate from the pathology of the past. The use of the familiar phrase 'Never Again' (strongly associated with Holocaust remembering) re-emphasizes the ANC's connection between apartheid and the Holocaust. Voicing this cry works both to code apartheid as a categorical evil and to identify the ANC and its allies as the custodians of the newly recovered present. I would argue that establishing this difference and strong separation between past and present is one of the ANC's main litmus tests for securing its legitimacy as a ruling party. Identifying itself with the mission to 'immunize' the present from the past may also be a way to symbolically respond to the fact that economically speaking, little seems to have changed in the new South Africa.

Again, by way of contrast, the National Party's submission tries to show that the past of apartheid and the present of democracy are actually linked together by a long series of events that reflect the country's progressive enlightenment. It argues for multiple political, economic, social and cultural connections between the two periods and asserts that the present was not possible without the past – indeed, it maintains that the former period of apartheid led inevitably to the current period of negotiation and democratization. This portrait of continual progress and improvement argues that the present has never been held prisoner by the past. 'Mistakes' are admitted, but rather than becoming pathological, these mistakes simply form the ground out of which enlightened social and political solutions are discovered.

The ANC submission rejects this historicist approach and instead argues that the apartheid past was a period of evil that must be worked through from the perspective of the present and defended against. The intent of the ANC submission is to begin this work of national therapy so that in reckoning with the past, the past, and all of its pathological consequences, can be put back where it belongs, 'never to return'.

Therapy, Legitimacy and the New South Africa(n State)

Having outlined some of the ways the ANC's historical submission takes on the contours of the therapeutic ethic, I will conclude by suggesting that in this writing of a therapeutic, or what could be called a 'post-traumatic' history, the traumatic memory of victims becomes the privileged source of memory for writing history. The therapeutic ethic seems to provide a unique avenue for memory's transformation into history, a transformation effected not through stories of great triumphs or even of great losses, but of individual losses, private losses that nonetheless continue to infringe on the present and need to be made public. Evidence that this might be the case can be seen in the treatment of victim testimony in TRC hearings. In many of the amnesty hearings where victims were allowed to confront perpetrators and testify either in support and against the amnesty application, their testimony was often the only testimony not subjected to the legalistic interrogation and hair-splitting suffered by other witnesses. In fact, though accusations ranging from political bias to outright corruption were levelled at nearly every class of TRC participant (commissioner, witness, audience, media, counsellors, lawyers, perpetrators, etc.), the victims and their testimony seemed to have been, with only a few exceptions, essentially off-limits. The perception among some that the 'emotional' testimony of victims was not being sufficiently challenged and confirmed in the hearings was strong enough to prompt the National Party to protest the 'skewed perception of the conflict, based as [it was] on the highly emotive testimony of victims' at least twice in a follow-up report.[47]

What we find then is the beginning of an historiographical ethic centred on the conversion of traumatized and traumatic memories into narrative memories, sharable by the nation. A history whose narrative conventions and self-justifications are organized around the narrative conventions and self-justifications of the psychotherapy of traumatized individuals. And a history that places the memory of these victims at the center of its historical imagination.

The next question that seems to present itself, then, is *why* the South African state, and to an extent its citizens, have chosen to use this therapeutic model of history as one of the ways it is organizing its sociopolitical reconstruction. There does seem to be a trend among many nation-states to portray the confrontation with a tragic or shameful past as the appropriate work of national historiography. This confrontation becomes a means of both crafting a newly legitimate national history and of identifying a new role for the (legitimate) state to play, that of provider of therapeutic services to the nation. What to make of this development, then? Is this the most proper, most 'healthy', most ethical posture towards the past? Is it the obvious or most humane way of dealing with the integration of countries long divided internally? These questions become especially difficult when asked of a country with little history of (this kind of) therapy, in an area of the world where all the categories we think we have abstracted into the thin air of postmodern insecurity – truth, sin, history, identity – are often *embodied* and *enacted* in ways strikingly at odds with some of the principles of the therapeutic ethos.[48] In the struggle to find for history a source of legitimate, authentic memory, the therapeutic ethos provides a cast of characters and a set of therapeutic practices centred on 'memory worth talking about – memory of trauma'. What new kind of political or historical subjectivity, if any, this therapeutic model might engender in South African political culture remains to be seen.

Notes

1 Andre DuToit, 'Justice and/or Truth', *South African Outlook* 125:6 (1995), p. 64 and Jody Kollapen, 'Comment from the National Director: Kollapen Encouraged by Truth Commission Appointment Process', *Rights* 13 (1995), p. 4.
2 Ian Liebenberg, 'The Truth and Reconciliation Commission in South Africa: Context, Future and Some Imponderables', *SA Public Law* 2:1 (1996), p. 133.
3 Premesh Lalu and Brent Harris, 'Journeys from the Horizons of History: Text, Trial and Tales in the Construction of Narratives of Pain', *Current Writing* 8:2 (1996), p. 33.
4 Desmond Tutu, 'Statement by Archbishop Tutu on his appointment to the Truth and Reconciliation Commission', 30 November 1995, online posting, newsgroup list. Available email: trcinfo-owner@listbot.com.
5 Desmond Tutu, 'Archbishop Tutu's address to the first gathering of the Truth and Reconciliation Commission', 16 December 1995, online posting, newsgroup list. Available email: trcinfo-owner@listbot.com.
6 Truth and Reconciliation Commission, *Interim Report* (Cape Town: Truth and Reconciliation Commission, 1996), par. 2.
7 Ibid., par. 1.6.
8 Andre DuToit, 'Laying the Past to Rest', *Indicator SA* 11:4 (1994), p. 67.
9 Lloyd Vogelman, 'It's Hard to Forgive – Even Harder to Forget', *Work In Progress* 9 (1993), p. 16.
10 Russel Botman and Robin Petersen (eds), *To Remember and Heal: Theological and Psychological Reflections on Truth and Reconciliation* (Cape Town: Human and Rousseau, 1996), p. 120.
11 Cited in Liebenberg, p. 155.
12 Truth and Reconciliation Commission, *Register of Reconciliation* (Cape Town: Truth and Reconciliation Commission, 1997), Entry #87.
13 Tutu, 'Address', par. 3.
14 TRC, *Interim*, par. 3.3.
15 Brandon Hamber, *The Burdens of Truth: An Evaluation of the Psychological Support Services and Initiatives Undertaken by the South African Truth and Reconciliation Commission* (Johannesburg: Centre for the Study of Violence and Reconciliation, 1997), p. 14.
16 TRC, *Policy Framework for Urgent Interim Reparation Measures* (Cape Town: Truth and Reconciliation Commission, 1996), par. C.
17 Paul Antze and Michael Lambek (eds), *Tense Past: Cultural Essays in Trauma and Memory* (New York: Routledge, 1996), p. xii.

18   Kirby Farrell, *Post-traumatic Culture: Injury and Interpretation in the Nineties* (Baltimore: Johns Hopkins University Press, 1998), pp. 1–33.

19   The description below is of what seems to be the TRC's general imagination of the therapeutic process. Though it draws from various psychological theories and treatments, it does not represent any particular psychological approach in practice. Nor does it address more recent changes in trauma theory and treatment that may be at odds with the TRC's emphasis on reliving and cathartic release.

20   Marcia Cavell, *The Psychoanalytic Mind: From Freud to Philosophy* (Cambridge, Mass.: Harvard University Press, 1993), p. 94.

21   Allan Young, *The Harmony of Illusions: Inventing Post-Traumatic Stress Disorder* (Princeton: Princeton University Press, 1995), p. 142.

22   Hamber, pp. 3–5.

23   Young, *The Harmony of Illusions*, p. 140.

24   Ruth Leys, 'Traumatic Cures: Shellshock, Janet and the Question of Memory', in Paul Antze and Michael Lambek (eds), *Tense Past: Cultural Essays in Trauma and Memory* (New York: Routledge, 1996), p. 120. This last quotation in its emphasis on narrative means of recovery refers in particular to Janet's model of trauma and recovery. This distinction between traumatic memory and narrative memory (developed differently by Freud) was picked up by recent trauma theorists (Judith Herman in particular) and has become a common element of contemporary trauma theory. See Ruth Leys's article (cited above) for a valuable analysis of the historical development of Freud and Janet's thought regarding trauma and its treatment.

25   Antze and Lambek, p. xii.

26   African National Congress, *Statement to the Truth and Reconciliation Commission* (Cape Town: African National Congress, 1996), Preface.

27   The Sharpeville Massacre was a confrontation between South African police and demonstrators protesting government pass laws that left 69 protestors dead and eventually resulted in the banning of the ANC and the PAC (Pan Africanist Congress).

28   ANC, Sect. 2.1.

29   Ibid., Preface.

30   Ibid.

31   Ibid., Sect. 3.1, emphasis mine.

32   Ibid., Sect. 3.4.

33   Ibid., Sect. 3.4.

34   Ibid., Sect. 3.4.

35   Cited in Marita Wenzel, 'The "Other" Side of History as Depicted in Isabel Allende's "Of Love and Shadows"', *Literator* 17:3 (1996), p. 12.

36   Carina Perelli, 'Memoria de Sangre', in Jonathan Boyarin (ed.), *Remapping Memory: The Politics of Time and Space* (Minneapolis: University of Minnesota Press, 1994), p. 110.

37   Michael Taussig, *Shamanism, Colonialism, and the Wild Man: A Study in Terror and Healing* (Chicago: University of Chicago Press, 1986).

38   ANC, Preface.

39   Ibid.

40   Ibid.

41   Ibid.

42   Young, *The Harmony of Illusions*.

43 Kristin Ann Hass, *Carried to the Wall: American Memory and the Vietnam Veterans Memorial* (Berkeley: University of California Press, 1998).
44 National Party, *Second Submission to the Truth and Reconciliation Commission* (Cape Town: National Party, 1996).
45 Hamber, p. 3.
46 ANC, Sect. 7.3.
47 National Party, par. 7.
48 These questions of the *embodiment* and the *performance* of memory are central to exploring alternative modes of suffering and healing that may be at work in the South African context.

PART IV
NACHTRÄGLICHKEIT:
HISTORY AND
AFTERWARDSNESS

10 History and Trauma: Reviewing *Forrest Gump*[1]

SUSANNAH RADSTONE

Trauma has recently been receiving much scholarly attention in the humanities. Since first coming to the fore in the field of Holocaust studies,[2] and in debates surrounding the prominence, in contemporary popular culture, of concerns with recovered memory, child sexual abuse and 'survivor culture',[3] the term has been taken up in many fields including those of history, literature and cultural studies. Yet though there is widespread interest in, fascination with, or even fetishism of trauma, more than one understanding of the concept underlies what looks set to become 'trauma studies'. Using as my example the film *Forrest Gump*[4] the aim of what follows, therefore, is to distinguish between two widely divergent understandings of trauma and to show how each of these understandings produces radically different analyses of their object of study.

One explanation for trauma's rise to prominence within the humanities, resides in an apparent compatibility between certain theories of trauma and postmodernist critiques of history. Though such critiques are wide-ranging, and too complex to be summarized here,[5] it is possible to point to the two issues which are arguably central to this critique. Firstly, postmodernist critiques of history argue that the attempt to give meaning to events must now be regarded as deeply problematic, if not impossible. Given the profound complexity of the contemporary world and the enormous scale of historical phenomena such as the Holocaust, the very notion of discrete events caused by identifiable agents must now be regarded as out-of-date. As Hayden White has argued, this is not to say that events do not happen, but it is to acknowledge, rather, that the task of achieving a consensus as to the meaning of contemporary events must be regarded as an impossible one.[6] Secondly, postmodernist critiques of history problematize 'traditional' historiography's claims to legitimacy by questioning that practice's reliance on realism, empiricism, documentarism and objectivism,[7] positions which assume a capacity to stand 'outside' history/events and to tell an authoritative story about them. While

177

some postmodernist critiques of history would argue that such a stance was *always* predicated on an authority linked to unacknowledged power, others would propose that though such a stance might once have been legitimate, the scale and complexity of the contemporary world and its events must now render it obsolete.

As Hayden White has argued, the concept of trauma can appear consonant with such postmodernist critiques of history. Indeed, in his well-known essay 'The Modernist Event',[8] White links what I would term postmodernist representational strategies, such as the blurring of boundaries between both the 'real' and the 'imagined' and 'fact' and 'fiction' with what he calls 'holocaustal' events – 'the two World Wars, the Great Depression … programmes of genocide …'[9] and continues, by arguing that such events:

> function in the consciousness of certain groups exactly as infantile traumas are conceived to function in the psyche of neurotic individuals. This means that they cannot be simply forgotten and put out of mind, but neither can they be adequately remembered, which is to say clearly and unambiguously identified as to their meaning and contextualised in the group memory in such a way as to reduce the shadow they cast over the group's capacities to go into its present and envision a future free of their debilitating effects.[10]

Pitting himself against those, like Fredric Jameson, who lament postmodernist historiography's blurring of the boundaries between the 'real' and the 'imagined', 'fact' and 'fiction', White advocates such strategies as appropriate to the representation of holocaustal events, which, like infantile traumas, resist 'inherited categories and conventions for assigning them meanings'.[11] Citing the work of Eric Santner,[12] White insists, moreover, that the attempt to *assign* meaning to such events works against the need to understand them. The assignment of meaning may provide what White, following Santner, calls 'intellectual mastery',[13] but such mastery is illusory – it provides, that is, a fetish that stands in the way of experiencing the pain which accompanies any acknowledgement of loss of certainty concerning what can be known. In place of narrative strategies which provide such 'intellectual mastery', White advocates postmodernist representational strategies which, in acknowledging the blurred boundaries between the 'real' and the 'imagined', 'fact' and fiction', enable some psychic mastery of contemporary experiences, which, like infantile traumas, resist the assignment of meaning.

Though the work of Hayden White reveals consonances between certain understandings of trauma and postmodernist critiques of history, in what follows, I propose that an alternative view of trauma is currently gaining ground within the humanities. Though this view of trauma arguably pays lip service to postmodernist critiques of history, its roots arguably link it with psychiatric understandings of trauma[14] in play in popular culture – particularly in those popular narratives that concern themselves with survivor movements, such as those attached to recovered memory and childhood sexual abuse. In what follows, then, I will be arguing that the psychiatric understanding of trauma in play in popular culture, as well as in some work within the humanities, stresses the possibility of linking trauma to an ultimately comprehensible event.

On this account, the term trauma refers to an event which, due to its shocking and initially incomprehensible nature, prompts a shut-down in normal processes of assimilating or 'digesting' experiences. In such cases, this undigested experience is understood to come to occupy a walled-off area of the memory, giving rise to symptoms commonly referred to as post-traumatic stress disorder (PTSD). Though a very wide variety of symptoms are now commonly attributed to PTSD, its aetiology is inextricably tied to the 'toxicity' of the event and the difficulties and costs of the struggle to confine this event within a separated-off part of the memory. Unlike postmodernist critiques of history, this psychiatric approach to trauma distinguishes clearly between the 'inside' and the 'outside'. Speaking of historiography, Hayden White insists that the task must now be to find modes of representation that are adequate to the postmodernist realization that the boundary between the 'outside', by which he means events, and the 'inside' by which he means the meanings attributed to events, is a permeable one.[15] Psychiatric understandings of trauma suggest that 'undigested' events become deposited in walled-off parts of the mind. Parts of the 'outside', in other words, become hidden away 'inside'. Psychoanalytic understandings of trauma argue, rather, that though events do 'happen', in practice, the 'outside' and the 'inside' cannot be distinguished from each other, since memory (already a form of representation, rather than a reflection of events), will itself always be refracted by fantasy. In theorizing the links between traumatic memory and fantasy, psychoanalytic understandings of trauma produce an understanding of trauma in keeping with postmodernist critiques of history. Conversely, understandings of trauma influenced by US psychiatry and survivor movements are less compatible with such critiques.

In what follows, I will be contrasting an approach to *Forrest Gump* informed by psychiatric understandings of trauma, with an analysis informed by psychoanalytic understandings of traumatic memory. In so doing, I aim to show that while the former approach is shaped by defensive fantasies producing an illusory intellectual mastery, the second approach shows that the film *Forrest*

Gump may be aiding in the struggle towards psychic mastery, rather than knowledge of the past.

Two Approaches to Trauma: *Forrest Gump* and its Critics

Forrest Gump is a perplexing film. Its seemingly unfathomable placing of a 'dim-wit'[16] at history's heart begs questions about the pleasure, for the audience, of getting 'to see the images that shaped a nation's consciousness'[17] accompanied by the 'glazed look'[18] and 'utter vacancy'[19] of its central protagonist. In their press reviews of the film, the critics queried the phenomenal appeal of Forrest, a 'doe-eyed man-cub',[20] into whose figure the film 'conflates some 30 years of US history'.[21] The headlines for these reviews – 'Transatlantic Gumption'[22] and 'The Gumping of America' – sum up the critical consensus that *Forrest Gump* was brainwashing America by implanting Forrest's anodyne, or even false memories of its tortuous and traumatic recent history. These reviews, which attacked the film for implanting memories suffused by an idiot's common sense ('gump' is an American colloquialism meaning 'common sense') are arguably suffused, themselves, by *another* common-sense, a common sense which *believes* both in the overwhelming power of the media, and in the audience's passive vulnerability in the face of this power. In these reviews, critics construct the film's audience as passively and helplessly falling under the 'evil' spell of *Forrest Gump* and on this arguably paranoid reading, the audience emerge either as passive victims, or as credulous fools.

The common sense that suffuses these reviews is, I want to argue, the common sense of 'survivor culture' – that culture which, according to sociologists and cultural critics, is centrally concerned with popular narratives and life stories in which the causes of problems, difficulties and symptoms come to be attributed solely to ultimately *knowable* external agents and events. Survivor culture has been linked both with millennial fever[23] and with the fragmentation and ungraspability of authority and power in contemporary Western society.[24] Accounts concur, however, that the accusatory scenarios and the emphasis upon external events shared by, for instance, the recovered memory movement and sufferers from chronic fatigue syndrome result from an inability to acknowledge the part played by fantasy in shaping our apprehension of the world. In place of the acknowledgement of the part played by the inevitably refractory internal world in the shaping of lives, survivor culture seeks cause and cure for disappointment, shortcomings, or even 'simple unhappiness ... firmly outside the self'.[25] Thus, in survivor culture, the boundaries between the 'real' and the 'imagined', 'fact' and 'fiction' are resolutely and firmly maintained. At the heart of survivor culture lies a particular understanding of *trauma* and its effects. This understanding of trauma posits, in the words of one commentator, 'the existence of a dissociated mental realm that contains, and to an extent seals off recollections of things too painful to bear …'[26] and is currently informing not only popular narratives and life histories, but psychiatry and academic work, too.

Forrest Gump's reviews are marked by various aspects of survivor culture. The audience is attributed with the passive vulnerability of the trauma victim, and the film is imbued with the extraordinary, overwhelming powers of the traumatic event. Moreover, reviews of *Forrest Gump* imply, too, that the film forms part of a generalized conspiracy to hide the historical *truth* from its audience: remember the headline 'The Gumping Of America'. In her book *Hystories*, Elaine Showalter argues that this type of conspiracy theory is frequently found in the popular narratives of what I am calling survivor culture. Whether in the popular narratives and social movements surrounding the 'traumas' of satanic abuse, alien abduction, or, most famously, sexual abuse, a belief in a powerful conspiracy surrounded by a wall of silence holds sway. How can the contemporary influence of survivor culture and its attendant concerns with trauma and fantasies of conspiracy best be understood?

Taken together, Showalter's *Hystories* and Ian Craib's *The Importance Of Disappointment* suggest that the appeal of survivor culture, and, I would add, of the trauma theories that underpin it, can best be understood in relation to a defensive and fragmented psychosocial culture that lacks adequate containment and within which authority, responsibility and agency have become increasingly complex and diffuse. In this context, the inevitably conflictual nature of the inner world becomes hard to bear, leading to paranoid conspiracy fantasies peopled by innocent victims and wicked perpetrators. The certainties of the trauma theory circulating in survivor culture arguably substitute a fetishistic and illusory sense of intellectual mastery for a more nuanced sense of psychic mastery – a mastery which would acknowledge the limited nature of any capacity to assign meaning to experience and the inevitable mixing, in any representation of experience, of 'the imaginary' with 'the happened'. On Showalter's and Craib's reading, trauma theory's emphasis upon the impact of external events upon passive victims is replaced by an emphasis upon the mind's *mediation* of cultural and social circumstances: the Manichean universe of conspiracy fantasies defends against the acknowledgement of 'ordinary' inner conflicts made intolerable by the uncontaining nature of the fragmented postmodern social world.

Reviews of *Forrest Gump* are shaped by conspiracy fantasies supported by survivor culture. Such reviews emphasize the film's capacity to overwhelm its audiences, but, like the trauma theories that underpin victim culture, they oversimplify the relation between the external and the inner world by stressing the film's impact upon a passive audience. Though *critiques* of survivor culture such as Showalter's and Craib's substitute a psychoanalytic emphasis upon the mind's mediation of external reality for trauma theory's stress upon the impact of the event upon the mind, in what follows I want to suggest, rather, that the paranoid conspiracy theories fuelling survivor culture in general, and reviews of *Forrest Gump* in particular, can best be understood in relation to a psychoanalytic understanding of *traumatic memory*. Critiques of survivor culture such as those of Craib and Showalter replace trauma theory's emphasis upon dissociative memory with a psychoanalytic emphasis upon the mind's mediation of external reality via fantasy. A psychoanalytic understanding of traumatic memory, however, retains an emphasis upon *both* fantasy *and* memory.

The psychoanalytic understanding of memory encompasses two related fields: those of temporality and symbolization. The term that is most central to the psychoanalytic understanding of the temporality of memory is *Nachträglichkeit*, or 'afterwardsness'.[27] This concept refers to a process of deferred revision, where 'experiences, impressions and memory-traces may be revised at a later date to fit in with fresh experiences or with the attainment of a new stage of development'.[28] On this reading, then, memories constitute revisions prompted by later events. For Freud, the revisions thus prompted were understood to be more closely related to primal *fantasies* than to historical reality. However, though 'memories' are thus understood to be related to fantasies, Freud's famous revisions of his 'seduction theory' did not simply substitute fantasy for the memory of traumatic events. Rather, in Freud's later writings on traumatic memory, fantasy and memory come to be conceived of not as binary opposites, but as complexly related terms. On this view, traumatic symptoms emerge where a seemingly innocuous event prompts memories of an earlier event that now becomes associated with inadmissable *fantasies*. Pathogeny derives not from the remembered event itself, but from the attempt to defend against the fantasies that now emerge in association with such memories: 'it is only *as a memory* that the first event becomes pathogenic by deferred action'.[29]

Two crucial differences separate the trauma theory that informs survivor culture from this psychoanalytic understanding of traumatic memory: its models of temporality, and of the relation between an external event and its registration within the inner world of psychical reality. Like traditional historiography, theories of traumatic memory and PTSD remain wedded to a linear model of temporality and a reflectionist understanding of the mind's relation to external events. At stake across both these differences is the issue of the mediation of the 'outside' by the 'inside' – the inner world's *mediation* of the external world, a mediation which is foregrounded by psychoanalytic theory, as well as by postmodernist critiques of history and minimized by trauma theory. Where temporality is at issue, the psychoanalytic concept of 'afterwardsness' posits traumatic memory not as the registration of an event, but as the outcome of a complex process of revision shaped by the promptings from the present. Trauma theory, on the other hand, posits the linear registration of events as they happen, albeit that such registrations may be secreted away through dissociation. Where the relation between an event and 'psychical reality' is at issue, psychoanalytic theory suggests that what is at stake in the formation of traumatic memory is the relation between the triggering second events and the *'phantasies they activate'*.[30] Conversely, trauma theories associate trauma not with the effects of triggered associations but with the ontologically unbearable nature of the event itself.

I have already suggested that, unlike Showalter and Craib, whose critiques of survivor culture substitute a psychoanalytic emphasis upon the mind's mediation of *fantasies* for trauma theory's emphasis upon the mind's registration of trauma in dissociated *memories*, my own approach to reviews of *Forrest Gump* will, like psychoanalytic understandings of traumatic memory, *integrate* questions of memory and fantasy.

I have already pointed out that those reviews are, like the victim narratives studied by Elaine Showalter, suffused by paranoid conspiracy theories that attribute great power to the film and utter helplessness to that film's audience. One psychoanalyst and writer has argued that this type of fantasy is, itself, a *symptom* of traumatic memory. Christopher Bollas's essay 'The Functions of History' argues for an approach that can acknowledge elements of fantasy and memory in clinical material. To this end, Bollas distinguishes between an ordinary and a traumatized sense of development. In healthy development, argues Bollas, there is a sense 'of one's development inside a structure ... derived from the self'.[31] In a traumatized development, on the other hand, there is a sense of 'one's development inside a structure *imposed on the self*'.[32] Bollas derives this distinction from Winnicott's fascinating child observations, in which the latter noted the initially unbearable nature of that which is presented for the first time (a new object, an unexpected event). The child responds to the unthinkable nature of 'the real' by looking away, creating a remembered 'blank nothing' that testifies to this impact. In the right circumstances, the event can be returned to, explored and woven into the unconscious material that constitutes our sense of self. But where circumstances preclude such a return – where the environment remains unstable, or uncontaining, for instance, these 'blanks' remain, creating a sense of developing within a structure imposed upon the self. To my mind, Bollas's Winnicottian understanding of the links between fantasy and traumatic memory reveals the links between trauma and conspiracy theories, which, as fantasies, testify, in distorted ways, to the arrest of unconscious dissemination by the impact of an 'unthinkable' event.

Christopher Bollas associates this paranoid fantasy of imposition upon the self with a sense of temporal suspension and the arrest of psychical dissemination. In contrast to trauma theory's concept of dissociation, however, which stresses only the impact of an event, Bollas's Winnicottian understanding of trauma describes a *remembered* gap constituted by *looking* away, a psychic *act* which leaves its trace, and can, depending upon the quality of the environment, be followed by *Nachträglichkeit* – by those enlivening acts of revision which begin to transform an inert past [33] and release its subject from its unthought burden. Whereas, in trauma theory, then, trauma is understood to impact upon a passive 'object', in Bollas's psychoanalysis, trauma impacts upon a subject who responds with a psychical *act* – albeit an act of looking away – and it is this psychical activity which leaves its mark, both as a gap and as a predisposition towards paranoid and conspiratorial fantasies, since the subject cannot make this 'lost' material – these 'dumb facts', to use Bollas's term – their own.

Psychoanalysis would seek answers to its questions about what inhibited the *revision* of such 'dumb facts' in the early environment and its failures. My question, however, concerns culture, rather than an individual. If I am right, and the paranoia in the film reviews I am discussing can be understood as conspiracy fantasy triggered by traumatic cultural memory, what is it about contemporary culture that is inhibiting the flow of association and revision that would temper paranoia? Ian Craib's thesis moves us precisely from a consideration of the environments of infancy or clinical psychoanalysis to a consideration of the quality of environment produced by contemporary social relations, politics and authority. For Craib, it is precisely the fragmented, confusing and uncontaining nature of the postmodern environment that fosters a predisposition towards conspiracy theory. Craib's emphasis falls upon the sheer difficulty, in this environment, of acknowledging inner conflict and uncertainty. His argument suggests that in place of such acknowledgement, the contemporary environment fosters a predisposition towards the projection of inner conflict and uncertainty, so that one's own 'destructiveness' and losses become sited in others. My emphasis falls rather upon the part played by that same environment in inhibiting *Nachträglichkeit*. But this is not an argument that proposes the impact upon passive subjects of a 'paralysing' environment. I am suggesting, rather, that in this environment, paranoid and conspiratorial *fantasies* take the place of *Nachträglichkeit*.

The reviews of *Forrest Gump* to which I referred earlier trade in paranoia and conspiracy theory and have been formed in a culture within which fantasies of innocent victims and wicked perpetrators hold sway. Culture, however, is neither uniform nor undifferentiated and a change of perspective can reveal a different landscape. By way of conclusion, then, I will discuss not a review, but a scholarly analysis of *Forrest Gump* and, in so doing, I want to contrast that analysis' indebtedness to trauma theory with my own analysis of the film – an analysis informed not by trauma theory, but by a psychoanalytic understanding of traumatic memory.

Robert Burgoyne's implicitly Foucauldian analysis of *Forrest Gump*[34] argues that the film seeks to implant a prosthetic memory of recent US history – a memory that can 'float free of the historical traumas of the 1960s and 1970s'[35] while forgetting what Burgoyne sees as the most important memory of all – the memory of political *agency* which he associates with this period. Burgoyne's emphasis upon the cinematic 'implantation' of memory and the immense power of the media is consonant with survivor culture's sense of overwhelming and yet diffuse structures of power[36] and a sense of a structure imposed upon the self. The concept of 'prosthetic memory' evokes, indeed, the claims and counterclaims concerning the eliciting of 'false memories' of sexual abuse otherwise known as the 'memory wars'[37] – an association which underlines further the links between this film analysis and 'survivor culture'. Most telling, however, particularly in the context of film theory's long-sustained emphasis upon the activity, as well as the passivity of film spectatorship, is the entirely passive model of spectatorship implied by Burgoyne's deployment of the term 'prosthetic memory'. It is ironic, though utterly understandable, that in this Foucauldian analysis, whose framework is the opposition between memory and history, what comes into view is the film's forgetting of potentially resistant memories of historical agency. Rendered inaccessible, or 'forgotten' within this framework, however, are cinepsychoanalytic insights concerning fantasy and the agency of spectators – insights whose inaccessibility is related to that splitting-off of memory from fantasy which is itself symptomatic of contemporary culture's imbrication with traumatic memory. In short, what gets forgotten, here, are psychoanalytic understandings concerning the mediation – the shaping power – of the unconscious in the production of memory. How would an analysis of *Forrest Gump* informed by such insights diverge from Burgoyne's reading of the film as 'implanted' 'prosthetic memory'?

For many commentators, the conjunction of Forrest's blankness with the film's address to a more understanding audience is deemed internally contradictory. As one reviewer puts this: '[i]t's one of the movie's paradoxes that such knowing, audience-flattering jokes are so at odds with the protagonist's supposed "innocence"'.[38] But *Forrest Gump*'s morphing of the fictional Forrest into archive footage of recent US history invites the spectator to identify with his uncomprehending witnessing of a series of painful events: Vietnam, Kennedy's assassination, Watergate. As Burgoyne himself puts it, Forrest appears 'impervious to the historical events that erupt in his immediate proximity'.[39] At the same time, and as many commentaries have pointed out, this incomprehension gains its dramatic force, whether understood in relation to irony, or to poignant humour, or both, from the audience's understanding of Forrest's experience. In short, the film's overall legibility and appeal depends upon its juxtaposition of memory prompts – its address, that is, to a relatively understanding audience – with the identification it invites with the uncomprehending, or even 'ignorant' Forrest. This ambiguous identification, which weaves together understanding and incomprehension contributes to what so many reviewers have seen as *Forrest Gump*'s unaccountable capacity to move. While so many critics jumped to the conclusion that the film's affect was linked only to Forrest's ignorance, and that the film was therefore trading in a historical common sense or 'gump' that might be likened to 'false memory', psychoanalysis provides another view of the force of this affective identification.

Forrest Gump's 'memories' of recent US history are constructed by means of the insertion of its 1990s 'hero' into archive footage of earlier decades. The 'doe-eyed'[40] Forrest looks on vacantly as 'history' unfolds. From a perspective informed by a psychoanalytic understanding of traumatic memory, I want to suggest that this morphing of Forrest into the archive constitutes not the construction of a false memory for implantation, but the visual literalization of *Nachträglichkeit* – of that complex 'afterwardsness' of remembrance represented by the phrase 'but we didn't know that then'.[41] This psychoanalytic reading of *Forrest Gump*'s temporality reverses that of Robert Burgoyne. His suggestion that the film 'wipe[s] the slate clean ... in an effort to disengage cultural memory from public history'[42] assumes that this engagement had already been made – an assumption that overlooks the psychoanalytic understanding of the inherent latency of trauma. While identification with Forrest encompasses an acknowledgement, then, of the 'gap' or 'blankness' of a remembered looking away, the film's comprehension depends upon a successful address to the audience's capacity to remember. On this reading, then, *Forrest Gump* emerges not as 'false memory', but as a point of affective identification through which traumatic memory begins to be worked through. Moreover, what needs to be understood, here, is the difference between 'remembrance' and 'knowledge', since what I am proposing is that the remembrance prompted by *Forrest Gump* is a remembrance of loss of certainty, of loss of belief in the capacity to assign meaning. This, if you like, is the 'knowledge' begun to be acknowledged by the film. If, on Burgoyne's Foucauldian reading, *Forrest Gump* implants, in my own quote from Foucault 'what they *must* remember having been',[43] a reading informed by psychoanalytic understandings of memory's temporality suggests, rather, that the film begins to acknowledge 'what they *couldn't* have known then'.[44] On this reading, moreover, new technology, which constitutes an aspect of that ungraspable environment which Ian Craib believes to be inhibiting reality-testing and promoting false selves, emerges here not only in relation to pathology, but also to the struggle towards understanding. Though for reviewers, as well as for Burgoyne, then, *Forrest Gump* is viewed as a film that 'doesn't wake people up to their times',[45] this psychoanalytically informed reading of the film's temporality of *Nachträglichkeit* suggests, rather, that the film remembers both an initial 'looking away' as well as the beginnings of remembrance – a reading that suggests an analogy with 'waking' rather than with 'dreaming', or by extension fantasy. *Forrest Gump*, that is, works towards psychic mastery, rather than towards the illusory intellectual mastery that underpins the conspiracy theories framing so many of the film's reviews.

This reading of *Forrest Gump* has suggested that Burgoyne's view of the film's 'implantation' of memory is influenced by 'survivor culture', which is, itself, a symptom of a traumatized society's inability to acknowledge the activities and conflicts of the inner world. In opposition to this view, a reading informed by psychoanalytic understandings of memory's temporality has been proposed. On this reading, what comes into view is *Forrest Gump*'s address to a spectator moving between an initial 'looking away' and the beginnings of revision – a spectator, that is, caught up in the movement, affect and activity of *Nachträglichkeit*. This rereading pits Burgoyne's emphasis upon the film's excision of memories of historical agency against its engagement with psychical acts of revision.

But a psychoanalytic reading that attends to the fantasies as well as the temporality put in play by *Forrest Gump* reveals that this process is an uneven one. The appeal of Forrest's 'blankness' can certainly be associated with an identification suspended between an initial ignorance and a later remembrance: 'what we remember', as Nicola King has put it, 'are events which took place in a kind of *innocence*'.[46] Yet in *Forrest Gump,* Forrest's incomprehension and innocence go hand in hand with his central, albeit uncomprehending role in major events of recent US history. The appeal of this apparently paradoxical combination of innocence and implication, of passivity and activity, can be explained however, by reference to fantasy structures familiar within psychoanalysis: specifically those fantasies that typify narcissism. According to psychoanalysis, this convergence of passivity and omnipotence is anything but paradoxical, but constitutes, rather, two sides of narcissism's coin. Infantile narcissism is understood by psychoanalysis as a necessary developmental stage in which the child experiences itself as part of the parent, who is fantasized as all-powerful. This fantasy of omnipotence can then be drawn upon to counter a growing awareness of insufficiency, incompleteness and dependency. In adulthood and at times of stress, such fantasies may be re-evoked. As we have already seen, Ian Craib points to the convergence in contemporary Western culture of fantasies of innocent victimhood with fantasies of omnipotence. The convergence, indeed, of this classically narcissistic pairing arguably typifies what I have described as the defensive fantasy structure mobilized by survivor culture. I have already referred to Ian Craib's eloquent description of the social conditions which are currently fostering these defensive fantasies of omnipotent passivity in a culture rendered incapable of grasping the power and limits of both unconscious fantasy and conscious will. What I am now suggesting is that the emergence of these fantasy structures alongside *Forrest Gump*'s *Nachträglichkeit*-like temporality suggests a struggle over what we clumsily refer to as 'the past'. *Forrest Gump* certainly addresses itself to an audience moving towards a remembrance that promises a degree of psychical mastery of loss. Yet its appeal to fantasies of narcissism arguably registers a resistance to such remembrance, a resistance registered, too, by the promise of intellectual mastery offered by the trauma theories which inform many of the film's reviews.

Notes

1   For a longer version of this essay, see Susannah Radstone, 'Screening Trauma: *Forrest Gump*, Film and Memory', in Susannah Radstone (ed.), *Memory and Methodology* (London and New York: Berg, 2000), pp. 79–107.

2   See, for instance, Shoshana Felman and Dori Laub, *Testimony: Crises of Witnessing in Literature, Psychoanalysis and History* (New York: Routledge, 1992).

3   Paul Antze and Michael Lambek, 'Introduction: Forecasting Memory' in Paul Antze and Michael Lambek (eds), *Tense Past: Cultural Essays in Trauma and Memory* (New York: Routledge, 1996); Elaine Showalter, *Hystories: Hysterical Epidemics in Modern Media* (New York: Columbia University Press, 1992).

4   Robert Zemeckis, US, 1994.

5   For a useful introduction to postmodernist critiques of history, see Keith Jenkins, *Re-Thinking History* (London: Routledge, 1991); see also Keith Jenkins (ed.), *The Postmodern History Reader* (London: Routledge, 1997).

6   Hayden White, 'The Modernist Event', in Vivian Sobchack (ed.), *The Persistence of History: Cinema, Television and the Modern Event* (New York: Routledge, 1996), pp. 17–38.

7   Jenkins (ed.), *The Postmodern History Reader*, p. 13.

8   White, op. cit.

9   White, p. 20.

10 Ibid.

11 White, p. 21.

12 Eric Santner, 'History beyond the Pleasure Principle', in Saul Friedländer (ed.), *Probing the Limits of Representation: Nazism and the 'Final Solution'* (Cambridge, Mass.: Harvard University Press, 1992).

13 White, p. 31.

14 Here, I refer to definitions of trauma published in the fourth edition of the highly influential US psychiatric nosology, *The Diagnostic and Statistical Manual of Mental Disorders* (Washington DC: American Psychiatric Association, 1994).

15 White, esp. p. 29ff.

16 Clive Barnes, 'The Gumping of America', *Evening Standard*, 17 August 1994, p. 13.

17 Monica Zetlin, review of *Forrest Gump*, *Cinema Papers* 102 (1994), pp. 68–9.

18 J. Hoberman, review of *Forrest Gump*, *Village Voice*, 12 July 1994, p. 41.

19 Jonathan Romney, 'Transatlantic Gumption', *New Statesman and Society*, 14 August 1994, p. 41.

20 Ibid.

21 Ibid.

22 Ibid.

23 Showalter, op. cit.

24 Ian Craib, *The Importance of Disappointment* (London: Routledge, 1994).

25 Showalter, p. 4.

26 Michael G. Kenny, 'Trauma, Time, Illness and Culture: An Anthropological Approach to Traumatic Memory', in Antze and Lambek (eds), pp. 151–71.

27 Jean Laplanche, 'Notes on Afterwardsness', in John Fletcher and Martin Stanton (eds), *Jean Laplanche: Seduction, Translation and the Drives* (London: ICA, 1992), pp. 217–23.

28 Jean Laplanche and J.-B. Pontalis, *The Language of Psycho-analysis*, trans. Donald Nicholson-Smith (London: Karnac Books, 1988), p. 111.

29 Ibid., p. 467 (authors' italics).

30 Ibid., p. 468 (my italics).

31 Christopher Bollas, *Cracking Up: The Work of Unconscious Experience* (London: Routledge 1995), p. 114.

32 Ibid. (my italics).

33 Ibid., p. 143.

34 Robert Burgoyne, *Film Nation: Hollywood Looks at US History* (Minneapolis: University of Minnesota Press, 1997).

35 Ibid., p. 107.

36 Craib, op. cit.

37 Here I refer to the scholarly and judicial battles that have recently been waged concerning whether or not memories (particularly of sexual abuse) can be completely dissociated and then 'recovered'. In the main, the academic version of this 'memory war' has been fought out between those whose understandings of traumatic memory are shaped by Freudian ideas of repression and those who believe, rather, that trauma prompts dissociation. For an account of the scholarly version of this 'memory war' edited by an avowed anti-Freudian, see Frederick Crews, *The Memory Wars: Freud's Legacy In Dispute* (New York: *New York Review of Books*, 1995).

38 Tom Charity, review of *Forrest Gump*, *Time Out*, 5–12 October 1994, p. 67.

39 Burgoyne, p. 108.

40 Romney, p. 41.

41 Nicola King, 'Autobiography as Cultural Memory: Three case-studies', *New Formations* 30 (1997), p. 50.

42 Burgoyne, p. 14.

43 Michel Foucault, 'Film and Popular Memory', *Foucault Live: Interviews 1966–1984* (New York: semiotext(e), 1989), p. 92 (my italics).

44 King, p. 50.

45 Alexander Walker, review of *Forrest Gump*, *Evening Standard*, 6 October 1994, p. 32.

46 King, p. 51 (my italics).

11 Traumatic Memories of Remembering and Forgetting

ELIZABETH COWIE

I

Trauma is outside memory, and outside history. It is the unrepresentable, and thus it is 'The unrememberable and the unforgettable'.[1] In the discussion which follows I explore some of the ways in which film as a mode of representation 'remembers' trauma and I will suggest that it does so not only as a repeated return to the unremembered but also by instituting a forgetting which enables trauma to pass into memory and thus some level of resolution. My discussion will centre on two films: an early, silent documentary about 'shell-shocked' soldiers in the First World War, *War Neuroses, Netley 1917 and Seale Hayne Military Hospital, 1918* (Pathé, 1918)[2] and Marguerite Duras's and Alain Resnais's *Hiroshima mon amour* (1959). *War Neuroses* juxtaposes a certain reality and a certain fiction, involving two modes of the real, on the one hand the filmed reality of shell-shocked soldiers, and on the other hand the documentary real of trauma, of the 'real' in Lacan's tripartite division of the real, the symbolic, and the imaginary. *Hiroshima mon amour*, too, imbricates fiction and nonfiction with questions of trauma and here again it is through the fictional that the real of trauma can be apprehended, ironically and scandalously through the story of a passionate and erotic love affair.

Trauma is a subjective, individual, but also unknown, experience. How, then, can its unrepresentability be represented? How can we come to know trauma, and can we know the other's trauma? My questions here parallel the enquiry undertaken by Cathy Caruth in her important study, *Unclaimed Experience*, in which she also considers *Hiroshima mon amour.* Where Caruth finds history, however, I posit the real, in the Lacanian sense. That is, for Caruth trauma consists in an historical 'real'. History here is the story of what cannot be understood, or, as she says 'What returns to haunt the victim, these stories tell us, is not only the reality of the violent event but also the reality of the way that its violence has not yet been fully known.'[3] This should not

191

imply that the not-fully known experience can be fully known, as if it were simply something that presently escapes our understanding, but which could come to be a fully-grasped experience by completing the missing in our understanding. As Caruth says, 'The story of trauma, then, as the narrative of a belated experience, far from telling of an escape from reality – the escape from a death, or from its referential force – rather attests to its endless impact on a life.'[4] Trauma thus produces the subject, it is its history. This in the sense, however, of time as duration, of the subject enduring, rather than a series of events in a causal relation.[5] From trauma two stories emerge, Caruth argues, a 'story of the unbearable nature of an event and the story of the unbearable nature of its survival'.[6] Insofar as these *are* stories, however, they are not – or no longer – trauma. It is the sense of time proposed by psychoanalysis in Freud's concept of *Nachträglichkeit* which might allow us to understand the workings of time and memory here. Jean Laplanche has argued that *Nachträglichkeit*, translated by Strachey as 'deferred action', but which Laplanche suggests is better understood in English as 'afterwardsness', is a key term for understanding how the significance or meaning of the past – as events or facts of an individual's history – may change or only emerge subsequently through later events and experiences.

> I want to account for this problem of the different directions, to and fro, by arguing that, right at the start, there is something that goes in the direction of the past to the future, from the other to the individual in question, that is in the direction from the adult to the baby, which I call the implantation of the enigmatic message. This message is then retranslated, following a temporal direction which is, in an alternating fashion, by turns retrogressive and progressive (according to my general model of translation-detranslation-retranslation).[7]

For Laplanche it is what he terms the enigmatic message which intrudes or penetrates – 'seducing' – the child, which produces trauma. Laplanche hereby reintroduces sexuality into the understanding of trauma, but not – as in Freud – as an organized meaning, the Oedipal complex.[8] Rather it is a seduction without meaning, and it is in this very senselessness that trauma inheres. What we have instead is a process of becoming understood, a translation, in the words of Jean Laplanche, and a narrativization. It is in this sense that I will continue to pose history against the real of trauma.

II

> No matter how different the subjective responses, trauma is due to the intrusion
> of the raw facticity of facts that bypass any principle of pleasure or reality and
> by the *haeccitas* of loss before any loss or absence can be acknowledged.[9]

Let me distinguish the 'unrepresentability' suggested above from the sense of
the unrepresentable sometimes put forward in relation to the Holocaust
(literally, the burning), the attempted extermination of the Jewish people (as
well as other groups) in Europe by the Nazis, or the Shoah, the catastrophe,
the term used by Claude Lanzmann in his filmed record of testimony from
Jewish survivors. It is claimed that the inhumanity of the Shoah requires that
it remain outside of any human understanding. Lanzmann makes this demand
explicitly when he writes of his approach in making *Shoah* (1985), 'It is enough
to formulate the question in simplistic terms – Why have the Jews been killed?
– for the question to reveal right away its obscenity. There is an absolute
obscenity in the very project of understanding.'[10] Lanzmann implies that to
understand is to somehow accept – and thus forgive, to make ordinary and
part of everyday life – what is clearly so unacceptable. As a result Lanzmann
rejects images of the events of the Shoah, whether reconstructed and fictional,
or the photographic documents made by the Nazis, or those of the Allied
forces after the concentration camps were finally liberated. There is behind
this contemporary iconoclasm perhaps the assumption that images could fully
or sufficiently represent the 'unrepresentable', and a fear that film, by appearing
as the 'real thing', might usurp the place of the actual event. The
unrepresentability of this trauma is thus sustained by taboo; and it is represented
in the failure of representation – the inability to show or to speak it – which is
drawn forth from many of his Jewish survivor witnesses, even over and above,
or against, the palpable pain and reluctance of these witnesses. It is as if they
must remain traumatized in order for the trauma of the Shoah to remain
unrepresentable, unthinkable, and thus free from historicization, relativization,
and forgetting.

The unrepresentable of both *War Neuroses* and *Hiroshima mon amour*,
by contrast, is not the horrific event but the subjects' relation to that event.
What is presented in each film is a traumatic forgetting which thereby also
traces for the spectator a remembering of trauma-as-unrepresentable. This
unrepresentable real is unconscious but it continues to bear on the psyche
through mechanisms of return, producing very real effects – notably the
hysterical symptoms of Freud's first patients. These are also the symptoms of

the 'shell-shocked' soldiers of the First World War. Indeed the contagion – as it was often perceived – of shell-shock was a contingency threatening the war-effort of allies and enemy alike while equally undermining the theoretical premises of both traditional physiological psychology and aspects of the new psychoanalysis of the Freudians.[11] Conventional psychiatry was forced to acknowledge the unconscious, while the Freudian view of the unconscious as formed from repressed *sexual* wishes, arising, for example, from the Oedipal complex, now seemed inadequate to understand the hysterical and neurasthenic symptoms of the stricken soldiers. Freud addressed these questions by initially positing a conflict within the ego between aggressivity and self-protection which gave rise to war neuroses, but later he reorganized his view of the role of the drives and sexuality to propose his most debated and notorious concept of the death drive as an incontrovertible element of the psyche, in order to account for the compulsion to repeat unpleasure in the obsessive return to the traumatic event and for self-aggression, which characterizes traumatic neurosis.[12]

Jacques Lacan has extended the challenge to a simple division of reality versus fantasy in Freud's notion of the unconscious through his distinction between the real, the imaginary and the symbolic. None of these terms relate straightforwardly to what is commonly termed everyday reality, while it is in his concept of the 'real' that Lacan incorporates those phenomena of human suffering which Freud termed the death drive. For Lacan the apprehension of the 'real' is the encounter with the contingent, impossible element of reality which is unapprehendable as signifying, that is, it is 'senseless'.[13] The givenness of reality, and of our look which finds and possesses the world through our images, is suddenly addressed as such. In *War Neuroses* this 'real' is not the war and the death and destruction it wrought, but the *unrepresentability* of war for the subjects of the film, the 'shell-shocked' soldiers, and for the viewing subjects of the film.

War Neuroses is a medical documentary film made under the supervision of Dr A.F. Hurst (later Sir Arthur Hurst) and Dr J.L. Symms with the production company, Pathé. It shows the work in 1917 and 1918 in two British military hospitals with 'shell-shocked' soldiers displaying a variety of hysterical symptoms in response to post-traumatic stress. As a medical documentary, *War Neuroses* functions as visible evidence, portraying the men's physical symptoms within the categories of psychiatric and physical medicine of the time; the recorded images present indexically the men's symptoms which are now *medical* categories.[14] *War Neuroses* is a *spectacle* of knowledge, which reassuringly affirms for the spectator the knowability of reality. At the same time the film *novelizes*, presenting its medical categorization of the soldiers within a narrative of cure, showing the men before treatment and afterwards, now relieved of their symptoms. These images of bodily symptoms also constitute a *filmic* discourse in as much as they signify as well the disturbed and disrupted minds of the soldiers; the film's discourse is therefore fully symbolic, both as scientific knowledge, and in its images of the grotesque contortions produced on the bodies of the soldiers which metaphorically stand in as an image of the injury wrought on the human mind. As such the images signify an unrepresented which is also unrepresentable, namely the absent trauma of war.

The 'real' of *War Neuroses* is encountered not in the film as represented, however, but as representing, that is, in so far as it is a process in the subject-spectator. Central to this becoming-process is the film's coda, in which the newly-cured men enact themselves as soldiers moving out of trenches to attack the enemy under shellfire. They thus replay the scene of trauma that had caused their bodies to act outside of their conscious knowledge and control – producing their hysterical symptoms. In the context of the discourse of psychiatry in the film, this re-enactment signals the successful abreaction of the men's symptoms of trauma. The battle replayed is consciously acted for the camera,[15] but whereas earlier the horror of their war experiences was signified – albeit by displacement – in the hysterical symptoms the men displayed, it is now repressed in their performance of *successful* soldiering. The place of the unconscious is figured by this repression, it is made absent, just as it was absent in the medical account of their bodily symptoms. The battle performed is also an *enactment* of their cure, that is, the men also act or play 'cured', so that we can discern here the repetition, replaying and representing of the subject's relation to trauma, that is, to the 'real'.[16] Thus precisely because it is *fictionally* enacted, the *reality* of war is given representation. At the same time, while the 'real' of trauma remains absent, it is figured in the picturing of cure which is the mimetic double of the source of the disorder – the battle. Two knowledges jostle side-by-side; the *before* of the men's traumatization through war that is represented *after* as cured in the enacted battle. This acted battle now successfully endured produces an oscillation between two realities for the cure never fully displaces its cause – the war – which itself is used to signify the cure. Thus, too, the 'after' of symbolization (cure) never fully displaces the 'before' of the 'real'. War is here not only a documentary reality but it also functions metaphorically to figure the scene of a psychological encounter for the men – it is a metaphor of the trauma of the 'real'. This *mock* battle serves terrifyingly well, therefore, to demonstrate the relation of the real and the symbolic whereby the 'before' of the 'real' is the *effect* and not the cause of the 'after' of symbolization, namely war as a product of the civilized democracies of Europe.

In *War Neuroses* we encounter two modes of remembering: the 'hysterical' symptoms of the shell-shocked men; and their enacting of a battle in which they perform the gestures and movements which, we may infer, they had earlier carried out on the real battlefields and trenches of Flanders and northern France. As such the re-enactment constitutes an extraordinary *document* of remembering by the formerly shell-shocked infantrymen, for in it they are not only remembering their earlier soldiering – a conscious remembering – they are also figuring for the spectator a 'remembering' of the scene of their trauma but of which, like their hysterical symptoms, they remain unconscious.

III

Hiroshima mon amour is similarly a document of remembering through filmed actuality and fiction in which the film's remembered is both personal history and public history. History is the past brought back before us through some form of argument, presented in a statement. History depends on facts or events in the past, but the meaning of these arises not inherently but through the historian's arguments which constitute the past as history, namely the causes and effects of past events. 'Hiroshima' names an historical event, not because of the numbers of people who died there from allied bombing, but because they died as a result of the first use of a new weapon – the atomic bomb. History always thus betrays the past, it is always partial. Film, as an indexical trace of reality, appears to give us the past in the present, denying time and overcoming death. Filmed actuality is thus always a 'remembering' of the past. To become (hi)story, however, it must be narrated, given a logic of cause and effect, in sum, it must become meaning(ful). It must change, that is, from the 'flashback' – in the sense used for the mental flashbacks experienced by trauma victims – to the flashback of classical cinema (on which the former sense is based), firmly secured within a film's causal narrative structure.

Memory is central to perception, and our understanding of the world arises not so much from what we see, optically, but from what is recognized – as like or unlike what we have seen and known from the past. Memory enables recognition at both a conscious and non-conscious or 'automatic' level and, as such, it is also central to cinema, not only for recognizing objects and actions, characters and locations, but also in understanding the combination of sounds and images as sequences, whether narrative or non-narrative – that is, of editing or montage in film. Film thus engages the viewer in a process of memory but it does so as a present-tense narration; insofar as film *shows* rather than *tells* it does so as an ongoing present which unfolds before our eyes. History itself is a form of memory, of remembering, which is a knowing of the past in the present. It is a cultural 'memory' handed down to us and evoked in the exhortation to remember. What we are asked to remember is a knowledge – which we might call an historical account or a myth – namely, 'here our nation was at its lowest ebb/triumphed'. Such remembering is not a call upon our personal experience. There is a gap between remembering one's own past and remembering a public past, a learned history, and both of these are distinct from memory as affect. If memory is thus also a feeling, is it caused by or does it cause the remembering of the words, images, or meanings also remembered? An emotion, of wishfulness or of loss surrounding an event might lead to something – an image or phrase or person – being remembered. The image remembered (but perhaps not the affect) subsequently points to the affect, but it is not the 'truth' of the affect, it does not have an indexical relation to the affect, as the photograph has to the object which it records. Thus knowing the image, or the event, cannot 'explain' the emotional response. For Freud, psychoanalysis is not concerned with uncovering the truth of memories – or of dreams – as a meaning to be decoded, rather it is concerned with the meaning of the processes of remembering, and of what brings one to remember something incompletely and thus to remember something as forgotten. To remember is to bring back to the present something of the past, but it is also to remember the pastness of the event and the meanings – and emotions – related to its pastness. Through *Nachträglichkeit*, the meaning of the past is continually remade in the present of remembering. Traumatic remembering, however, is an oxymoron, and when Freud says that 'hysterics suffer mainly from reminiscences', he means by this a remembering which is unconscious; the body 'speaks' trauma where the mind cannot.[17] Trauma is not a remembering but a return of the past as unremembered, a repetition. *Hiroshima mon amour* is not only about remembering, it is also about forgetting – without which memory itself would not be possible – such that I want to say it presents two kinds of memory and forgetting – the traumatic and the memorializing or mourning.

Hiroshima mon amour presents both a contamination of trauma and sexuality, and a positing of trauma as an issue of the unrepresentable. At the same time the film is, I will suggest, a work of transformation through translation, the translation of trauma into tale, of the memorialized unrepresentable spoken as forgotten. In this the spectator, as well as the film's two central characters, are implicated.[18] *Hiroshima mon amour* presents us with two past, *traumatic,* events, both of which are narrated by a Frenchwoman to her Japanese lover (the characters, unnamed in the film, are played by Emmanuelle Riva and Eiji Okada), one of which is fictional, while the other is a real historical event, namely, the atomic bombing of Hiroshima. The fictional trauma is the Frenchwoman's story of the shooting and death of her wartime lover, a young German soldier, on the day her hometown of Nevers is liberated by the allies. Her story of Hiroshima comes first, however, at the beginning of the film. Her Japanese lover says 'You saw nothing in Hiroshima. Nothing', to which she replies 'I saw everything, everything. I saw the hospital, for instance ....'[19] Her words are heard over images, on the one hand of the two lovers, naked, embracing, and on the other hand images – a documentary film – whose reality confirms the truth of her words. This visual record involves remnants which attest to the force and destruction of the bombing – twisted iron girders, which she describes as 'iron become vulnerable as flesh', burnt bricks and stones, or the shards of flesh preserved in bottles. It also involves *records* – photographs, statements of witnesses and victims, and statistics, of the heat created by the fireball, of the number and kinds of injuries and causes of death, as well as revealing the startling regeneration in nature as flowers of all kinds spring up in the ground between the crushed buildings and shattered lives of Hiroshima's remaining citizens. She describes, as well, the 'reconstructions, since there is nothing else ... descriptions, since there is nothing else ...' and that 'the illusion, quite simply, is so perfect ... that tourists weep ....People may be scornful ... But what can a tourist do, other than weep?' What is at stake for these reconstructions, these mementos, is how to remember Hiroshima. The name of the city now stands not only for the horror of atomic annihilation, that is, death, but also the horror of a living death to which the survivors are condemned: the horror of the traces of the bomb which continue not only as the wounds and physical traumas of the immediate bombing and its resultant fireball, but also as the silent and unseen effects of the radiation fall-out, traced in the emerging sicknesses, cancers, malformed foetuses aborted, and the deformed children conceived or born after the bombing.

The film presents two love affairs, one in the past, the other in the present. The passionate encounter of the Frenchwoman and her Japanese lover which occurs in the present-time of the film is immediately haunted by impending loss – for after their lovemaking she tells him that she is flying home to France the next morning, following the completion of work in the French movie she is making and which is the reason she came to Hiroshima. He asks her to stay, but she refuses. Later that day he goes to find her at the film location and they leave together, but are caught in a parade demonstrating against the testing of nuclear weapons. Making their escape, they arrive at his home (his wife, he says, is away) where they make love again. The second love affair narrated, which in chronological time is really the first, is the story she then tells her Japanese lover of her earlier, lost love, the German soldier shot as he waited to leave Nevers with her. Both the trauma of Hiroshima and of Nevers are recounted by the Frenchwoman but *shown* to the film's audience, functioning as flashbacks. While the cinematic flashback signals a past time, what is shown is in the present tense, and the events shown, although motivated as the subjective knowledge or memory of a character, are rarely shown through subjective camera, that is, through the optical point-of-view of the character. Instead the character remembering is also shown within the scene (the camera's look is therefore 'objective'), thus she is split, she is the object of the visual narration in the past while she is the subject of her story spoken over the images in the film's present-time.[20]

In each of her narrations the Japanese man acts as an interlocutor, but whereas he denies her discourse on Hiroshima, he takes up a position within her story of Nevers as her dead German lover. How should we understand his denial? And how should we understand his identification? Nevers is a spoken personal trauma for her, while Hiroshima is presented as a 'public' trauma – a portrayed horror, though it is also the man's trauma for while he was absent from the city, fighting, his family were there. He, however, is never the subject of this trauma. What is the relation of Nevers and Hiroshima? Shockingly, it is death and desire. The film begins its contamination of the traumatic and the erotic in the opening shots of the film which shows two intertwined and naked bodies. At first, the bodies are seen becoming drenched in a fine sand which accumulates in the crevices of their bodies; the image then dissolves to show the bodies oiled and gleaming; after another dissolve the bodies appear glistening with beads of sweat. The images suggest both the passage of time through the dissolves and an accompanying state of transformation in the bodies. A third dissolve reveals the bodies from a new angle, matt and unadorned. Their embracing now becomes the present-time diegetic image, alternating with the documentary shots which accompany her story of Hiroshima's bombing and which might at first be read as flashbacks from her point of view.[21] She says she has invented nothing, but he counters her claim saying she has invented everything. She replies, saying again, 'Nothing.' The Japanese man's denials are a rhetorical device by which we are challenged to think about her claims, and how possible it is to know catastrophe, trauma.

She continues 'Just as love has its illusions … The illusion that you will never be able to forget … so I had the illusion, faced with Hiroshima, that I will never forget … Listen to me, like you I know what it is to forget', to which he replies, 'No, you don't know what it is to forget.' Over the exterior of a gift shot she continues, 'Like you, I am endowed with memory. I know what it is to forget.' He says, 'No. You are not endowed with memory.' She continues, as we see tourists around a stone monument, 'like you I have fought with all my might against forgetfulness. Like you, I wanted an inconsolable memory, a memory of stone and shadow.' There is a series of shots of a tourist bus seen going around the sites of the city as she says, 'Each day I fought with all my might against the horror … of no longer knowing … the reason for remembering … like you, I have forgotten.' 'Why deny the obvious necessity for memory?' The problem of knowledge and memory are thus explicitly posed by the film. Its answer is to institute a certain mode of forgetting.

After describing how another Hiroshima will happen, her voice-over changes tone as she begins to describe Hiroshima, its estuary, its tides. The camera cuts from their bodies to a car travelling through the city she is describing and she says 'I meet you. I remember you. Who are you? You are killing me. You are good for me. How could I have known that this town was made for love?' Imbricating Hiroshima's story with her erotic passion she says, 'What sweetness. You cannot possibly understand. You are killing me. You are good for me ….' She repeats these words again, then says, 'I have the time. I beg you please … consume me, make me hideous.' What should we make of her words here? Where before the images gave support to her claims, despite his denials, now there is merely more views of the city. No doubt we do not take her words literally, but rather as signs of her desire, her ecstatic pleasure, yet, spoken so soon after the images of other killings, other – mutilated – bodies made hideous, are we not shocked by this juxtaposition? And can Duras and Resnais really want us to accept as somehow interchangeable, as comparable, the two traumas: the horror of Hiroshima and the Frenchwoman's murdered lover? On the one hand, the second trauma is a story of young lovers and their secret meetings, on the other hand the lover is an enemy, a German soldier and part of an occupying force which had sent thousands of French people to Germany as slave-workers. Duras clearly intended that the love affair be tainted by impropriety, marked as transgressive if not traitorous, for in her original text the girl's mother was described as Jewish and herself in hiding from the Nazis and their French collaborators.[22]

It is not, however, as simple analogy that I think Duras and Resnais are posing the conjunction of death and desire.[23] The trauma of the Frenchwoman in Nevers is not that of the mutilated victims of Hiroshima, that is, it does not have the historical status of Hiroshima; nor is she the subject of the physical infraction, instead her trauma is loss, it is the abrupt cessation of all that she imagined and hoped for her future, and cessation of all that she enjoyed in their love. But none of these are necessarily traumatic. If her trauma is not supported by any conventional verisimilitude, we must suppose it arises in some other way. And indeed this is what psychoanalysis has urged us to understand, namely that it is not the event as shock which produces trauma but something in the way the subject knows this shock. The belatedness of trauma here concerns not the event but the 'understanding' of the event, that is, the unconscious apprehension of the shock which sets in train processes of detranslation and retranslation of earlier enigmatic, and thus traumatic, messages. The trauma of the love story of Nevers involves not only loss, but loss as punishment for transgressive desire, and insofar as desire is necessarily transgressive, this losing is a punishment of desire. The trauma is not, then, the loss of her German soldier-lover but the intrusion of an arbitrary power which denies *jouissance* to her. By the narration of her trauma the French-woman – and her Japanese lover as interlocutor, and ourselves as spectators – become engaged in a process of traumatic remembering and forgetting.

The film imbricates a public history and a private memory, so that our relationship to the one becomes our relationship to the other. And the remembering, and forgetting, of that death in Nevers by her is made equivalent to or parallel to the work of remembering, and forgetting, which we are asked to undertake by the film in relation to Hiroshima's traumatic deaths. Marie-Claire Ropas-Wuilleumier has described the film as staging the gap between seeing and knowing. Seeing exhausts itself in the process of self-affirmation, of this, and this, and this.[24] Knowing translates the seen into a reading, an understanding, which deciphers the trace, the real, into a written, into a spoken and a stated, and thereby obliterates the trace as trace. For the Frenchwoman, remembering her German lover becomes a forgetting, a losing of him in forgetting the searing physical yearning and pain of loss she felt. In this second, Japanese, 'impossible' (she will leave tomorrow) love affair she 'remembers' the first, it is doubled and therefore it loses its singularity, its uniqueness. But for her Japanese lover, too, as well as for the spectator, the film narrates a love as impossibly lost. At the end of the film, memorially, he is Hiroshima, and she is Nevers. Ropars-Wuilleumier writes

> The film obliges us to acknowledge the mechanisms of an exchange in which we participate. In making the spectators take on, within the filmic perception,

the burden of the transference and the modulation of remembrance-oblivion, *Hiroshima mon amour* demands that we realize, in every meaning of the word, the ambiguity of a historicization which the textual mediation renders necessarily indirect and thus uncertain. Unless it is inscribed in bodies, History leads to the museum; the trace is at once an aid to readability and a sign of the unfamiliar; and if the reading still remains to be done, the writing-reading reminds us, by its surplus and its overflowing, of the loss of substance that the acquisition of meaning costs.[25]

It is the thing-in-itself of the memory/event as trauma, as affect, which the love affair represents, and it is this thing-in-itself which is the memory we can never have of Hiroshima, or of Auschwitz. Its very representation in 'history' effaces it as memory, becoming knowledge not affect. To remember trauma we make a detour through a woman's loss so that we arrive at memory as affect only to – with her, as well as with her Japanese lover – lose this too. What had been trauma is now forgotten and therefore can now be remembered.

Notes

1   Max Hernandez, 'Winnicott's "Fear of Breakdown": On and beyond Trauma', *Diacritics* 28:4 (Winter 1998), p. 139. Hernandez is referring here to the work of Alvin Frank in 'The Unrememberable and the Unforgettable: Passive Primal Repression', *The Psychoanalytic Study of the Child* 24 (1969), pp. 48–77.
2   The discussion here draws upon my more extended consideration of this film and the documentary real in 'The Spectacle of Actuality' in Jane M. Gaines and Michael Renov (eds), *Collecting Visible Evidence* (Minneapolis: University of Minnesota Press, 1999).
3   Cathy Caruth, *Unclaimed Experience: Trauma, Narrative, and History* (Baltimore: Johns Hopkins University Press, 1996), p. 6. Caruth does, however, write of trauma as 'experiences not yet completely grasped' (ibid., p. 56).
4   Ibid, p. 6.
5   Instead of time as something measured in units (hours, minutes and seconds), as a progression moment by moment in which the past falls irrevocably away from the newly-made present in the next and the next and the next, Henri Bergson proposed *duration*. This is time experienced by consciousness; duration is continuous, like a melody in music in which the elements are blended and experienced as a whole rather than heard as just notes. Time, however, is the division of duration into perceptible moments, it is a calibration of duration. Past, present and future are neither radically disjunct nor a continuum; rather each is made and re-made through the present experience of duration. This is undertaken through memory, recollection. Such a notion of time is important in Resnais's work, and is of course central to Gilles Deleuze's discussion of Resnais's film in *Cinema 2, The Time-Image*, trans. Hugh Tomlinson and Robert Galeta (Minneapolis: University of Minnesota Press, 1989), pp. 116–25.

6 Caruth, *Unclaimed Experience*, p. 7.

7 Jean Laplanche, 'Notes on Afterwardsness', in *Essays on Otherness*, ed. John Fletcher (London: Routledge, 1999), p. 265. See also Jean Laplanche in John Fletcher and Martin Stanton (eds), *Jean Laplanche: Seduction, Translation and the Drives* (London: ICA, 1992) and Andrew Benjamin's illuminating essay in that volume, 'The Unconscious: Structuring as a Translation', pp. 137–57.

8 Laplanche argues that his theory of seduction 'affirms the priority of the other in the constitution of the human being and of its sexuality. Not the Lacanian Other, but the concrete other: the adult facing the child. A perverse adult? Yes, one must say; but intrinisically perverse because his [or her] messages are "compromised" by his own unconscious', 'Masochism and the General Theory of Seduction', in *Essays on Otherness*, p. 212.

9 Hernandez, p. 140.

10 Caruth (, *Unclaimed Experience*, pp. 123–4) cites Lanzmann as saying, 'Not to understand was my iron law during all the eleven years of the production of *Shoah*. I had clung to this refusal of understanding as the only possible ethical, and at the same time the only possible operative, attitude' (quoted from Bernard Cuau et al., *Au sujet de Shoah: Le film de Claude Lanzmann* [Paris: Belin, 1990]).

  Miriam Bratu Hansen ('*Schindler's List* Is Not *Shoah*: The Second Commandment, Popular Modernism, and Public Memory', *Critical Inquiry* 22 (Winter 1996), p. 301), discussing the issue of *Schindler's List* (Spielberg, 1993), and its violation of the taboo on representation in its attempt to give an 'image of the unimaginable', cites Lanzmann's accusation that film fails to respect the unique and absolute status of the Holocaust, 'unique in that it erects a ring of fire around itself, a borderline that cannot be crossed because there is a certain ultimate degree of horror that cannot be transmitted. To claim it is possible to do so is to be guilty of the most serius transgression.' Lanzmann was writing in *The Guardian Weekly*, 9 April 1994, p. 14.

11 Martin Stone, ('Shellshock and the Psychologists', in W.F. Bynum, Roy Porter and Michael Shepherd (eds), *The Anatomy of Madness: Essays in the history of psychiatry* [Cambridge: Cambridge University Press, 1985], pp. 242–71) has argued that this arose as the result of an article by the psychologist and anthropologist, W.H. Rivers, 'Freud's Psychology of the Unconscious', which appeared in the *Lancet*, the main British journal of medicine, in 1917.

12 Sigmund Freud, *Beyond the Pleasure Principle* (1920) in *The Standard Edition of the Complete Works of Sigmund Freud*, vol. XVIII (London: The Hogarth Press, 1955), pp. 3–84. See in particular pp. 14–17, Freud's discussion of the *fort-da* game he observed his small grandson playing through which the child replayed the loss and return of his mother, represented by the cotton reel thrown away, *fort* and retrieved, *da*. He observes that the child's attention was focussed especially on the mother-gone, rather than her return to him.

13 Jacques Lacan, *The Four Fundamental Concepts of Psycho-Analysis* (Harmondsworth: Penguin Books, 1977), p. 53. Lacan notes that the real 'first presented itself in the history of psycho-analysis in a form that was in itself already enough to arouse our attention, that of the trauma' (p. 54).

14 *War Neuroses* continues to be used as visual evidence within medical teaching.

15 A contemporary account of the film claims that the re-enactment was at the men's suggestion.

16 Hal Foster in his discussion of repetition in Andy Warhol's works (*The Return of the Real* [Cambridge, Mass.: MIT Press, 1996], p. 132) describes the paradoxical role of the real: 'Somehow in these repetitions, then, several contradictory things occur at the same time: a warding away of traumatic significance *and* an opening out to it, a defending against traumatic affect *and* a producing of it.'

17 Freud, *Beyond the Pleasure Principle*, p. 13.

18 Or entangled, a term used by Cathy Caruth. See on this, Petar Ramadonovic, 'When "To die in freedom" is written in English', *Diacritics* 28:4 (Winter 1998), pp. 54–67.

19 The dialogue here is the translation used in the film's subtitles in the vhs video version available in Britain. Duras's script has been published in French, *Hiroshima mon amour* (Paris: Gallimard, 1960); and in English, Marguerite Duras and Alain Resnais, *Hiroshima mon amour*, trans. Richard Seaver (New York: Grove Press, 1961).

20 The term 'flashback' came to be used to describe sequences showing events which we are asked to understand as past, as distinct from imagined events or the present-time of the film. Flashbacks, by giving story information out of chronological order, typically disorder the story events. *Hiroshima mon amour* uses just such an 'objective' camera in the flashback that shows the Frenchwoman, as young girl in Nevers, running down steps to join her lover, she is looking frame left, horrified, and in the next shot, we see what she sees, namely her lover dying, but then the camera pans quickly to the balcony of a house overlooking the river embankment from which the fatal shot might have come. With the pan the shot ceases to be her look. The flashbacks are not in Duras's original text but were discussed extensively by Duras and Resnais. Maureen Turim discusses the history of the cinematic flashback and its use in *Hiroshima mon amour* in *Flashbacks in Film* (London: Routledge, 1989).

21 The first shots appear to be subjective camera, travelling down a hospital corridor, then turning into a ward where the injured patients initially stare at the camera, but then look away as if rejecting the camera's observation, or, perhaps, her tourist's look.

22 In the film the spectator is alerted to this fact much earlier than in the script, in a flashback to his death where we can see that he is wearing the uniform of a German soldier. This flashback is like the mental flashback of war neurosis and post-traumatic stress in that it is a single shot, and the shot-reverse-shot of her looking and a shot of her Japanese lover's hand moving as he sleeps suggests that this motivates the cut to a close-up of another man's hand, but the camera's rapid pan across him which reveals his German uniform, rests briefly to show a woman in a floral cotton dress – the Frenchwoman as the young girl she once was, lying across him, holding his bleeding head – implies a look which in seeing her as well as what she sees is not restricted to her view.

23 Duras and Resnais, in allying desire and trauma, are also returning to Freud's privileging of sexuality in the understanding of psychical trauma, a relation which had been challenged by the cases of the war neuroses in the First World War.

24 Marie-Claire Ropars-Wuilleumier, 'How History Begets Meaning: Alain Resnais' *Hiroshima mon amour* (1959)', in Susan Hayward and Ginette Vincendeau (eds), *French Film: Texts and contexts* (London: Routledge, 1990), p. 183.

25 Ropars-Wuilleumier, p. 182.

12 Aftermath: Pastiche, the Postmodern and the End of History in Angela Carter's *Nights at the Circus*

RACHEL CARROLL

Fredric Jameson has written that 'postmodernism' is the name given to an era which has witnessed the 'disappearance of a sense of history'.[1] The ubiquity of pastiche in postmodern culture is, he argues, 'an alarming and pathological symptom of a society incapable of dealing with time and history':[2] a society suffering from 'historical amnesia'.[3] A postmodern text such as Angela Carter's *fin de siècle* fantasy *Nights at the Circus* – which self-consciously evokes the textuality of history through historical and literary pastiche – is undoubtedly vulnerable to the Jamesonian charge of reducing history to a travesty of parodic gestures and costumes and evading a more complex and ethical encounter with the otherness of the past. Jameson remarks upon the 'flat', 'blank' or 'depthless' quality of pastiche; indeed, the self-referential nature of pastiche renders it peculiarly resistant to critical analysis. It is notable that the most credible and influential critical approach to pastiche – as historiographic metafiction[4] – is itself a metacritical discourse; it would seem that the self-conscious remove from history which pastiche enacts is self-perpetuating. However, pastiche does have dimensions, dimensions which its 'flat', 'blank' and 'depthless' effects conceal: principally, it has a distinctively temporal dimension of return and repetition. The temporal dimension of postmodern pastiche is addressed by Hal Foster in his study of neo-avant-garde art, *The Return of the Real*; Foster opens this temporal dimension by employing a Lacanian psychoanalytical model. Foster suggests that the modernist shock of the new could be understood as a missed encounter with the real:[5] it is only in its traumatized repetition that the encounter is registered. Hence, Foster, in a bold application of the Lacanian concept of trauma to the history of modern art in the twentieth century, proposes that 'if the historical avant garde was *repressed* institutionally, it was *repeated* in the first neo-avant-garde rather than, in the Freudian distinction, *recollected*, its contradictions worked through'.[6] Postmodern recoveries and returns, then, might be understood as a form of deferred action: 'rather than break with the fundamental practises and discourses of modernity, the signal practises and discourses of postmodernity have advanced in a *nachträglich* relation to them'.[7] The preoccupation with the past, and its parodic repetition, which is evident in much postmodern fiction could easily be read as a symptom of the pathological nostalgia which Jameson finds throughout postmodern culture. However, I intend to read a postmodern fiction, Angela Carter's *Nights at the Circus*, with Foster's understanding of pastiche in mind: that is, to attempt to disclose the complex temporality of return and repetition in order to break open the impasse in which much modern/postmodern debate seems suspended.

'Not all people exist in the same Now'[8]

> The very idea of modernity is closely correlated with the principle that it is both possible and necessary to break with tradition and institute absolutely new ways of living and thinking.
>   We now suspect that this 'rupture' is in fact a way of forgetting or repressing the past, that is, repeating and not surpassing it.[9]

Whilst for Jameson it is postmodern culture which is culpable of 'historical amnesia,' for Lyotard it is modernity which is founded on repressions. The unacknowledged 'forgetting' and 'repressing' of these origins by modernity is the condition for their later discovery; as Susan Buck-Morss has suggested 'it is no accident that early modernity feels an affinity for the primitive and the archaic'.[10] Angela Carter's *Nights at the Circus*, set at 'the cusp of the modern age, the hinge of the nineteenth century',[11] emphatically anticipates the new century as an era of radical change and revolution. As the momentum of the narrative gathers pace, its trajectory finds fitting expression as the circus boards the Trans Siberian Express; the railway's 'annihilation of time and space'[12] becoming identified with the inauguration of a new calendar. However, simultaneous to this break or rupture with the past in Carter's text is a recurrent motion of return: the 'prehistory' of the modern is 'discovered' – and discovered to be constructed by the discourses of modernism – in motifs of nature, animals, childhood, sexual difference, pre-industrial cultures and the colonial 'others' of empire. The catastrophic train crash which the travelling circus suffers is the culmination of this dynamic of return; the circus, and the narrative, are plunged into the wilderness of Siberia, a space in which Western history and time have no meaning.

By returning its passengers to a state of origin, the locomotive heralds uncanny encounters between the archaic and modern, the primitive and the technologically advanced. Wolfgang Schivelbusch illustrates the 'disorientation experienced by the traditional space-time consciousness when confronted by the new technology'[13] by quoting Heinrich Heine: 'I feel as if the mountains and forests of all countries were advancing on Paris. Even now, I can smell the German linden trees; the North Sea's breakers are rolling against my door.'[14] The sense that the locomotive travels a liminal threshold between organic nature and industrial culture is expressed in *Nights at the Circus* when Fevvers – herself a monstrous hybrid thrown up by an age of revolutions – comments on the incongruity of travelling through a 'pre-Adamite world' in the splendour of an 'Empire drawing room':[15] she views the barren landscape through a frame of tassels and brocade. Schivelbusch's insight into the assumption by modern innovations of disguising facades seems pertinent here. Accounting for the excessive upholstery of the railway interior, he suggests that it reveals a function other than that of comfort: its function is to camouflage the industrial origins of bourgeois wealth and privilege. Moreover, it is designed to conceal from the passenger his absorption into the circulation of goods. As Schivelbusch writes:

> the jolt to be softened is no longer physical but mental: the memory of the industrial origin of objects, from railway stations or exhibition halls constructed out of steel, to chairs constructed out of wood. The opulent baroque and Renaissance fronts that cover the steel girders are nothing but, on a larger scale, the braided and tasseled upholstery cushions that render the true construction of the armchair or sofa invisible and thus forgettable.[16]

The railway, then, is a symbol of transition between 'old' and 'new' nature. Moreover, it is an agent of the crisis of subjectivity which modernity inaugurates; it initiates the human body into the modern era by its revolutionary technological achievement – the 'annihilation of time and space'.[17] The bourgeois interior of the carriage conspires with the apparently effortless passage of the locomotive to assure the traveller that s/he has not left home. However, the hurtling pace with which the engine thrusts its cargo into other times and places attests to the violence immanent in the explosive charges of modernity.[18] The force latent in this 'annihilation' reveals its power in the train crash in *Nights at the Circus*, which shatters identity as well as time and space.

Clinical theories of shock originated in the nineteenth century with accounts of the delayed symptoms suffered by survivors of railway accidents; Freud himself employed such a collision to illustrate his theory of latency in *Moses and Monotheism*.[19] Hal Foster has remarked upon the significance of this surprising encounter between the origins of industrial technology and the origins of psychoanalytic theory:

> The discourse of shock was developed in the nineteenth century partly in relation to railway accidents, the traumatic effects of which were regarded first physiologically, then psychologically, and finally psychoanalytically. In short, shock is an alternate route to the unconscious, the discovery of which is so often traced first to hysteria, then to dreams.[20]

To read the railway as the alternate 'royal road' to the unconscious is to begin to comprehend its significance in Carter's narrative: it is a route to other worlds of consciousness, both subjective and historical.[21]

Homesickness for the Future

> History is no entity advancing along a single line, in which capitalism for instance, as the final stage, has resolved all the previous ones; but it is a polyrhythmic and multi-spatial entity, with enough unmastered and as yet no means revealed and resolved corners.[22]

The transforming magic inflicted on 'authentic history'[23] in Carter's narrative amounts to the conjuring of these polyrthymic and multispatial dimensions as if from the unconscious. When the circus is plunged into the Siberian wilderness it initially appears that a millennial vision of the future has been substituted by the inescapability of origin; uneasily, the narrative regresses, succumbing to the dead time of the state of nature, as if disillusion with the progress of history has borne a nihilistic primitivism. However, the backwards glance which arrests the novel – suspending time and transfixing the 'locomotive of history'[24] – might be interpreted as the culmination of a keening homesickness, most poignantly expressed in Mignon's rendition of Schubert's 'Kennst Du Das Land',[25] which pervades the novel. This is not a homesickness which pines for the restitution of an idyllic state comparable to childhood. Indeed, in *Nights at the Circus*, childhood is a perilous state afflicted by neglect and abuse: Fevvers's youth is marked by abandonment and abduction; both Mignon and Ivan witness parental violence and murder; Mignon suffers destitution and exploitation by Herr M; the circus stable boy flees persecution for his sexual identity only to be murdered by the Strong Man. There are no homes in *Nights at the Circus*, as its world is one of dispossession. The dreaming of 'elsewheres' does not convey a fatalistic melancholy so much as a radical yearning for the future: it is a nostalgia for a utopian future anticipated but not yet comprehended. The state signified by 'home' occupies a powerful place in utopian thinking: it is 'the house in which one would be at home, inside, no longer estranged'.[26] Adorno is describing its significance in the philosophy of Ernst Bloch, who transforms a subjective affect into a vehicle of materialist enlightenment:

> Once man has comprehended himself and has established his own domain in real democracy, without depersonalisation and alienation, something arises in the world which all men have glimpsed in childhood: a place and a state in which no one has yet been. And the name of this something is home ...[27]

The backwards glance, in this account of utopian thought and in the narrative of *Nights at the Circus*, is a safeguard against forgetfulness. It prepares the way for the future by confronting the contradictions of the past. As Susan Buck-Morss writes:

> A construction of history that looks backward, rather than forward, at the destruction of material nature as it *has actually taken place*, provides dialectical contrast to the futurist myth of historical progress (which can only be sustained by forgetting what happened).[28]

Bloch's 'home' is both familiar and unknown; familiar to the utopian yearnings of humanity throughout time, but unknown as it has yet to be made a reality.[29]

A concept of history which emphasizes the recovery of the past, the persistence of memory, and the importance of remembering, has an affinity with the project of psychoanalytic thought. Commenting on this analogy, Maud Ellmann notes the pervasive 'prohibition of the backward glance' in the classical mythology to which Freud's writing is so indebted: 'Lot's wife turns into a pillar of salt when she looks back at her homeland left behind; Orpheus is permitted to conduct Eurydice out of the underworld only under the condition that he does not look back at her.'[30] The revolution effected by psychoanalysis is to defy this prohibition: a return to the past is ventured which braves the risk of blinding and dismemberment. Ellmann writes that it is in the '*process of discovery rather than the crimes revealed*'[31] that the power of psychoanalysis resides: 'its terror lies in the interpretative activity itself, the sheer audacity of looking back into the past and rediscovering the violence of childhood'.[32]

As the narrative leaves London, Walser adopts the tone of a dilettantish host – 'let me invite you to spend a few nights at the circus'[33] – presiding over an evening of light diversion; indeed, a panoramic procession of scenes from the past are summoned as if projected by a magic lantern.[34] However, the catastrophe of the railway crash explodes any sense of complacent spectatorship. Moreover, it is the culmination of glimpses of horror on which the course of the narrative has already stalled. Incidental to the picaresque progress of the novel are a sequence of scenes of women's oppression. These tableaux represent images of women frozen in postures of subjection. Fevvers boards the train to escape assimilation into the Archduke's collection of automata; the train is identical to the miniature model revealed in the final Fabergé-style egg.[35] The vestal hearth of Ma Nelson's rational brothel, with its 'brace of buxom, smiling goddesses',[36] is succeeded by the crypt and 'black theatre'[37] of Madame Schreck's 'museum of woman monsters',[38] who stand in 'profane altars',[39] by Rosencreutz's Gothic mansion in which Fevvers's symbolism renders her expendable, by the alcove in which Mignon 'impersonate[s] the dead'[40] and by the cells 'lit up like so many small theatres'[41] in the women's asylum. The staging and banishing of these dramas might be modelled upon the outline of revolutionary historical progress articulated in Marx's 'Eighteenth Brumaire of Louis Bonaparte'. Marx famously asserts that the 'tradition of all the dead generations weighs like a nightmare on the brain of the living;'[42] he implies that in order to achieve a revolution which is genuinely radical, the ghosts of past oppression must be exorcized – it is to this end that the past is revisited in Carter's narrative. *Nights at the Circus* is certainly haunted by history, though some of its ghosts are not yet dead and one significant spectre about to be born.[43]

At the turn of the twentieth century, the rapid and escalating pace of modernity consigns even the recent past – that of the preceding generation – to historical redundancy. For Walter Benjamin, the peculiar enchantment of outmoded forms in the disenchanted modern world attest to the haunting power of the past and the radical potential of the irrational.[44] Benjamin attributes the discovery of the category of the outmoded to André Breton and the Surrealists, who enlisted both Freud and Marx to their *avant garde* project. The Surrealists returned with wonder to the lost world of their childhood. This return echoes throughout Carter's narrative, which is itself set within the metamorphic transition of the nineteenth century into the modern era – that is, the mythical world of the Surrealists' childhood.[45] Benjamin writes:

[Breton] was the first to perceive the revolutionary energies that appear in the 'outmoded', in the first iron constructions, the first factory buildings, the earliest photos, the objects that have begun to be extinct ... No one before these visionaries and augurs perceived how destitution – not only social but architectonic, the poverty of interiors, enslaved and enslaving objects – can be suddenly transformed into revolutionary nihilism.[46]

These are the interiors of Fevvers's youth, past but not dead; they still cast such a baleful spell that to return to them, even in memory, is to undergo a harrowing of the past. The compressed force of history lies revealed in the 'outmoded': in the outmoded is revealed modernity's capacity to throw up revolutions in form and to consign them swiftly to extinction.

Benjamin's 'One-Way Street' tours the densely claustrophobic bourgeois home by nauseous gaslight. The apprehension of ill-concealed secrets is comparable to that evoked by the damasked, velvet interior of Ma Nelson's brothel and, moreover, the draped and bandaged facade of Madame Schreck's 'black theatre': 'What things were interred and sacrificed amid magic incantations, what horrible cabinet of curiosities lies there below, where the deepest shafts are reserved for what is most commonplace'.[47] Carter's cabinet of curiosities is the 'lumber room of femininity'[48] in which men who are pillars of the patriarchal establishment act out their authority in perverse form beneath the foundations of Victorian propriety. Benjamin's 'horror of apartments' also evokes the cruelties inflicted in *Nights at the Circus*, amid dense curtains and shadowy alcoves, by Herr M. The suffocating interiors surreptitiously extinguish life just as surely as the epidemics out of which Herr M's ghost photography profits:

> The bourgeois interior of the 1860s to the 1890s, with its gigantic sideboards distended with carvings, the sunless corners where palms stand, the balcony embattled behind its balustrade, and the long corridors with their singing gas flames, fittingly houses only the corpse.[49]

In *Nights at the Circus,* the corpse is the child-woman Mignon: made to mimic the living dead, weeping over the memory of her dead mother traced in her own portrait and beaten back into infancy by abuse.

The past is conjured in *Nights at the Circus* not to borrow its costumes but rather to dispense with them. Scenes are relived not to perpetuate their oppressive effects but to reform them; the return is made in the name of a departure. So it is in Marx's model that the imprisoning cycle of repetition must be exploded:

> The social revolution of the nineteenth century cannot draw its poetry from the past, but only from the future. It cannot begin with itself before it has stripped off all superstition in regard to the past. Earlier revolutions required recollections of past world history in order to drug themselves concerning their own content. In order to arrive at its own content, the revolution of the nineteenth century must let the dead bury their dead ... Society now seems to have fallen back behind its point of departure; it has in truth first to create for itself the revolutionary point of departure, the situation, the relations, the conditions under which alone modern revolution becomes serious.[50]

The narrative of *Nights at the Circus* falls back behind its point of departure in order to gather its forces for a revolutionary projection into the future. This point of departure is arrived at by shedding the past and by a necessary shattering of consciousness: Walser's kaleidoscopic vision is wiped clean as a slate, Fevvers's panorama fragmented. Hence, as Marx himself indicates, this model of history serves as a model for a revolution in identity:

> The reformation of consciousness only consists in letting the world enter one's consciousness, in waking up the world from the dream about itself, in explaining its own actions to itself ... Then it can be shown that it does not concern a large hyphen between past and future but the completion of the idea of the past.[51]

This 'completion of the idea of the past' is a function which Bloch attributes to the utopian impulse and its 'anticipatory illumination' of the future in the past. As Christopher Norris has written of Bloch's philosophy, it detects the '"not yet" or token of unredeemed promise ... in every manifestation of past and present culture'.[52] Carter's purpose in returning to scenes of the past is to plunder it of its subversive content as it is concealed in the archaic or outmoded.[53] Her narrative returns to the past not only to exorcize its horrors but also to appropriate its utopian anticipations of the future.

The 'spiralling tornado' of laughter with which the narrative ends gathers together in its progress the moments of ecstasy, vertigo or disorientation in which time is suspended: the storm which blows the clowns 'off the face of the earth'; the 'breath of stale night air' which 'ripple[s]' the seats and 'stroke[s]' the cherubs at the theatre as Fevvers limbers up for flight; the 'wind of wonder' of the audience's awe; the beating of Fevvers's wings which 'ruffle' Walser's notes; the 'sharp gusts' of scent and powder in Fevvers's dressing-room as she slams home a point of her narrative; the swish of Fevvers's eyelashes which disturbs Walser's pages; the sound of beating of wings which inspire Fevvers's first attempt at flight; the wind which sends Fevvers's hair into a 'wide flaxen arc' and threatens to 'whirl [her] away'; the 'glow' and 'sizzle' of the baboushka's fire at the mention of St. Petersburg; the 'draught' which threatens to lift the Colonel's 'flimsy, impermanent, wonderful tent .... up and off'; the 'little spectral eddies and scurries' of windblown snow which herald the discovery of the Maestro's house; the 'wind of wonder' of the villagers' 'expelled breaths' which saves Fevvers in the shaman's god-hut; the 'vertiginous sensation' which Walser experiences under the spell of Lizzie's suspension of time and in the presence of the Princess's and Mignon's music, the 'dizzying' sensation when looking into the Professor's eyes, and the 'erotic vertigo' prompted by Fevvers's presence.[54] Thus, the novel ends not with closure but on a threshold; Carter's 'storm of time'[55] irresistibly recalls Benjamin's meditations on the storm of progress as depicted in Klee's 'Angelus Novus':

> This is how one pictures the angel of history. His face is turned toward the past. Where we perceive a chain of events, he sees one single catastrophe which keeps piling wreckage upon wreckage and hurls it in front of his feet. The angel would like to stay, awaken the dead, and make whole what has been smashed. But a storm is blowing from Paradise; it has got caught in his wings with such violence that the angel can no longer close them. This storm irresistibly propels him into the future to which his back is turned, while the pile of debris before him grows skyward. This storm is what we call progress.[56]

Fevvers is Carter's 'angel of history': facing the devastation of the past, she is projected into the future by the storm of her own laughter.

Aftermath: 'I am a woman dating from last century'[57]

Fevvers is a woman dated to the last century but dating from the future; in my reading of *Nights at the Circus*, I have attempted to disclose a temporal dynamic which is at least double: the linear trajectory through time and space finds itself turning towards the past, but this return is not a regressive evasion of historical change but rather a transformative preparation for the future. Having opened this paper with reference to a mode of thinking that, within only decades of its inception, may now seem 'outmoded' – Fredric Jameson's periodizing definition of postmodernism – I nevertheless intend to conclude by returning to this impasse in thinking about modernity and the postmodern.

Where debates about modernism and postmodernism have become most entrenched and polarized, this impasse could be traced to the almost tautological issue of causality. For the modernist, the modern is the originating cause and the postmodern a degraded imitation; for the postmodernist, anticipatory signs of the postmodern in the past legitimize the concept in the present. For example, Carter's representation of the turn of the century could be interpreted as demonstrating that the discourses of modernity contained their own critique, rendering the postmodern critique belated and redundant. Equally, it could be read as revealing how the postmodern is anticipated, even vindicated, in the counter discourses of modernity. The tautology is caught in the ambiguity not only of the prefix 'post-' but also of the terms 'after' and 'following'. The prefix 'post-' in relation to the modern may be interpreted as meaning 'after the end or death of' the modern, but may also imply 'following the inception of the modern' – in which case the narrow twentieth century parameters of the modern/postmodern debate are justly exploded. The fact that 'after' and 'following' can mean both 'behind' and 'in front' further complicates any understanding of the past in purely linear and chronological terms.

Two ways of understanding the relationship between past and present inform this impasse: one is deterministic, in that the past determines the present, the other retrospective, in that the past is constructed by the present. I would here like to introduce, as a threshold onto a further way of interrogating this impasse, Jean Laplanche's interrogation of the dominant usages of the term 'deferred action' and the understanding of time which they assume. Laplanche comments on how applications of Freud's notion of 'deferred action' tend to fall into two apparently opposing, but mutually reinforcing categories: the deterministic and the retrospective. Laplanche argues that Strachey's translation of Freud's *Nachträglichkeit* misleadingly retains a element of causality – one that is merely delayed. He proposes instead the term 'afterwardsness' as one which not only acknowledges a complex temporality but which also sustains the sense that 'the past already has something in it that demands to be deciphered'.[58] That is, it is neither an authentic origin whose loss we are forever mourning, nor a retrospective projection in which the present is endlessly re-enacted.

Jameson's comments on postmodern culture, subsequently canonized as a founding intervention in the postmodern debate, categorizes the postmodern condition as one in need of diagnosis. It would seem that the postmodern subject, like Freud's hysterics, 'suffer[s] mainly from reminiscences';[59] if so, it is perhaps in the recognition of the 'enigmatic message' (Laplanche) which the past transmits to the present, rather than the pathological fixation with the past by which the present seeks to legitimize itself, that we might find a way of thinking an ethical relation to history.

Notes

1 Frederic Jameson, 'Postmodernism and Consumer Society', in Peter Brooker (ed.), *Modernism/Postmodernism* (London: Longman, 1992), p. 179.

2 Jameson, 'Postmodernism and Consumer Society', p. 171.

3 Jameson, 'Postmodernism and Consumer Society', p. 179.

4 See Linda Hutcheon, *The Politics of Postmodernism* (New York: Routledge, 1989).

5 See Jacques Lacan, 'The Unconscious and Repetition', in *The Four Fundamental Concepts of Psychoanalysis*, trans. Alan Sheridan, ed. Jacques-Alain Miller (New York: Norton, 1978).

6 Hal Foster, *The Return of the Real: The Avant Garde at the End of the Century* (Cambridge, Mass.: MIT Press, 1996), p. 21.

7 Foster, *The Return of the Real*, p. 32.

8 Ernst Bloch, *Heritage of Our Times*, trans. Neville and Stephen Plaice (Cambridge: Polity Press, 1991), p. 97.

9 Jean-François Lyotard, 'Note on the Meaning of "Post-"', in Thomas Docherty (ed.), *Postmodernism: A Reader* (Hemel Hempstead: Harvester Wheatsheaf, 1993), p. 48.

10 Susan Buck-Morss, *The Dialectics of Seeing: Walter Benjamin and the Arcades Project* (London: MIT Press, 1989), p. 70.

11 References to Angela Carter, *Nights at the Circus* (London: Picador, 1985), hereafter abbreviated as *NC*.

12 Wolfgang Schivelbusch, *The Railway Journey: Trains and Travel in the Nineteenth Century*, trans. Anselm Hollo (Oxford: Blackwell, 1977), p. 13.

13 Schivelbusch, p. 44.

14 Ibid.

15 *NC*, p. 199.

16 Schivelbusch, p. 124.

17 Schivelbusch, p. 13.

18 Carter evokes this conjunction of modernity and shock when she describes Walser as a 'kaleidoscope equipped with consciousness' (*NC*, p. 10); her phrase irresistibly recalls Walter Benjamin's Baudelairean metaphor ('On Some Motifs in Baudelaire', *Illuminations*, trans. Harry Zohn [London: Fontana, 1992], pp. 157–202, p. 171) of the consciousness assailed by the shocks of modernity as a 'kaleidoscope equipped with consciousness'.

19 Freud defines latency as follows: 'the emergence of unintelligible manifestations calling for an explanation and an early, and later forgotten, event as a necessary determinant.' Sigmund Freud, *Moses and Monotheism* (1939), in *The Standard Edition of the Complete Psychological Works of Sigmund Freud*, trans. and ed. James Strachey, vol. 23 (London: The Hogarth Press, 1955), pp. 3–137. See also Cathy Caruth, 'Unclaimed Experience: Trauma and the Possibility of History', in Cathy Caruth, *Unclaimed Experience: Trauma, Narrative, and History* (Baltimore: Johns Hopkins University Press, 1996), pp. 10–24.

20 Hal Foster, *Compulsive Beauty* (Cambridge, Mass.: MIT Press, 1993), pp. 48–9.

21 'The interpretation of dreams is the royal road to a knowledge of the unconscious activities of the mind', Sigmund Freud, *The Interpretation of Dreams,* second part (1900), in *The Standard Edition of the Complete Psychological Works of Sigmund Freud*, trans. and ed. James Strachey, vol. 5 (London: The Hogarth Press, 1955), pp. 339–627, p. 608.

22 Bloch, *Heritage of Our Times*, p. 62.

23 *NC*, p. 97.

24 The image of the suspended train recalls René Magritte's 'Time Suspended'. Moreover, the engine stalled in the wilderness and absorbed into nature evokes the 'photograph of a speeding locomotive abandoned for years to the delirium of a virgin forest' with which Breton illustrated his concept of 'convulsive beauty' (quoted in Foster, *Compulsive Beauty*, p. 25).

25 Carolyn Steedman suggests a resemblance between Schubert's 'Kennst Du Das Land' and 'Home Sweet Home' and explores the motivation behind a widespread scholarly impulse to identify Mignon: 'The search for Mignon's origins ... is about the desire to give the child a home: to find her a home in the world: to give her a history, a psychology' ('New Time: Mignon and her Meanings', in *Fin de siècle/Fin du Globe: Fears and Fantasies of the Late Nineteenth Century*, ed. John Stokes [Basingstoke: Macmillan, 1992], p. 111).

26 Theodor Adorno, 'Ernst Bloch's "Spuren": On The Revised Edition of 1959', *Notes to Literature*, vol. 1 (New York: Columbia University Press, 1991), p. 205.

27 Ernst Bloch, *On Karl Marx* (New York: Herder and Herder, 1971), pp. 44–5.

28 Buck-Morss, p. 95.

29 See Anson Rabinbach, 'Unclaimed Heritage: Ernst Bloch's *Heritage Of Our Times* and the Theory of Fascism', *New German Critique* 11 (1977), pp. 5–21: '[It is] a critique of nihilism and a restoration of utopia to its original meaning as an immanent force, a "waking dream" of the possible ... Nihilism accepts only the homelessness of mankind and resigns itself before the loss of the other worldly' (pp. 7–8).

30 Maud Ellmann, Introduction, *Psychoanalytic Literary Criticism*, ed. Maud Ellmann (London: Longman, 1994), p. 9.

31 Ellmann, pp. 8–9.

32 Ellmann, p. 9.

33 *NC*, p. 91.

34 'As the traveler steps out of that space, it beomes a stage setting, or a series of such pictures or scenes created by the continously changing perspective. Panoramic perception, in contrast to traditional perception, no longer belongs to the same space as the perceived objects' (Schivelbusch, p. 66).

35 This egg has a historical precedent. Fabergé were commissioned to present the Tsarina and Dowager Empress with Easter eggs every year: an egg containing a model of the Trans Siberian Express was crafted to commemorate its opening. See Sofka Zinovieff, 'The Jewel in the Crowd: How Fabergé's extraordinary art of the ordinary heralded the end for European nobility', *Times Literary Supplement*, 18 February 1994, pp. 16–17.

36 *NC*, p. 26.

37 *NC*, p. 61.

38 *NC*, p. 55.

39 *NC*, p. 61.

40 *NC*, p. 138.

41 *NC*, p. 211.

42 Karl Marx, 'The Eighteenth Brumaire of Louis Bonaparte,' *Selected Works* (London: Lawrence and Wishart, 1968), p. 96.

43 'A spectre is haunting Europe – the spectre of Communism' (Karl Marx and Friedrich Engels, *The Communist Manifesto* [Harmondsworth: Penguin, 1967], p. 78).

44 Margaret Cohen designates Benjamin's thought as Gothic Marxism: the term describes a 'genealogy fascinated with the irrational aspects of social process, a genealogy that both investigates how the irrational pervades existing society and dreams of using it to effect

social change' (*Profane Illuminations: Walter Benjamin and the Paris of Surrealist Revolution* [London: University of California Press, 1993], pp. 1–2).

45 In 'The Alchemy of the Word', Carter professes an affinity with Surrealism; the range of the marvellous in the narrative of *Nights at the Circus* certainly seems infused with a Surrealist spirit: 'Surrealism celebrated wonder, the capacity for seeing the world as if for the first time which, in its purest state, is the prerogative of children and madmen, but more than that, it celebrated wonder itself as an essential means of perception. Yet not a naive wonder. The surrealists did not live in naive times. A premonition of the imminent end of the world is always a shot in the arm for the arts; if the world has, in fact, just ended, what then? The 1914–18 war was, in many respects, for France and Germany, indeed the end of the world ... However, the Russian Revolution of 1917 suggested the end of one world might mark the commencement of another world. ...' (Carter, *Expletives Deleted: Selected Writings* [London: Chatto and Windus, 1992], p. 67). In the 'somewhere, elsewhere' (*NC*, p. 249) of Carter's text, there might be heard an echo of the concluding declaration of Breton's 1924 'Manifesto of Surrealism': 'Existence is elsewhere' (André Breton, *Manifestoes of Surrealism*, trans. Richard Seaver and Helen R. Lane [Ann Arbor: University of Michigan Press, 1972], p. 47).

46 Walter Benjamin, 'Surrealism: The Last Snapshot of the European Intelligentsia', *One-Way Street and Other Writings*, trans. Edmund Jephcott and Kingsley Shorter (London: Verso, 1979), p. 229.

47 Benjamin, *One-Way Street*, p. 46.

48 *NC*, p. 69.

49 Benjamin, *One-Way Street*, pp. 48–9.

50 Marx, 'Eighteenth Brumaire', pp. 98–9.

51 Marx quoted in Bloch, *Utopian Function in Art and Literature: Selected Essays*, trans. Jack Zipes and Frank Mecklenburg (Cambridge, Mass.: MIT Press, 1993), p. 51.

52 Christopher Norris, 'Marxist or Utopian? – The Philosophy of Ernst Bloch', *Literature and History* 9:2 (1983), pp. 240–5, p. 242.

53 Frederic Jameson (*Marxism and Form: Twentieth-Century Dialectical Theories of Literature* [Princeton: Princeton University Press, 1971], p. 119) has described Bloch's philosophical project as proceeding by an 'expropriation of apparently alien or antagonistic cultural monuments'.

54 *NC*, pp. 295, 243, 15, 16, 90, 100, 245, 290, 87, 110, 143.

55 Ibid., p. 29.

56 Benjamin, 'Theses on the Philosophy of History', *Illuminations*, pp. 255–66, p. 249.

57 Sigmund Freud and Josef Breuer, *Studies on Hysteria*, trans. James and Alix Strachey (Harmondsworth: Pelican, 1974): 'On the occasion when I first visited her [Frau Emmy Von N.] I asked her old she was and she answered quite seriously: "I am a woman dating from last century." Some weeks later she explained to me she had been thinking at the time in her delirium of a beautiful old cupboard which, as a connoisseur of old furniture, she had bought on her travels. It was to this cupboard that her answer had referred when my question about her age raised the topic of dates' (p. 107). The female patient, not for the first time, offers a solution to the analyst's consternation; her answer simultaneously vindicates the psychoanalytic technique and mocks it – her wandering thoughts anticipating her own straying from Freud. This explanation acts as a pretext to evade the complex relationship between femininity, memory and temporality: an issue I hope to explore in a future paper.

58 Jean Laplanche, 'Notes on Afterwardsness', in *Essays on Otherness*, ed. John Fletcher, (London: Routledge, 1999), pp. 260–5, p. 265.

59 Freud and Breuer, 58.

Bibliography

Adorno, Theodor W., *Negative Dialectics*, trans. E.B. Ashton (London: Routledge & Kegan Paul, 1973).

Adorno, Theodor W., *Notes to Literature*, vol. 1, trans. Shierry Weber Nicholsen (New York: Columbia University Press, 1991).

Adorno, Theodor W. and Max Horkheimer, *Dialectic of Enlightenment*, trans. John Cumming (London: Verso, 1979).

African National Congress, *Statement to the Truth and Reconciliation Commission* (Cape Town: African National Congress, 1996).

Allen, Beverley, *Rape Warfare: The Hidden Genocide in Bosnia-Herzegovina and Croatia* (Minneapolis: University of Minnesota Press, 1996).

Allen, Jim, 'Port Arthur Site Museum, Australia: Its Preservation and Historical Perspectives', *Museum* 28:2 (1976), pp. 98–105.

Althusser, Louis, 'Ideology and Ideological State Apparatuses (Notes towards an Investigation)' in *Mapping Ideology*, ed. Slavoj Žižek (London: Verso, 1994), pp. 100–140.

American Psychiatric Association, *Diagnostic and Statistical Manual of Mental Disorders*, 4th edn (Washington, DC: American Psychiatric Association, 1994).

Améry, Jean, *At the Mind's Limits: contemplations by a survivor on Auschwitz and its realities*, trans. Sidney Rosenfeld (London: Granta, 1999).

Antze, Paul and Michael Lambek (eds), *Tense Past: Cultural Essays in Trauma and Memory* (New York: Routledge, 1996).

Augustine, *The City of God against the Pagans*, 7 vols (Cambridge, Mass.: Harvard University Press and London: William Heinemann, 1988), iii.

Barnes, Clive, 'The Gumping of America', *Evening Standard*, 17 August 1994, p. 13.

Baudelaire, Charles, *Les Fleurs du mal*, ed. Jacques Dupont (Paris: Flammarion, 1991).

Beckett, Samuel, 'Proust', in *Proust and Three Dialogues* (London: John Calder, 1987), pp. 11–93.

Bender, John, *Imagining the Penitentiary: Fiction and the Architecture of Mind in Eighteenth-Century England* (Chicago: University of Chicago Press, 1987).

Benjamin, Andrew, 'The Unconscious: Structuring as a Translation', in Fletcher and Stanton (eds), pp. 137–57.

Benjamin, Walter, 'Die Aufgabe des Übersetzers', in *Gesammelte Schriften*, ed. Rolf Tiedemann and Hermann Schweppenhäuser, vol. 4.1, ed. Tillman Rexroth (Frankfurt am Main: Suhrkamp, 1972), pp. 9–21.

Benjamin, Walter, *The Origin of German Tragic Drama*, trans. John Osborne (London: NLB, 1977).

Benjamin, Walter, *One-Way Street and Other Writings*, trans. Edmund Jephcott and Kingsley Shorter (London: Verso, 1979).

Benjamin, Walter, *Illuminations*, trans. Harry Zohn (New York: Schocken Books, 1969; London: Fontana, 1992).

Benjamin, Walter, *Selected Writings: Volume 1, 1913–1926*, ed. Marcus Bullock and Michael W. Jennings (Cambridge, Mass.: Harvard University Press, 1996).

Bennett, Tony, 'History on the Rocks', in *Australian Cultural Studies: A Reader*, ed. John Frow and Meaghan Morris (Sydney: Allen and Unwin, 1993), pp. 222–40.

Bentham, Jeremy, 'Principles of Penal Law, Part II: Rationale of Punishment' [1830], *The Works of Jeremy Bentham, Vol. 1*, ed. John Bowring (Edinburgh: William Tait, 1843).

Bernstein, J.M., 'Why Rescue Semblance? Metaphysical Experience and the Possibility of Ethics', in *The Semblance of Subjectivity: Essays in Adorno's Aesthetic Theory*, ed. Tom Huhn and Lambert Zuidervaart (Cambridge, Mass. and London: MIT Press, 1997), pp. 177–212.

Bloch, Ernst, *On Karl Marx* (New York: Herder and Herder, 1971).

Bloch, Ernst, *Heritage of Our Times*, trans. Neville and Stephen Plaice (Cambridge: Polity Press, 1991).

Bloch, Ernst, *Utopian Function in Art and Literature: Selected Essays*, trans. Jack Zipes and Frank Mecklenburg (Cambridge, Mass.: MIT Press, 1993).

Bloch, Ernst et al., *Aesthetics and Politics*, Afterword Fredric Jameson (1977: London: Verso, 1980).

Bloom, Harold, *Agon: Towards a Theory of Revisionism* (New York: Oxford University Press, 1982).

Bollas, Christopher, *Cracking Up: The Work of Unconscious Experience* (London: Routledge 1995).

Botman, Russel, and Robin Petersen (eds), *To Remember and Heal: Theological and Psychological Reflections on Truth and Reconciliation* (Cape Town: Human and Rousseau, 1996).

Bowie, Malcolm, *Psychoanalysis and the Future of Theory* (Oxford: Blackwell, 1993).

Boyle, Robert, *A Free Enquiry into the Vulgarly Received Notion of Nature*, ed. Edward B. Davis and Michael Hunter (Cambridge: Cambridge University Press, 1996).

Bracher, N., 'Faces of History, Figures of Violence', *Zeitschrift für Französische Sprache und Literatur* 102:3 (1992), pp. 252–62.

Brand, Ian, *The 'Separate' or 'Model' Prison, Port Arthur* (Launceston: Regal Publications, n.d.).

Breton, André, *Manifestoes of Surrealism*, trans. Richard Seaver and Helen R. Lane (Ann Arbor: University of Michigan Press, 1972).

Bronfen, Elisabeth, 'Eine Frau verschwindet: Sophie Freud und Jenseits des Lustprinzips', *Psyche* 47:6 (January 1993).

Buck-Morss, Susan, *The Dialectics of Seeing: Walter Benjamin and the Arcades Project* (London: MIT Press, 1989).

Burgoyne, Robert, *Film Nation: Hollywood Looks at US History* (Minneapolis: University of Minnesota Press, 1997).

Buse, Peter and Andrew Stott (eds), *Ghosts: Deconstruction, Psychoanalysis, History* Basingstoke: Macmillan, 1999).

Calling the Ghosts, dir. Mandy Jacobson and Karmen Jelincic (Bowery Productions, 1997).

Carter, Angela, *Nights at the Circus* (London: Picador, 1985).

Carter, Angela, *Expletives Deleted: Selected Writings* (London: Chatto and Windus, 1992).

Caruth, Cathy, *Unclaimed Experience: Trauma, Narrative, and History* (Baltimore: Johns Hopkins University Press, 1996).

Caruth, Cathy (ed.), *Trauma: Explorations in Memory* (Baltimore: Johns Hopkins University Press, 1995).

Cavell, Marcia, *The Psychoanalytic Mind: From Freud to Philosophy* (Cambridge, Mass.: Harvard University Press, 1993).

Caygill, Howard, *Walter Benjamin: The Colour of Experience* (London: Routledge, 1998).

Charity, Tom, review of *Forrest Gump*, *Time Out*, 5–12 October 1994, p. 67.

Clarke, Marcus, 'Port Arthur Nos. 1, 2, and 3' [1873], in *Marcus Clarke*, ed. Michael Wilding (St Lucia: University of Queensland Press, 1976), pp. 511–30.

Cohen, Margaret, *Profane Illuminations: Walter Benjamin and the Paris of Surrealist Revolution* (London: University of California Press, 1993).

Corliss, Richard. Rev. of *Forrest Gump*. *Time* 1 Aug. 1994: 41–42.

Cowie, Elizabeth, 'The Spectacle of Actuality', in *Collecting Visible Evidence*, ed. Jane M. Gaines and Michael Renov (Minneapolis: University of Minnesota Press, 1999).

Craib, Ian, *The Importance of Disappointment* (London: Routledge, 1994).

Crews, Frederick, *The Memory Wars: Freud's Legacy In Dispute* (New York: *New York Review of Books*, 1995).

Cuau, Bernard et al., *Au sujet de Shoah: Le film de Claude Lanzmann* (Paris: Belin, 1990).

Culler, Jonathan, *The Pursuit of Signs. Semiotics, Literature, Deconstruction* (London: Routledge & Kegan Paul, 1981).

Daniels, Kay, 'Cults of Nature, Cults of History', *Island Magazine* 16 (Spring 1983), pp. 3–8.

Davidson, Jim, 'Port Arthur: A Tourist History', *Australian Historical Studies* 26:105 (October 1995), pp. 653–65.

de Certeau, Michel, *Heterologies: Discourse on the Other*, trans. Brian Massumi, Foreword Wlad Godzich (Manchester: Manchester University Press, 1986).

de Certeau, Michel, *The Writing of History*, trans. Tom Conley (New York: Columbia University Press, 1988).

Delbo, Charlotte, *Days and Memory*, trans. Rosette Lamont (Vermont: Marlboro Press, 1990).

Delbo, Charlotte, *Auschwitz and After*, trans. Rosette Lamont, introd. Lawrence Langer (New Haven: Yale University Press, 1995).

Delbo, Charlotte, *Convoy to Auschwitz: Women of the French Resistance*, trans. Carol Cosman, introd. John Felstiner (Boston: Northeastern University Press, 1997).

Deleuze, Gilles, *Cinema 2, The Time-Image*, trans. Hugh Tomlinson and Robert Galeta (Minneapolis: University of Minnesota Press, 1989).

de Man, Paul, 'Semiology and Rhetoric', in *Allegories of Reading: Figural Language in Rousseau, Nietzsche, Rilke, and Proust* (New Haven: Yale University Press, 1979), pp. 3–19.

de Man, Paul, 'A Letter from Paul de Man', *Critical Inquiry* 8:3 (Spring 1982), pp. 509–13.

de Man, Paul, 'Anthropomorphism and Trope in the Lyric', in *The Rhetoric of Romanticism* (New York: Columbia University Press, 1984), pp. 239–62.

de Man, Paul, 'Conclusions: Walter Benjamin's "The Task of the Translator"', *Yale French Studies* 69 (1985), pp. 25–46.

de Man, Paul, *The Resistance to Theory*, Foreword Wlad Godzich (Minneapolis: University of Minnesota Press, 1986).

de Man, Paul, *Critical Writings, 1953–1978*, ed. Lindsay Waters (Minneapolis: University of Minnesota Press, 1989).

de Man, Paul, *Romanticism and Contemporary Criticism: The Gauss Seminar and Other Papers*, ed. E.S. Burt, Kevin Newmark and Andrzej Warminski (Baltimore: Johns Hopkins University Press, 1993).

de Man, Paul, *Aesthetic Ideology*, ed. Andrzej Warminski (Minneapolis: University of Minnesota Press, 1996).

de Man, Paul, 'Autobiography As De-Facement', in *The Rhetoric of Romanticism* (New York: Columbia University Press, 1984), pp. 67–81.

de Man, Paul, '"Conclusions": Walter Benjamin's "The Task of the Translator"', *Yale French Studies* 69 (1985), pp. 25–46.

Derrida, Jacques, *Writing and Difference*, trans. Alan Bass (London: Routledge, 1978).

Derrida, Jacques, *Glas*, trans. John P. Leavey Jr and Richard Rand (Lincoln: University of Nebraska Press, 1986).

Derrida, Jacques, 'To Speculate – on "Freud"', in *The Post Card: From Socrates to Freud and Beyond* , trans. Alan Bass (Chicago: University of Chicago Press, 1987), pp. 257–409.

The Diagnostic and Statistical Manual of Mental Disorders (Washington, DC: American Psychiatric Association, 1994).

Duras, Marguerite, *Hiroshima mon amour* (Paris: Gallimard, 1960).

Duras, Marguerite and Alain Resnais, *Hiroshima mon amour*, trans. Richard Seaver (New York: Grove Press, 1961).

DuToit, Andre, 'Laying the Past to Rest', *Indicator SA* 11:4 (1994), pp. 63–68.

DuToit, Andre, 'Justice and/or Truth', *South African Outlook* 125:6 (1995), pp. 52–65.

Dwork, Deborah, *Children with a Star* (New Haven: Yale University Press, 1991).

Easthope, Anthony, 'History and Psychoanalysis', *Textual Practice* 9:2 (Summer 1995), pp. 349–63.

Ellmann, Maud, *Psychoanalytic Literary Criticism* (London: Longman, 1994).

Evans, Richard J., *In Defence of History* (London: Granta, 1997).

Evans, Robin, *The Fabrication of Virtue: English Prison Architecture, 1750–1840* (Cambridge: Cambridge University Press, 1982).

Farrell, Kirby, *Post-traumatic Culture: Injury and Interpretation in the Nineties* (Baltimore: Johns Hopkins University Press, 1998).

Felman, Shoshana, 'Postal Survival: The Question of the Navel', *Yale French Studies* 69 (1985), pp. 49–72.

Felman, Shoshana, and Dori Laub, *Testimony: Crises of Witnessing in Literature, Psychoanalysis and History* (New York: Routledge, 1992).

Flanagan, Richard, 'Crowbar History: Panel Games and Port Arthur', *Australian Society* 9:8 (1990), pp. 35–37.

Fletcher, John, and Martin Stanton (eds), *Jean Laplanche: Seduction, Translation and the Drives* (London: ICA, 1992).

Flint, Valerie I.H., *The Rise of Magic in Early Medieval Europe* (Oxford: Clarendon Press, 1991).

Fludernik, Monika, 'Carceral topography: spatiality, liminality and corporality in the literary prison', *Textual Practice* 13:1 (1999), pp. 43–77.

Forrest Gump, dir. Robert Zemeckis (USA, 1994).

Foster, Hal, *Compulsive Beauty* (Cambridge, Mass.: MIT Press, 1993).

Foster, Hal, *The Return of the Real* (Cambridge, Mass.: MIT Press, 1996).

Foucault, Michel, *Discipline and Punish: The Birth of the Prison*, trans. Alan Sheridan (Harmondsworth: Penguin, 1979).

Foucault, Michel, 'Film and Popular Memory', *Foucault Live: Interviews 1966–1984* (New York: semiotext(e), 1989), pp. 89–106.

Frank, Alvin, 'The Unrememberable and the Unforgettable: Passive Primal Repression', *The Psychoanalytic Study of the Child* 24 (1969), pp. 48–77.

Freud, Sigmund, *Studienausgabe* (Frankfurt am Main: Fischer Verlag, 1969–79), Band III.

Freud, Sigmund, *The Standard Edition of the Complete Psychological Works of Sigmund Freud*, trans. and ed. James Strachey, 24 vols (London: The Hogarth Press, 1953–74).

Freud, Sigmund, *The Project for a Scientific Psychology* (1895), in *The Standard Edition of the Complete Psychological Works of Sigmund Freud*, trans. and ed. James Strachey, vol. 1 (London: The Hogarth Press, 1966), pp. 283–398.

Freud, Sigmund, *Beyond the Pleasure Principle* (1920), in *The Standard Edition of the Complete Psychological Works of Sigmund Freud*, trans. and ed. James Strachey, vol. 18 (London: The Hogarth Press, 1955), pp. 3–64.

Freud, Sigmund, *Moses and Monotheism* (1939), in *The Standard Edition of the Complete Psychological Works of Sigmund Freud*, trans. and ed. James Strachey, vol. 23 (London: The Hogarth Press, 1955), pp. 3–137.

Freud, Sigmund, *The Interpretation of Dreams,* second part (1900), in *The Standard Edition of the Complete Psychological Works of Sigmund Freud*, trans. and ed. James Strachey, vol. 5 (London: The Hogarth Press, 1955), pp. 339–627.

Freud, Sigmund, 'Analysis of a Phobia in a Five-year-old Boy ("Little Hans")', *Case Histories I*, trans. James Strachey, ed. Angela Richards, Penguin Freud Library 8 (Harmondsworth: Penguin, 1977), pp. 167–303.

Freud, Sigmund, 'From the History of an Infantile Neurosis (The "Wolf Man")', *Case Histories II*, trans. James Strachey, ed. Angela Richards, Penguin Freud Library 9 (Harmondsworth: Penguin, 1991), pp. 227–366.

Freud, Sigmund, *The Interpretation of Dreams*, trans. James Strachey, ed. Angela Richards, Penguin Freud Library 4 (Harmondsworth: Penguin, 1991).

Freud, Sigmund and Josef Breuer, *Studies on Hysteria*, 1893–5, vol. 3 of *The Penguin Freud Library*, 15 vols, trans. James and Alix Strachey, ed. Angela Richards (1973–82); Albert Dickson (1982–) (Harmondsworth: Pelican, 1974).

Friedländer, Saul (ed.), *Probing the Limits of Representation: Nazism and the 'Final Solution'* (Cambridge, Mass.: Harvard University Press, 1992).

Frow, John, '*Toute la mémoire du monde*: Repetition and Forgetting', in *Time and Commodity Culture: Essays in Cultural Theory and Postmodernity* (Oxford: Clarendon Press, 1997), pp. 218–46.

Fuentes, Carlos, 'Centaur of the North', *Los Angeles Times Book Review,* Sunday 4 April 1999, p. 2.

Gasché, Rodolphe, 'The Witch Metapsychology', in Todd Dufresne (ed.), *Returns of the French Freud: Freud, Lacan, and Beyond* (New York: Routledge, 1997), pp. 169–207.

Godzich, Wlad, 'Foreword: The Tiger on the Paper Mat', in de Man, *The Resistance to Theory*, pp. ix–xviii.

Goldstein, Laurence, *Ruins and Empire: The Evolution of a Theme in Augustan and Romantic Literature* (Pittsburgh: University of Pittsburgh Press, 1977).

Green, Anna and Kathleen Troup (eds), *The Houses of History. A Critical Reader in Twentieth-Century History and Theory* (Manchester: Manchester University Press, 1999).

Griffiths, Tom, 'Past Silences: Aborigines and Convicts in our History-Making', *Australian Cultural History* 6 (1987), pp. 18–32.

Hacking, Ian, *Rewriting the Soul: Multiple Personality and the Sciences of Memory* (Princeton: Princeton University Press, 1995).

Hacking, Ian, 'Memory Sciences, Memory Politics', in Antze and Lambek (eds), pp. 67–87.

Hamacher, Werner, '"LECTIO": de Man's Imperative', in *Premises: Essays on Philosophy and Literature from Kant to Celan*, trans. Peter Fenves (Cambridge, Mass.: Harvard University Press, 1996), pp. 181–221.

Hamber, Brandon, *The Burdens of Truth: An Evaluation of the Psychological Support Services and Initiatives Undertaken by the South African Truth and Reconciliation Commission* (Johannesburg: Centre for the Study of Violence and Reconciliation, 1997).

Hamilton, Paul, *Historicism* (London: Routledge, 1996).

Hansen, Miriam Bratu, '*Schindler's List* Is Not *Shoah*: The Second Commandment, Popular Modernism, and Public Memory', *Critical Inquiry* 22 (Winter 1996), pp. 292–312.

Harrison, Peter, *Religion and 'Religions' in the English Enlightenment* (Cambridge: Cambridge University Press, 1990).

Hartman, Geoffrey H., 'Learning from the Survivors: The Yale Testimony Project', *Holocaust and Genocide Studies* 9 (1995), pp. 192–207.

Hass, Kristin Ann, *Carried to the Wall: American Memory and the Vietnam Veterans Memorial* (Berkeley: University of California Press, 1998).

Hegel, G.W.F., *Science of Logic*, trans. A.V. Miller (London: Allen & Unwin, 1969).

Hegel, G.W.F., *Phenomenology of Spirit*, trans. A.V. Miller (Oxford: Oxford University Press, 1977).

Heidegger, Martin, 'Letter on Humanism', in *Basic Writings*, ed. David Farrell Krell, revised edn (London: Routledge, 1993), pp. 217–65.

Henry, Michel, *Marx*, 2 vols (Paris: Gallimard, 1976).

Henry, Michel, *Phénomenologie matérielle* (Paris: Presses Universitaires de France, 1990).

Herman, Judith Lewis, *Trauma and Recovery* (New York: Basic Books, 1992).

Hernandez, Max, 'Winnicott's "Fear of Breakdown": On and beyond Trauma', *Diacritics* 28:4 (Winter 1998), pp. 134–43.

Hertz, Neil, 'Lurid Figures', in *Reading de Man Reading*, ed. Lindsay Waters and Wlad Godzich (Minneapolis: University of Minnesota Press, 1989), pp. 82–104.

Hertz, Neil, 'More Lurid Figures', *Diacritics* 20:3 (Fall 1990), pp. 2–27.

Hiroshima mon amour, dir. Alain Resnais (1957).

Hobbes, Thomas, *Leviathan*, ed. Richard Tuck (Cambridge: Cambridge University Press, 1991).

Hoberman, J., review of *Forrest Gump*, *Village Voice*, 12 July 1994, p. 41.

Hughes, Robert, *The Fatal Shore: A History of the Transportation of Convicts to Australia, 1787–1868* (London: Collins Harvill, 1987).

Hukanovic, Rezak, *The Tenth Circle of Hell: A Memoir of Life in the Death Camps of Bosnia* (New York: Basic Books, 1996).

Hutcheon, Linda, *The Politics of Postmodernism* (New York: Routledge, 1989).

Huyssen, Andreas, 'Monument and Memory in a Postmodern Age', in *The Art of Memory: Holocaust Memorials in History*, ed. James T. Young (Munich: Prestel-Verlag, 1994), pp. 9–17.

Ignatieff, Michael, *A Just Measure of Pain: The Penitentiary in the Industrial Revolution 1750–1850* (1978; reprinted London: Penguin, 1989).

Irigaray, Luce, *Sexes and Genealogies*, trans. Gillian C. Gill (New York: Columbia University Press, 1987).

Jacobs, Carol, 'The Monstrosity of Translation: "The Task of the Translator"', in *In the Language of Walter Benjamin* (Baltimore: Johns Hopkins University Press, 1999), pp. 75–90.

Jacobus, Mary, Preface, 'Trauma and Psychoanalysis', Special Issue, *Diacritics* 28:4 (Winter 1998), pp. 3–4.

Jameson, Fredric, *Marxism and Form: Twentieth-century Dialectical Theories of Literature* (Princeton: Princeton University Press, 1971).

Jameson, Fredric, 'Postmodernism, or the Cultural Logic of Late Capitalism', *New Left Review* 146 (1984), pp. 53–92.

Jameson, Fredric, *Late Marxism: Adorno, or, the persistence of the dialectic* (London: Verso, 1990).

Jameson, Fredric, 'Postmodernism and Consumer Society', in Peter Brooker (ed.), *Modernism/Postmodernism* (London: Longman, 1992), pp. 163–79.

Jameson, Fredric, *Postmodernism or The Cultural Logic of Late Capitalism* (London: Verso, 1991).

Jarvis, Simon, *Adorno: A Critical Introduction* (Cambridge: Polity Press, 1998).

Jenkins, Keith, *Re-Thinking History* (London: Routledge, 1991).

Jenkins, Keith (ed.), *The Postmodern History Reader* (London: Routledge, 1997).

Jones, Rhys, 'Appendix: Tasmanian Tribes', in Norman B. Tindale, *Aboriginal Tribes of Australia: Their Terrain, Environmental Controls, Distribution, Limits, and Proper Names* (Berkeley: University of California Press, 1974), pp. 317–54.

Kafka, Franz, 'In the Penal Colony', *The Complete Stories*, trans. Willa and Edwin Muir, ed. Nahum N. Glatzer (New York: Schocken Books, 1971).

Kant, Immanuel, *Critique of Judgment*, trans. Werner S. Pluhar (Indianapolis: Hackett, 1987).

Kant, Immanuel, *Critique of Pure Reason*, trans. Werner S. Pluhar (Indianapolis and Cambridge: Hackett, 1996).

Katz, Friedrich, *The Life and Times of Pancho Villa* (Stanford: Stanford University Press, 1999).

Kenny, Michael G., 'Trauma, Time, Illness, and Culture: An Anthropological Approach to Traumatic Memory', in Antze and Lambek (eds), pp. 151–71.

Kincaid, R.A., 'Charlotte Delbo's *Auschwitz et Après*: The Struggle for Signification', *Symposium* 45.4 (1992), pp. 255–72.

King, Nicola, 'Autobiography as Cultural Memory: Three case-studies', *Cultural Memory*, special issue of *New Formations* 30 (1997), pp. 50–62.

Klein, Kerwin Lee, 'On the Emergence of *Memory* in Historial Discourse', *Representations* 69 (Winter 2000), pp. 127–50.

Kollapen, Jody, 'Comment from the National Director: Kollapen Encouraged by Truth Commission Appointment Process', *Rights* 13 (1995), pp. 4–5.

Kostelnick, Charles, 'Wordsworth, Ruins, and the Aesthetics of Decay: From Surface to Noble Picturesque', *The Wordsworth Circle* 19:1 (1988), pp. 20–28.

Lacan, Jacques, *Écrits: A Selection*, trans. Alan Sheridan (London: Routledge, 1977).

Lacan, Jacques, *The Four Fundamental Concepts of Psycho-Analysis*, trans. Alan Sheridan, ed. Jacques-Alain Miller (Harmondsworth: Penguin Books, 1977 and New York: Norton, 1978).

LaCapra, Dominick, *Representing the Holocaust: History, theory, trauma* (Ithaca: Cornell University Press, 1994).

LaCapra, Dominick, 'Lanzmann's *Shoah*: "Here There Is No Why"', *Critical Inquiry* 23 (1997), pp. 231–69.

LaCapra, Dominick, *History and Memory After Auschwitz* (Ithaca: Cornell University Press, 1998).

Lalu, Premesh, and Brent Harris, 'Journeys from the Horizons of History: Text, Trial and Tales in the Construction of Narratives of Pain', *Current Writing* 8:2 (1996), pp. 24–38.

Landsberg, Alison, 'Prosthetic Memory: *Total Recall* and *Blade Runner*', in *Cyberspace/Cyberbodies/Cyberpunk: Cultures of Technological Embodiment*, ed. Mike Featherstone and Roger Burrows (London: Sage, 1995), pp. 175–89.

Lanzmann, Claude, 'Why Spielberg has Distorted the Truth', *The Guardian Weekly*, 9 April 1994, p. 14.

Lanzmann, Claude, 'The Obscenity of Understanding: An Evening with Claude Lanzmann', in Caruth (ed.), *Trauma: Explorations in Memory*, pp. 200–20.

Laplanche, Jean, *Life and Death in Psychoanalysis*, trans. and introd. Jeffrey Mehlman (Baltimore: Johns Hopkins University Press, 1970).

Laplanche, Jean, *Essays on Otherness*, ed. John Fletcher (London: Routledge, 1999).

Laplanche, Jean and J.-B. Pontalis, 'Fantasy and the Origins of Sexuality', *International Journal of Psychoanalysis* 49 (1968), pp. 1–18.

Laplanche, Jean and J.-B. Pontalis, *The Language of Psycho-analysis*, trans. Donald Nicholson-Smith, introd. Daniel Lagache (London: The Hogarth Press, 1973).

Levi, Primo, *The Drowned and the Saved*, trans. Raymond Rosenthal (London: Abacus, 1989).

Leys, Ruth, 'Traumatic Cures: Shellshock, Janet and the Question of Memory', in Antze and Lambek (eds), pp. 103–45.

Liebenberg, Ian, 'The Truth and Reconciliation Commission in South Africa: Context, Future and Some Imponderables', SA *Public Law* 2:1 (1996), pp. 123–59.

Lifton, Robert J., *Death in Life: Survivors of Hiroshima* (New York: Basic Books, 1967).

Lifton, Robert J., *The Broken Connection: Death and the Continuity of Life* (1979; New York: Basic Books, 1983).

Lyotard, Jean-François, *The Differend: Phrases in Dispute*, trans. Georges Van Den Abbeele (Manchester: Manchester University Press, 1988).

Lyotard, Jean-François, 'Note on the Meaning of "Post-"', in *Postmodernism: A Reader*, ed. Thomas Docherty (Hemel Hempstead: Harvester Wheatsheaf, 1993), pp. 47–50.

Marx, Karl, *Selected Works* (London: Lawrence and Wishart, 1968).

Marx, Karl, *Capital*, vol. 1, trans. Ben Fowkes (Harmondsworth: Penguin, 1976).

Marx, Karl and Friedrich Engels, 'Die Deutsche Ideologie', in *Werke*, 42 vols (Berlin: Dietz, 1962–71), iii.

Marx, Karl and Friedrich Engels, *The Communist Manifesto* (Harmondsworth: Penguin, 1967).

Marx, Karl and Friedrich Engels, *The German Ideology* (Amherst: Prometheus Books, 1998).

Masson, Jeffrey, *The Assault on Truth: Freud's Suppression of the Seduction Theory* (New York: Farrar Straus Giroux, 1984).

Mayhew, Henry and John Binny, *The Criminal Prisons of London, and Scenes of Prison Life* (1862; reprinted London: Frank Cass, 1968).

Meisel, Perry, 'Freud's Reflexive Realism' *October* 28 (Spring 1984).

Menton, Seymour, *Latin America's New Historical Novel* (Austin: University of Texas Press, 1993).

Moynihan, Robert, 'Interview with Paul de Man', *The Yale Review* 73:4 (Summer 1984), pp. 576–602.

National Party, *Second Submission to the Truth and Reconciliation Commission* (Cape Town: National Party, 1996).

Newmark, Kevin, 'Beyond Movement: Paul de Man's History', in *Beyond Symbolism: Textual History and the Future of Reading* (Ithaca: Cornell University Press, 1991), pp. 195–230.

Nora, Pierre, 'Between Memory and History: Les Lieux de Mémoire', *Representations* 26 (1989), pp. 7–25.

Nora, Pierre, 'L'Ère de la commémoration', *Les Lieux de Mémoire III: Les France, 3: De l'Archive à l'emblème*, ed. Pierre Nora (Paris: Gallimard, 1992), pp. 997–1012.

Nora, Pierre, 'Entre Mémoire et Histoire: La problématique des lieux' (1984), in *Les Lieux de Mémoire*, ed. Pierre Nora, 3 vols (Paris: Éditions Gallimard, 1997), i, pp. 23–43.

Nora, Pierre, *Realms of Memory: rethinking the French past*, English-Language Edition, ed. Lawrence D. Kritzman, trans. Arthur Goldhammer, 3 vols (New York: Columbia University Press, 1996–98).

Norris, Christopher, 'Marxist or Utopian? – The Philosophy of Ernst Bloch', *Literature and History* 9:2 (1983), pp. 240–5.

Pellón, Gustavo, 'The Spanish American Novel: Recent Developments, 1975–1990', in *The Cambridge History of Latin American Literature*, 3 vols, ed. Roberto González Echevarría and Enrique Pupo Walker (Cambridge: Cambridge University Press, 1996), ii, pp. 279–302.

Perelli, Carina, 'Memoria de Sangre', in *Remapping Memory: The Politics of Time and Space*, ed. Jonathan Boyarin (Minneapolis: University of Minnesota Press, 1994).

Rabinbach, Anson, 'Unclaimed Heritage: Ernst Bloch's *Heritage Of Our Times* and the Theory of Fascism', *New German Critique* 11 (1977), pp. 5–21.

Radstone, Susannah, 'Screening Trauma: *Forrest Gump*, Film and Memory', in *Memory and Methodology*, ed. Susannah Radstone (London and New York: Berg, 2000), pp. 79–107.

Ramadonovic, Petar, 'When "To die in freedom" is written in English', *Diacritics* 28:4 (Winter 1998), pp. 54–67.

Reynolds, Henry, '"That Hated Stain": The Aftermath of Transportation in Tasmania', *Historical Studies* 14:53 (October 1969), pp. 19–31.

Reynolds, Henry, *Fate of a Free People: A Radical Re-Examination of the Tasmanian Wars* (Ringwood: Penguin, 1995).

Romney, Jonathan, 'Transatlantic Gumption', *New Statesman and Society*, 14 August 1994, p. 41.

Ropars-Wuilleumier, Marie-Claire, 'How History Begets Meaning: Alain Resnais' *Hiroshima mon amour* (1959)', in *French Film: Texts and contexts*, ed. Susan Hayward and Ginette Vincendeau (London: Routledge, 1990), pp. 173–85.

Rose, Gillian, *Mourning Becomes the Law: Philosophy and Representation* (Cambridge: Cambridge University Press, 1996).

Rosso, Stefano, 'An Interview with Paul de Man' (1983), in de Man, *The Resistance to Theory*, pp. 115–21.

Ryan, Lyndall, *The Aboriginal Tasmanians* (St Lucia: University of Queensland Press, 1981).

Santner, Eric L., *Stranded Objects: Mourning, Memory, and Film in Postwar Germany* (New York: Cornell University Press, 1990).

Santner, Eric L., 'History beyond the Pleasure Principle', in Friedländer (ed.), pp.143–54.

Schivelbusch, Wolfgang, *The Railway Journey: Trains and Travel in the Nineteenth Century*, trans. Anselm Hollo (Oxford: Blackwell, 1977).

Scott, Margaret, *Port Arthur: A Story of Strength and Courage* (Milsons Point: Random House, 1997).

Showalter, Elaine, *Hystories: Hysterical Epidemics in Modern Media* (New York: Columbia University Press, 1992).

Sobchack, Vivian (ed.), *The Persistence of History: Cinema, television and the modern event* (New York: Routledge, 1996).

Solares, Ignacio, *Madero, el otro* (Mexico City: Joaquín Mortiz, 1989).

Solares, Ignacio, 'Madero en la historiografía de la Revolución mexicana', in *Literatura mexicana hoy. Del 68 al ocaso de la revolución*, ed. Karl Kohut (Frankfurt am Main: Vervuert Verlag, 1991), pp. 180–90.

Stafford, Barbara Maria, *Voyage Into Substance: Art, Science, Nature, and the Illustrated Travel Account, 1760–1840* (Cambridge, Mass.: MIT Press, 1984).

Steedman, Carolyn, 'New Time: Mignon and her Meanings', in John Stokes (ed.), *Fin de siècle/Fin du Globe: Fears and Fantasies of the Late Nineteenth Century* (Basingstoke: Macmillan, 1992), pp. 102–16.

Stiglmayer, Alexandra (ed.), *Mass Rape: The War Against Women in Bosnia Herzegovina* (Lincoln: University of Nebraska Press, 1994).

Stone, Martin, 'Shellshock and the Psychologists', in *The Anatomy of Madness: Essays in the history of psychiatry*, ed. W.F. Bynum, Roy Porter and Michael Shepherd (Cambridge: Cambridge University Press, 1985), pp. 242–71.

Stoney, Captain H. Butler, *A Residence in Tasmania: With a Descriptive Tour through the Island from Macquarie Harbour to Circular Head* (London: Smith, Elder and Co., 1856).

Taussig, Michael, *Shamanism, Colonialism, and the Wild Man: A Study in Terror and Healing* (Chicago: University of Chicago Press, 1986).

Thomä, Helmut and Neil Cheshire, 'Freud's *Nachträglichkeit* and Strachey's "Deferred Action": Trauma, Constructions and the Direction of Causality', *International Review of Psychoanalysis* 18 (1991), pp. 407–27.

Timpanaro, Sebastiano, *On Materialism*, trans. Lawrence Garner (London: NLB, 1975).

Tort, Patrick, *Marx et le problème de l'idéologie. Le modèle Égyptien* (Paris: Presses Universitaires de France, 1988).

Trollope, Anthony, *Australia*, ed. P.D. Edwards and R.B. Joyce (St Lucia: University of Queensland Press, 1967 [1873]).

Truth and Reconciliation Commission, *Interim Report* (Cape Town: Truth and Reconciliation Commission, 1996).

Truth and Reconciliation Commission, *Policy Framework for Urgent Interim Reparation Measures* (Cape Town: Truth and Reconciliation Commission, 1996).

Truth and Reconciliation Commission, *Register of Reconciliation* (Cape Town: Truth and Reconciliation Commission, 1997).

Turim, Maureen, *Flashbacks in Film* (London: Routledge, 1989).

Tutu, Desmond, 'Statement by Archbishop Tutu on his appointment to the Truth and Reconciliation Commission', 30 November 1995, online posting, newsgroup list. Available email: trcinfo-owner@listbot.com.

Tutu, Desmond, 'Archbishop Tutu's address to the first gathering of the Truth and Reconciliation Commission', 16 December 1995, online posting, newsgroup list. Available email: trcinfo-owner@listbot.com.

van der Kolk, Bessel A., 'Trauma and Memory', in *Traumatic Stress: The Effects of Overwhelming Experience on Mind, Body, and Society*, ed. Bessel A. van der Kolk, Alexander C. McFarlane and Lars Weisaeth (New York: The Guildford Press, 1996).

van der Kolk, Bessel A. and Onno van der Hart, 'The Intrusive Past: The Flexibility of Memory and the Engraving of Trauma', in Caruth (ed.), *Trauma: Explorations in Memory*, pp. 158–82.

Vogelman, Lloyd, 'It's Hard to Forgive – Even Harder to Forget', *Work In Progress* 9 (1993), pp. 14–16.

Walker, Alexander, review of *Forrest Gump*, *Evening Standard*, 6 October 1994, p. 32.

War Neuroses, Netley 1917 and Seale Military Hospital, 1918 (Pathé, 1918).

Warminski, Andrzej, 'Ending Up/Taking Back (with Two Postscripts on Paul de Man's Historical Materialism)', in *Critical Encounters: Reference and Responsibility in Deconstructive Writing*, ed. Cathy Caruth and Deborah Esch (New Brunswick: Rutgers University Press, 1995), pp. 11–41.

Warminski, Andrzej, 'Introduction: Allegories of Reference', in de Man, *Aesthetic Ideology*, pp. 1–33.

Waters, Lindsay, 'Introduction. Paul de Man: Life and Works', in de Man, *Critical Writings*, pp. ix–lxxiv.

Weber, Samuel, *The Legend of Freud* (Minneapolis: University of Minnesota Press, 1982).

Weber, Samuel, *Return to Freud: Jacques Lacan's Dislocation of Psychoanalysis*, trans. Michael Levine (Cambridge: Cambridge University Press, 1991).

Wenzel, Marita, 'The "Other" Side of History as Depicted in Isabel Allende's "Of Love and Shadows"', *Literator* 17:3 (1996), pp. 1–13.

White, Hayden, 'The Modernist Event', in Sobchack (ed.), pp. 17–38.

Whitehead, Anne, '"A still, small voice": Letter-writing, testimony and the project of address in Etty Hillesum's *Letters from Westerbork*', *Cultural Values* 5:1 (2001).

Wilson, Elizabeth, *Neural Geographies: Feminism and the Microstructure of Cognition* (London: Routledge, 1998).

Winnicott, D.W., *Playing and Reality* (London: Tavistock Publications, 1971).

Wordsworth, William, *The Thirteen-Book Prelude*, ed. Mark L. Reed, 2 vols (Ithaca: Cornell University Press, 1991).

Young, Allan, *The Harmony of Illusions: Inventing Post-Traumatic Stress Disorder* (Princeton: Princeton University Press, 1995).

Young, David, *Making Crime Pay: The Evolution of Convict Tourism in Tasmania* (Hobart: Tasmanian Historical Research Association, 1996).

Zetlin, Monica, review of *Forrest Gump*, *Cinema Papers* 102 (1994), pp. 68–9.

Zinovieff, Sofka, 'The Jewel in the Crowd: How Fabergé's extraordinary art of the ordinary heralded the end for European nobility', *Times Literary Supplement*, 18 February 1994, pp. 16–17.

Žižek, Slavoj, *The Sublime Object of Ideology* (London: Verso, 1989).

Index

Adorno, Theodor W. 14, 37, 39, 209
  Dialectic of Enlightenment 55
  Negative Dialectics 55
  Notes to Literature, Vol I 55, 216
African National Congress *see* ANC
'afterwardsness' *see Nachträglichkeit*
Allen, Beverley, *Rape Warfare: The Hidden
    Genocide in Bosnia-Herzegovina and
    Croatia* 110, 119
Allen, Jim 136, 137, 142
Allende, Isabel 165
Althusser, Louis 2, 3
  on ideology 29–30, 31, 37
Améry, Jean 104
  At the Mind's Limits 107
ANC (African National Congress) 9, 158
  and apartheid 162–7
  *Statement to the Truth and Reconciliation
    Commission* 172, 173
  testimony to TRC 162–9
'Angel of History' 14, 213
Antze, Paul 160
  *Tense Past: Cultural Essays in Trauma
    and Memory* 106, 171, 172, 189
apartheid
  and the ANC 162–7
  and historicism 167–8, 169
  and the NP 167–8
  and testimony 157
  and The Holocaust 164–5, 169
  therapeutic approach 167–71
  and trauma 164, 165
architecture, and punishment 131, 132
Arendt, Hannah 164
art, and testimony 108, 110–11, 118
Ashton, E.B. 55
Augustine, Saint, *City of God against the
    Pagans* 25, 27, 37
Auschwitz 98, 102, 103

Barnes, Clive 189
Bass, Alan 67, 71, 92
Baudelaire, Charles
  'Correspondances', analysis 44–6
  Les Fleurs du mal 56, 58
  Tableaux parisiens 57
Bauer, Otto 22
Beccaria, Cesare 131
Beckett, Samuel 6, 102
  Proust and Three Dialogues 106
Bender, John, *Imaging the Penitentiary:
    Fiction and the Architecture of Mind
    in Eighteenth-Century England* 141
Benítez, Fernando 144
Benjamin, Andrew 203
Benjamin, Walter 2, 4, 14, 39, 210–11, 213
  Gesammelte Schriften 57
  Illuminations 18, 57, 215
  One-Way Street and other Writings 217
  Selected Writings: Volume I, 1913–1926
    55, 57
  The Origin of German Tragic Drama 57
  on translation 47–54, 57
Bennett, Tony 137, 142
Bentham, Jeremy
  The Rationale of Punishment 127
  The Works of Jeremy Bentham, Vol. I 140
Bergson, Henry 202
Bernstein, J.M. 55
Binny, John 141
Bloch, Ernst 209, 212
  Heritage of Our Times 215, 216
  On Karl Marx 216
  *Utopian Function in Art and Literature:
    Selected Essays* 217
Bloom, Harold, *Agon: Towards a Theory of
    Revisionism* 93, 95
Bollas, Christopher 183, 184
  *Cracking Up: The Work of Unconscious
    Experience* 190

Bosnia
  ethnic-cleansing 110
  genocide 110
  rape 7, 109, 110, 118
Botman, Russel, *To Remember and Heal:*
  Theological and Psychological
  Reflections on Truth and
  Reconciliation 171
Bowie, Malcolm, *Psychoanalysis and the*
  Future of Theory 72–3
Bowring, John 140
Boyarin, Jonathan, *Remapping Memory: The*
  Politics of Time and Space 172
Boyle, Robert
  Free Enquiry into the Vulgarly Received
  Notion of Nature 28, 37
  on nature 35
Bracher, N. 106
Brand, Ian 129
  The 'Separate' or 'Model' Prison, Port
  Arthur 140
Brand, Robert 159
Breton, André 210, 216
  Manifestoes of Surrealism 217
Breuer, Josef 217, 218
Bronfen, Elisabeth 95
Brooker, Peter, *Modernism/Postmodernism*
  215
Brot, meaning, compared with *pain* 49
Bryant, Martin 124, 125, 139
Buck-Morss, Susan 206, 209
  The Dialectics of Seeing: Walter
  Benjamin and the Arcades Project
  215, 216
Bullock, Marcus 55
Burgoyne, Robert 185, 186, 187
  Film Nation: Hollywood Looks at US
  History 190
Buse, Peter, *Ghosts: Deconstruction,*
  Psychoanalysis, History 17

Calling the Ghosts 119
  as testimony 109, 110, 111, 114, 115,
  116–17
  and trauma theory 7, 16
Cárdenas, Francisco 154
Carroll, Rachel 9, 13–14, 16, 18

Carter, Angela 9
  Expletives Deleted: Selected Writings 217
  Nights at the Circus 13–14, 18, 215
  as a postmodernist text 205–14
  and Surrealism 217
Caruth, Cathy 105, 107, 119, 123, 203, 204
  Critical Encounters: Reference and
  Responsibility in Deconstructive
  Writing 55
  on nightmare 5–6
  Trauma: Explorations in Memory 5, 15,
  106, 118
  Unclaimed Experience: Trauma,
  Narrative and History 5, 15, 18, 92,
  95, 106, 107, 140, 191–2, 202, 215
  on urban violence 6
catharsis, and therapy 161
Cavell, Marcia, *The Psychoanalytic Mind:*
  From Freud to Philosophy 172
Caygill, Howard, *Walter Benjamin: The*
  Colour of Experience 55, 58
Centre for the Study of Violence and
  Reconciliation 159
Charity, Tom 190
Cheshire, Neil 17
children, and trauma, support mechanisms
  84–8
chronic fatigue syndrome 180
Church Fathers, and idolatry 27–8
Clarke, Marcus, *Marcus Clarke ... UQP*
  Australian Authors 142
Cohen, Margaret, *Profane Illuminations:*
  Walter Benjamin and the Paris of
  Surrealist Revolution 217
colonialism 2
Colvin, Christopher 9–10, 18
Comte, Auguste 31
Conley, Tom 156
Connors, Clare 2, 4, 5
consciousness
  and materialism 41
  and Sigmund Freud 70, 79–80
conspiracy theories
  and *Forrest Gump* 182, 183, 184–5
  and *Nachträglichkeit* 185
  and postmodernism 184–5
constancy principle, the, and neurones 65–6
Cosman, Carol 106

Cowie, Elizabeth 7, 12, 13, 16, 18
Craib, Ian 182, 183, 184, 187, 188
  The Importance of Disappointment 181,
    189, 190
Crews, Frederick, *The Memory Wars:*
    Freud's Legacy in Dispute 190
Cuau, Bernard, *Au sujet de Shoah: Le film de*
    Claude Lanzmann 203
Culler, Jonathan, *The Pursuit of Signs,*
    Semiotics, Literature, Deconstruction
    156
cultural artefacts, and ideology 25
Cumming, John 55

Daniels, Kay 141, 142
Davidson, Jim 141
Davis, Edward B. 37
de Certeau, Michel 9
  Heterologies: Discourse on the Other
    144, 145, 146, 147, 148, 149, 150,
    155, 156
  on historiography 144–50, 154–5
  The Writing of History 144, 145, 146,
    148, 149, 150, 155, 156
de Man, Paul 2, 38, 39
  Aesthetic Ideology 37, 54, 55, 56, 58
  Allegories of Reading: Figural Language
    in Rousseau, Nietzsche, Rilke, and
    Proust 55, 56
  Critical Writings, 1953–1978 57
  on ideology 32, 42–3
  influence 5
  on Kant's materialism 32–4, 37
  on language 16, 42–54
  on Marx 3–4
  Romanticism and Contemporary
    Criticism: The Gauss Seminar and
    Other Papers 54, 58
  The Resistance to Theory 15, 55, 56
  The Rhetoric of Romanticism 15, 56
  on Walter Benjamin 47–54
de Tracy, Destutt 22, 23, 32
death, and life 80–1, 82–4, 88, 90, 93, 95, 96
death drive, the, and Sigmund Freud 194
deconstruction 3
  and ideology 31
  and trauma theory 5
  use 4

del Paso, Fernando, *Noticias del Imperio*
    143–4
Delbo, Charlotte 7, 16–17
  Auschwitz and After 98, 101, 105, 106,
    107
  Convoy to Auschwitz 106
  Days and Memory 6, 16, 98, 101, 106
  Le Convoi du 24 janvier 98, 106
  life 97–8
  and trauma representation 97–105
Deleuze, Gilles, *Cinema 2, The Time-Image*
    202
Derrida, Jacques 43, 60, 67, 69, 72, 73
  Glas 56
  on Sigmund Freud 94, 95
  The Post Card: From Socrates to Freud
    and Beyond 92
  Writing and Difference 71
  The Diagnostic and Statistical Manual of
    Mental Disorders 189
Díaz, Porfirio 143
differend, meaning 59, 71
disenchantment
  and ideology 23, 25, 34
  and materialism 34, 36
Docherty, Thomas, *Postmodernism: A*
    Reader 215
dreams
  function 77
  and Sigmund Freud 77
Dudach, Georges 97–8
Dufresne, Todd, *Returns of the French*
    Freud: Freud, Lacan, and Beyond 92
Dupont, Jacques 56
Duras, Marguerite 191, 200, 204
DuToit, Andre 171
Dwork, Deborah 103
  Children with a Star 106

Easthope, Antony 59, 64, 71
Echevarría, Roberto González 155
economics, and metaphysics 45
Edwards, P.D. 141
Ellmann, Maud 209
  Psychoanalytic Literary Criticism 216
Engels, Friedrich 3, 21–2, 24, 25, 30, 31, 37,
    39, 55, 216
Esch, Deborah 55

ethics, and metaphysics 1
ethnic-cleansing, Bosnia 110
Evans, Richard J. *In Defence of History* 156
Evans, Robin 131
  The Fabrication of Culture: English Prison Architecture, 1750–1840 140, 141

Farrell, Kirby 160
  Post-Traumatic Culture: Injury and Interpretation in the Nineties 172
Felman, Shoshana 5, 108, 110–11
  Testimony: Crises of Witnessing in Literature, Psychoanalysis and History 15, 16, 105, 106, 118, 119, 189
Fenves, Peter 56
Feuerbach, Ludwig Andreas 2, 22, 24, 28, 41
fiction, and history 9, 144, 147, 155
Fiddian, Robin 9
film
  flashbacks 204
  and memory 197
  and *Nachträglichkeit* 11–13
  and trauma theory 7, 12–13, 191
  see also *Calling the Ghosts*; *Forrest Gump*; *Hiroshima mon amour*; *Schindler's List*; *Shoah*; *War Neuroses*
Flanagan, Richard 139, 141
Fletcher, John 218
  Jean Laplanche: Seduction, Translation and the Drives 189, 203
Fliess, Wilhelm 61
Flinders Island 140
Flint, Valerie I.H. *The Rise of Magic in Early Medieval Europe* 37
Fludernik, Monika 130, 140
Forrest Gump
  analysis 180–8
  and conspiracy theories 182, 183, 184–5
  and *Nachträglichkeit* 11–12, 17, 18, 186–8
  and narcissism 188
  reviews 181, 182, 183, 188, 189
  see also film

fort-da game
  significance 5–6, 78, 88–9, 91–2, 92–3, 203
  and trauma theory 78–9, 81–4, 89–91, 94
Foster, Hal 208
  Compulsive Beauty 215, 216
  The Return of the Real: The Avant Garde at the End of the Century 203, 205–6, 215
Foucault, Michel 131, 187
  Discipline and Punish: The Birth of the Prison 141
  Foucault Live: Interviews 1966–1984 190
Fowkes, Ben 37
Fowler, T.W. 136
Frank, Alvin 202
Freud, Anna 91
Freud, Sigmund 2, 73
  analysis 60–71
  Beyond the Pleasure Principle 5–6, 72, 77, 78, 81, 84, 90, 91, 92, 93, 95, 96, 203
  Case Histories I & II 17
  Civilization and Its Discontents 95
  on consciousness 70, 79–80
  and the death drive 194
  on dreams 77
  on life and death 80–1, 93, 95
  Moses and Monotheism 5, 18, 91, 92, 95, 96, 105, 106, 215
  and *Nachträglichkeit* 12, 17, 182, 192, 197, 214
  Project for a Scientific Psychology 4, 59
  on repression 148, 149, 150
  Studienausgabe 91
  Studies on Hysteria 217, 218
  The Ego and the Id 95
  The Interpretation of Dreams 17, 215
  The Standard Edition of the Complete Psychological Works of Sigmund Freud 71, 91, 203, 215
  and trauma theory 6, 7, 79–81, 88–91, 93
  and the unconscious 194
Friedländer, Saul, *Probing the Limits of Representation: Nazism and the 'Final Solution'* 189

Frow, John 8, 9
   Australian Cultural Studies: A Reader
      142
   *Time and Commodity Culture: Essays in
      Cultural Theory and Postmodernity*
      17, 140
Fuentes, Carlos 156
   La muerte de Artemio Cruz 151
   The Old Gringo 144

Gadamer, Hans Georg 47
Gaines, Jane M., *Collecting Visible Evidence*
   202
Garner, Lawrence 15
Gasché, Rodolphe 92
genocide, Bosnia 110
Gill, Gillian C. 95
Gilpin, William 135
   *Observations on ... the Mountains and
      Lakes of Cumberland* 141
Glatzer, Nahum N. 140
Godzich, Wlad 15, 56, 57, 156
Goldstein, Laurence, *Ruins and Empire: The
      Evolution of a Theme in Augustan
      and Romantic Literature* 141
Green, Anna, *The Houses of History, A
      Critical Reader in Twentieth-Century
      History and Theory* 156
Griffiths, Tom 141

Hacking, Ian, *Rewriting the Soul: Multiple
      Personality and the Sciences of
      Memory* 140
Hamacher, Werner, *Premises: Essays on
      Philosophy and Literature from Kant
      to Celan* 56
Hamber, Brandon, *The Burdens of Truth:
      An Evaluation of the Psychological
      Support Services and Initiatives
      Undertaken by the South African
      Truth and Reconciliation
      Commission* 171, 172, 173
Hamilton, Paul, *Historicism* 15
Hansen, Miriam Bratu 203
Harris, Brent 171
Harrison, Peter, *Religion and 'Religions' in
      the English Enlightenment* 37

Hartman, Geoffrey H. 105, 107
Hass, Kristin Ann, *Carried to the Wall:
      American Memory and the Vietnam
      Veterans Memorial* 173
Hayward, Susan, *French Film: Texts and
      contexts* 204
Hegel, Georg Wilhelm Friedrich 38
   Phenomenology of Spirit 70, 73
   Science of Logic 54
Hegelians 40, 42
Heidegger, Martin 53
   Basic Writings 58
Heine, Heinrich 207
Henry, Michel 30
   Marx 37
   Phénoménologie matérielle 37
heritage concept, and Port Arthur 137–8
Herman, Janet Lewis, *Trauma and Recovery*
      107
Hernandez, Max 202, 203
Hertz, Neil 15, 53–4, 57, 58
Hiroshima, and trauma theory 12–13, 93–4,
      198
Hiroshima mon amour 7, 12, 18, 93–4, 204
   analysis 196–202
   and memory 196, 197
   and trauma 191, 193, 197–8
   see also film
historicism 1, 15
   and apartheid 167–8, 169
   and Port Arthur 138–9
historiography, and Michel de Certeau
      144–50, 154–5
history
   criticism 15
   and fiction 9, 144, 147, 155
   and memory 1, 2, 77, 105, 170, 185
   and narrative 144, 170
   and postcolonial theory 144
   postmodernist critiques of 177–8
   and psychoanalysis 9, 59, 82, 144,
      147–50, 155
   theories 2
   and trauma 178
   and the unconscious 155
Hobbes, Thomas 2
   on idolatry 26–7, 28
   Leviathan 3, 25, 37

Hoberman, J. 189
Hollo, Anselm 215
Holocaust, The 16
    and apartheid 164–5, 169
    and memory 6, 99–102
    and survivor guilt 100–1
    and testimony 108–9
    and trauma 97–9, 193
Horkheimer, Max 55
Howard, John Winston 131
Hughes, Robert 127, 128
    The Fatal Shore: A History of
        Transportation of Convicts to
        Australia, 1787–1868 140
Huhn, Tom, *The Semblance of Subjectivity:*
        Essays in Adorno's Aesthetic Theory
    55
Hukanovic, Rezak, *The Tenth Circle of Hell:*
        A Memoir of Life in the Death Camps
        of Bosnia 119
Hunter, Michael 37
Hurst, A.F., Dr 194
Hutcheon, Linda, *The Politics of*
        Postmodernism 215
Huyssen, Andreas 15

idealism, and subjectivity 35
ideology
    and cultural artefacts 25
    and deconstruction 31
    and disenchantment 23, 25, 34
    and idolatry 21, 25, 28
    and Karl Marx 22–4, 30–1
    and Louis Althusser 29–30, 31, 37
    and materialism 21
    meaning 22, 29
    and mystification 22–3
    and Paul de Man 32, 42–3
    and priests 22–3
idolatry
    and the Church Fathers 27–8
    idea of 25–6
    and ideology 21, 25, 28
    and nature 28–9
    and Thomas Hobbes 26–7, 28
IFP (Inkatha Freedom Party, South Africa)
    158

Ignatieff, Michael 133
    A Just Measure of Pain: The Penitentiary
        in the Industrial Revolution 1750–
        1850 141
individualism, and Karl Marx 30
inertia
    meaning 62
    and neurones 61–2, 63–4, 69
Inkatha Freedom Party *see* IFP
insanity, and silence 132–3
Irigaray, Luce, *Sexes and Genealogies* 95

Jacobs, Carol 49, 51
    In the Language of Walter Benjamin 57
Jacobson, Mandy 109, 111, 115, 117, 118,
    119, 120
Jacobus, Mary 15
Jameson, Frederic 14, 45, 178, 205, 213,
    214, 215
    Late Marxism: Adorno, or, The
        Persistence of the Dialectic 56
    Marxism and Form: Twentieth Century
        Dialectical Theories of Literature 217
Janet, Pierre 103, 104, 107, 172
Jarvis, Simon 2, 3, 14
    Adorno: A Critical Introduction 37, 55
Jelincic, Karmen 109, 111, 115, 117, 118,
    119
Jenkins, Keith
    Rethinking History 189
    The Postmodern History Reader 156,
        189
Jennings, Michael W. 55
Jephcott, Edmund 217
Jewett, William 56
Jones, Rhys 139, 142
Joyce, R.B. 141

Kafka, Franz 8, 38
    Complete Stories 140
    'In the Penal Colony' 140
    meaning 127–8
    summary 125–6
Kant, Immanuel 38
    Critique of Judgement 3, 37
    Critique of Pure Reason 32, 54
    on materialism 32–4

Katz, Friedrich, *The Life and Times of Pancho Villa* 144, 154, 156
Keats, John, 'Ode to a Nightingale' 54
Keenan, Tom 120
Kenny, Michael G. 189
Kids Alive and Loved Oral History Archive 84–5, 94
Kincaid, R.A. 106
King, Nicola 188, 190
Klee, Paul 213
Klein, Kerwin Lee 15
Kohut, Karl *Literatura mexicana hoy. Del 68 al ocaso de la revolución* 156
Kollapen, Jody 171
Kostelnick, Charles 141
Krell, David Farrell 58, 60

Lacan, Jacques 10, 73, 191
    Écrits: A Selection 17, 92
    and reality 194
    The Four Fundamental Concepts of Psycho-Analysis 92, 203, 215
LaCapra, Dominick 109
    History and Memory After Auschwitz 119
    Representing the Holocaust: History, Theory, Trauma 16
Lalu, Premesh 171
Lambek, Michael 106, 160, 171, 172, 189
Lamont, Rosette 105, 106
Lane, Helen R. 217
Langer, Lawrence 105
language
    and memory 85, 87–8
    nature of 46, 55
    Paul de Man on 16, 42–54
    poetic 47
    pure 52–3
    and trauma 83–4
    William Wordsworth on 15–16
Lanzmann, Claude, and testimony concept 7, 16, 108–9, 115, 118, 119, 193, 203
Laplanche, Jean 10–11, 12, 13, 189, 192, 214
    Essays on Otherness 17, 203, 218
    Life and Death in Psychoanalysis 17, 93
    The Language of Psycho-analysis 17, 72, 190
Laub, Dori 16, 97, 101, 103, 105, 106, 118, 119, 189

Leavey, John P. 56
Leite, Bernadette 6, 84–7, 94, 95
Levi, Primo 100–1, 115
    The Drowned and the Saved 106
Levine, Michael 92
Leys, Ruth 104, 106, 107, 172
Liebenberg, Ian 171
life, and death 80–1, 82–4, 88, 90, 93, 95, 96
Lifton, Robert Jay 81, 98–9, 104–5, 106
    Death in Life: Survivors of Hiroshima 93
    The Broken Connection: Death and the Continuity of Life 92
loss, and trauma 201
Lukács, Georg 55
Lyotard, Jean-François 206, 215
    The Differend: Phrases in Dispute 71

McFarlane, Alexander C. 93
McGowan, W. 136
Madero, Francisco I. 9, 143
    personality 150–1
Magritte, René, *Time Suspended* 216
Mandela, Nelson 18, 158, 163
Mapp, Nigel 2, 3–4
Márquez, Gabriel García, *El general en su laberinto* 144, 154
Marx, Karl 2, 28
    Capital 23, 37
    on ideology 22–4, 30–1
    on individualism 30
    on the past 210, 211–12
    Selected Works 216
    The Communist Manifesto 216
    'The Eighteenth Brumaire of Louis Bonaparte' 210, 216, 217
    The German Ideology 3, 21–2, 24, 25, 30, 31, 37, 39, 55
    Werke 37
Massumi, Brian 156
Mastretta, Angeles, *Mal de Amores* 144
materialism 3, 15
    characteristics 34, 55
    and consciousness 41
    and disenchantment 34, 36
    and ideology 21
    and Immanuel Kant 32–4
    and nature 36

materialism (cont'd)
    and subjectivity 35
    and William Wordsworth 33, 34
Mayhew, Henry 132
    The Criminal Prisons of London, and
        Scenes of Prison Life 141
mechanics, and neurology 61
Mecklenburg, Frank 217
Meisl, Perry 95
memory
    collective 1–2, 123
    cultural 8, 9, 11
    and film 197
    and *Hiroshima mon amour* 196, 197
    and history 1, 2, 77, 105, 170, 185
    criticism 15
    and The Holocaust 6, 99–102
    and language 85, 87–8
    and Marcel Proust 6, 102
    meaning of 66, 196–7
    model of 8
    and *Nachträglichkeit* 11, 182–3, 192
    and neurones 66–9
    and perception 196
    and punishment 131, 133
    recovery of 185, 190
    and testimony 115
    and trauma theory 172, 202
    types of 6, 102–3, 172, 190
    and the unconscious 186
    and *War Neuroses* 195–6
Menton, Seymour, *Latin America's New*
    Historical Novel 155
metaphor 45
    and translation 48
metaphysics
    and economics 45
    and ethics 1
Michelet, Jules 149–50
Miller, A.V. 54, 73
Miller, Jacques-Alain 92, 215
mind, model of 81
models
    of memory 8
    of mind 81
modernism
    meaning 214
    and postmodernism 13, 213–14

More, Henry 28
    Divine Dialogues 37
Morris, Meaghan 142
Morrison, Toni
    Beloved 11
    Jazz 11
Moynihan, Robert 54
Muir, Willa and Edwin 140
mystification, and ideology 22–3

Nachträglichkeit
    and conspiracy theories 185
    and film 11–13
    and *Forrest Gump* 11–12, 17, 18, 186–8
    meaning of 10–11, 182, 184, 197
    and memory 11, 182–3, 192
    and *Nights at the Circus* 13–14, 18
    and postmodernism 13
    and Sigmund Freud 12, 17, 182, 192,
        197, 214
    and time 192, 202
    uses 11
    and *War Neuroses* 12
narcissism, and *Forrest Gump* 188
narrative
    and history 144, 170
    and trauma 116–17, 170, 172
    and trauma theory 10
National Party of South Africa *see* NP
nature
    and idolatry 28–9
    and materialism 36
    and Robert Boyle 35
Nessus, shirt of 15–16
neurology, and mechanics 61
neurones
    and the constancy principle 65–6
    and external stimuli 62–3, 64, 67
    and inertia 61–2, 63–4, 69
    meaning 72
    and memory 66–9
    and the psyche 61
Newmark, Kevin 46, 58
    Beyond Symbolism: Textual History and
        the Future of Reading 56
Nicholls, Peter 11, 17
Nicholsen, Shierry Weber 55
Nicholson-Smith, Donald 72

nightmare 5–6, 93
Nora, Pierre 1, 17, 105, 107, 138
    Les Lieux de Mémoire 8–9, 14–15, 123,
        140
Norris, Christopher 212, 217
novel, historical, developments 143–4
NP (National Party, South Africa) 9, 158
    Second Submission to the Truth and
        Reconciliation Commission 173
    testimony to TRC 167–8, 169, 170
    view of apartheid 167–8

Okada, Eiji 198
Omarska, prison camp 7, 110, 119
Osborne, John 57
Owen, W.J.B. *The Prose Works of William*
    Wordsworth 15

PAC (Pan Africanist Congress) 172
pain, meaning, compared with *Brot* 49
panopticon 126, 131
past, the
    alternative views 2
    and Karl Marx 210, 211–12
    recovery of 209–10
pastiche, and postmodernism 205
Pellón, Gustavo 155
Pentonville Prison 129, 132
perception, and memory 196
Perelli, Carina 165, 172
Petersen, Robin 171
Plaice, Neville & Stephen 215
Plato, on power 1
Pluhar, Werner S. 37, 54
Pontalis, J.-B. 10, 17, 72, 190
Port Arthur
    and heritage concept 137–8
    and historicism 138–9
    histories of 8–9
    mass shooting 124
    Model Prison 132–3, 139
    as penal settlement 125, 134
        preservation 136–8
        ruins 134–6
    punishment regimes 128–9
post-traumatic stress disorder 179
postcolonial theory, and history 144
postmodernism 3

and conspiracy theories 184–5
and critiques of history 177–8
meaning of 205, 213–14
and modernism 13, 213–14
and *Nachträglichkeit* 13
as pastiche 205
and trauma 177
power
    Plato on 1
    Thucydides on 1
priests, and ideology 22–3
prison, concept 130–131
Proust, Marcel, on memory 6, 102
psyche, the
    and neurones 61
    and time 69–71
psychiatry, and trauma 179
psychoanalysis
    and history 9, 59, 82, 144, 147–50, 155
    and trauma 179, 187
punishment
    and architecture 131, 132
    and memory 131, 133
    regimes, Port Arthur 128–9
    and silence 132

Rabinbach, Anson 216
Radstone, Susannah 11, 13, 18
    Memory and Methodology 189
railways, symbolism 207–8
Ramadonovic, Peter 204
Rand, Richard 56
rape
    Bosnia 7, 109, 110, 118
    and ethnic genocide 110
Ravensbrück 98
reality
    and Jacques Lacan 194
    and *War Neuroses* 194–5
Reed, Mark L. 37
religion, critique of 39–41
Renov, Michael 202
repression
    political, and psychological repression
        165–7
    psychological
        and political repression 165–7
        and Sigmund Freud 148, 149, 150

Resnais, Alain 191, 200, 204
Rexroth, Tillman 57
Reynolds, Henry 141
  *Fate of a Free People: A Radical
    Re-Examination of the Tasmanian
    Wars* 142
Richards, Angela 17
Ritter, Mark 55
Riva, Emmanuelle 198
Rivers, W.H. 203
Robinson, George 140
Romney, Jonathan 189
Ropas-Wuilleumier, Marie-Claire 201–2, 204
Rose, Gillian 1, 2, 3
  *Mourning Becomes the Law: Philosophy
    and Representation* 14, 15
Rose, Jacqueline, *The Haunting of Sylvia
    Plath* 11, 17
Rosenfeld, Sidney 107
Rosenthal, Raymond 106
Rosso, Stefano 55
Rottenberg, Elizabeth 94
Roudebush, Marc, *Realms of Memory:
    Rethinking the French past* 15
Rousseau, Jean Jacques 15
Rulfo, Juan, *Pedro Páramo* 152
Ryan, Lyndall, *The Aboriginal Tasmanians*
    142

Santner, Eric L. 178, 189
  *Stranded Objects: Mourning, Memory,
    and Film in Postwar Germany* 91–2
Schiller, 32
Schindler's List 203
  see also film
Schivelbusch, Wolfgang 207
  *The Railway Journey: Trains and Travel
    in the Nineteenth Century* 215
Schweppenhäuser, Hermann 57
Scott, Margaret 138–9
  *Port Arthur: A Story of Strength and
    Courage* 140, 142
Seaver, Richard 204, 217
Sharpeville Massacre (1960) 163, 164, 172
Sheridan, Alan 17, 92, 141, 215
Shoah 7, 108, 193
  see also film

Shorter, Kingsley 217
Showalter, Elaine, *Hystories: Hysterical
    Epidemics in Modern Media* 181,
    182, 183, 189
silence
  and insanity 132–3
  and punishment 132
Smyser, J.W. 15
Sobchack, Vivian, *The Persistence of
    History: Cinema, Television and the
    Modern Event* 189
Solares, Ignacio 9, 144, 156
  analysis 150–5
  Columbus 143
  El gran Elector 143
  El jefe máximo 143
  Madero, el otro 143, 144, 156
Spielberg, Steven 203
Stafford, Barbara Maria *Voyage Into
    Substance: Art, Science, Nature, and
    the Illustrated Travel Account, 1760–
    1840* 141
Stanner, W.E.H. 134
Stanton, Martin 189, 203
Steedman, Carolyn 216
Stewart, Victoria 6, 16, 17
Stiglmayer, Alexandra *Mass Rape: The War
    Against Women in Bosnia-
    Herzegovina* 119
Stirner, Max 22
Stokes, John *Fin Du Siècle/Fin Du Globe:
    Fears and Fantasies of the Late
    Nineteenth Century* 216
Stone, Matthew *The Anatomy of Madness:
    Essays in the history of psychiatry*
    203
Stoney, H. Butler, Capt. *A Residence in
    Tasmania: With a Descriptive Tour
    through the Ilsand from Macquarie
    Harbour to Circular Head* 141, 142
Stott, Andrew 17
Strachey, James 10, 17, 60, 67, 71, 72, 91,
    192, 214, 215
subjectivity
  and idealism 35
  and materialism 35
surrealism, and *Nights at the Circus* 217

surrealists 210
survivor culture 180–1
    and trauma 181
Symms, J.L., Dr 194

Tasman Peninsula 139–40
Taussig, Michael 165
    *Shamanism, Colonialism, and the Wild
        Man: A Study in Terror and Healing*
        172
testimony
    and apartheid 157
    and art 108, 110–11, 118
    and *Calling the Ghosts* 109, 110, 111,
        114, 115, 116–17
    and memory 115
    and The Holocaust 108–9
    and trauma 116, 117–18
*The Cambridge History of Latin American
    Literature* 155
*The Heritage of Australia: The Illustrated
    Register of the National Estate* 141
therapy
    and apartheid 167–71
    and catharsis 161
    purpose 161
    and trauma 160–2
Thomä, Helmut 10, 17
Thucydides, on power 1
Thurston, Luke 218
Tiedemann, Rolf 57
Tikkun 51
time
    and *Nachträglihkeit* 192, 202
    and the psyche 69–71
Timpanaro, Sebastiano *On Materialism* 15
Tindale, Norman B. *Aboriginal Tales of
    Australia: Their Terrain,
    Environmental Controls,
    Distribution, Limits, and Proper
    Names* 142
Tort, Patrick 22
    *Marx et le problème de l'idéologie. Le
        modèle Égyptien* 36
translation
    and metaphor 48
    nature of 48–9
    and Walter Benjamin 47–54, 57

trauma
    and apartheid 164, 165
    and children 84–8
    and *Hiroshima mon amour* 191, 193,
        197–8
    and history 178
    and The Holocaust 97–9, 193
    and language 83–4
    and loss 201
    meaning 82, 98–9, 177, 179, 192
    and narrative 116–17, 170, 172
    and postmodernism 177
    psychoanalytic approaches 179, 187
    representation of 97–105, 191–2, 193,
        203
    and survivor culture 181
    symptoms of 98, 106
    and testimony 116, 117–18
    and therapy 160–2
    and understanding 115
    and video-testimony 97, 105
    and *War Neuroses* 191
    see also trauma theory
trauma theory 1, 2
    and *Calling the Ghosts* 7, 16
    and deconstruction 5
    emergence 11
    and film 7, 12–13, 191
    and the *fort-da* game 78–9, 81–4, 89–91,
        94
    and Hiroshima 12–13, 93–4, 198
    and memory 172, 202
    and narrative 10
    scope 5, 15, 183
    and Sigmund Freud 6, 7, 79–81, 89–91
    see also trauma
TRC (Truth and Reconciliation Commission,
    South Africa) 9, 18
    ANC testimony 162–9
    composition 158
    Interim Report 171
    mission 157, 158
    *Policy Framework for Urgent Interim
        Reparation Measures* 171
    Register of Reconciliation 171
    therapeutic approach 159–62, 163
    victim testimony 170

Trollope, Anthony 134–5
   Australia 141
Troup, Kathleen 156
Tuck, Richard 37
Turim, Maureen, *Flashbacks in Film* 204
Tutu, Desmond 158, 159, 171
Tyson, Jan 91

unconscious, the
   and history 155
   and memory 186
   and Sigmund Freud 194
understanding, and trauma 115

Van Den Abbeele, Georges 71
van der Hart, Onno 103–4, 106, 107
van der Kolk, Bessel, A. 103–4, 106, 107
   *Traumatic Stress: The Effects of
      Overwhelming Experience on Mind,
      Body, and Society* 93
Vice, Sue 11
   Psychoanalytic Criticism: A Reader 17
video testimony, and trauma 97, 105
Villa, Pancho 153–4
Vincendeau, Ginette 204
violence, urban 6, 84–5
Vogelman, Lloyd 159, 171

Waldeyer, W. 72
Walker, Alexander 190
Walker, Enrique Pupo 155
War Neuroses
   analysis 195–6
   and memory 195–6
   and *Nachträglichkeit* 12
   and reality 194–5, 203
   and trauma 191, 193
   see also film
Warhol, Andy 203
Warminski, Andrzej 37, 46, 54, 55, 56
Waters, Lindsay, *Reading de Man Reading*
   57

Weber, Samuel
   *Return to Freud: Jacques Lacan's
      Dislocation of Psychoanalysis* 92
   The Legend of Freud 92, 95
Weisaeth, Lars 93
Wenzel, Marita 172
White, Hayden 177–8, 179, 189
Whitehead, Anne 95
Wilding, M. 142
Wilson, Elizabeth 60, 72
   *Neural Geographies: Feminism and the
      Microstructure of Cognition* 71
Winnicott, D.W. 183–4
   Playing and Reality 96
witnessing *see* testimony
Wordsworth, William
   Essays upon Epitaphs 15
   on language 15–16
   on materialism 33, 34
   The Thirteen-Book Prelude 37

Xenophanes 25

Yale Video Testimony Project 105
Young, Allan 165
   *The Harmony of Illusions: Inventing
      Post-Traumatic Stress Disorder* 172
Young, David *Making Crime Pay: The
      Evolution of Convict Tourism in
      Tasmania* 141
Young, James T *The Art of Memory:
      Holocaust Memorials in History* 15
Young, Stephenie 7

Zemeckis, Robert 189
Zeno 70
Zetlin, Monica 189
Zinovieff, Sofka 216
Zipes, Jack 217
Žižek, Slavoj
   Mapping Ideology 37
   The Sublime Object of Ideology 55
Zohn, Harry 18, 50, 52, 57, 215
Zuidervaart, Lambert 55